D1040611

GARDENING WITH HERBS

FOR FLAVOR AND FRAGRANCE

By

HELEN MORGENTHAU FOX

Drawings by

LOUISE MANSFIELD

DOVER PUBLICATIONS, INC.

New York

This 1970 edition is an unabridged and unaltered republication of the work originally published by The Macmillan Company in 1933.

Library of Congress Catalog Card Number
(Paperback edition): 71-99762

Standard Book Numbers:
Paperback edition: 486-22450-2
Hardcover trade edition: 8069 3914-1
Reinforced library edition: 8069 3915-X

Manufactured in the United States of America

To My Mother and Father

WHO BY THEIR ENCOURAGEMENT AND PRIDE IN MY WORK AS WELL AS THE EXAMPLE OF THEIR VIVID AND ADVENTUROUS LIVES HAVE BEEN AN INSPIRATION TO ME.

HELENAE FOX

Botanicae Doctae

Aestate priore te multa in horto optime fecisse miratus verbis dulcibus te tuumque librum laudavissem. Dulce fuisset tuae fronti coronam roseam imponere cum verbis magistri Horatii, sicut:

Nec flos purpureus rosae.

Sed hos menses ob strepitum mundanum lyra non modulatur et hieme nunc instante nil nisi haec verba frigida et flaccida fero: quae autem quamvis tristia aliquid possunt, nam prima vera ut virgulta tua revirescent. Quibus verbis, cara domina, dicere conor meam admirationem tui perennem esse.

Richardson Wright.

TO HELEN FOX

The Learned Herbalist

Last summer, in the ardor of my admiration for your gardening achievements, I would have sung honied phrases to laud you and this book. How pleasant, then, to have pressed a coronal on your brow with a grand gesture out of my master Horace, say:

Nec flos purpureus rosae.

But the world has clamored about my ears and the lyre remained untouched these many months. Now winter comes. Alas, all I offer you are these poor, faded, frost-bitten phrases.

Yet, though withered, virtue is still in them. They will spring up again, like your herbs, at the first touch of spring.

Which, dear lady, is my poor way of saying that my admiration for you is perennial.

Once Helen launched a thousand ships.
This Helen, gentler far, equips
Her argosy with cargo wrought
Of kindly herbs with fragrance fraught.
No battles here, no clash of arms;
Instead a wizardry of charms.
Ambrosias and aromas sweet
In tender strife and conflict meet.
Thyme, tarragon, bee balm and til,
Sweet iris, marjoram, and dill,
Sage, hyssop, coriander, bay,
Angelica and caraway,
The lavender, both spike and true,
Bush basil, rosemary, and rue,
The mints, the mustards, dittany,
Cloves, clary, chives—a litany
Of perfumes rare that shall their censers raise
To speak in incense sweet fair Helen's praise.

JULES ECKERT GOODMAN.

How shall one write a garland for this book
And there set down its measure of sweet praise
In which are gathered up for nose and tongue
For fancied ache and certain ill, the ways
Of ancient dames, of chemists of old days?

But I protest, care not for balms in buns,
For bergamot in soup, soufflés of rue,
Or risk my unsuspecting temper's rise
From draughts of caraway or midnight stew
Of moon-plucked dill,—and yet what may I do?

For here are onions, noble fruit, and chives,
Shallots and leeks, enough to fox away
Sad vapours from the mind, to purge my tongue
Of nonsense, so in this last line I lay
A wreath for Helen, if not made of bay!

BENJAMIN YOE MORRISON.

ADAM'S LUXURY AND EVE'S SALVATION

A House-wife hath great need of perfect knowledge of the Properties and Vertues of all manner of choyce Herbes and Simples and skill therewith. Her Garden should bee of good compasse and well set forth with them for Herbes ioyned with good Sense and Industrie maketh all things pleasant and wel as I doe well know and acknowledge. First there should bee alwaies good store of Herbes for the Kitchen for if her housbande return home in a mood curst and malicious and his Minde set agaynst his Victuals it is easie for the skilled House-wife by the Grace of God and the aide of such Herbes as Fennell, Basil and others to set before him what purporteth to be a new Dish *and so to soothe and admonish him to gentlenesse. But wanting such helpes she may suffer disaster.*

Also must she have thought ever for her beautie and Comelinesse and the softnesse and whitenesse of her skin. Diuers Herbes as Balm and Bergamot steeped in faire clean rain water yeeldeth sweet washing waters for the care of her bodie and so doth Lavender and Rosemary which softeneth and preseureth the skin and imparteth thereto a pleasant sweete Smell.

Also must she alwaies take thought for the health of her Household neyther neglect it for laughter or merrie-making or idlenesse. She should have knowledge of the very many strange effects and operations of Simples acting against all manner of Sicknesse, Soresnesse and diuers griefs as well venemous bitings and stingings, yeoxings and Melancholy, and of the making of lotions and medicines for the relief thereof. If she must send for an outlandish and Bombast Chirugeon she is none of my good House-wives.

There can be no humane thing more excellent, either for pleas-

ure or profit than a Garden well set forth with Herbes as shal be (God willing) proved in the treatise following by Mistress Fox, for what is laid down in this Boke is not the audacious attempt of an unskilled House-wife but the certain knowledge which comes from the long experience and trauell of the Author who workes for the unspeakable benefit of mankind.

Therefore leaving this let us come to the Herbes themselves, which are the chief fruites of her accomplisht labours.

—Mistress Wilder.

CONTENTS

ILLUSTRATIONS

GARDENING WITH HERBS FOR FLAVOR AND FRAGRANCE

I

THE BEGINNING

As I weed and cultivate the basils, savories, and thymes in my garden, touch their furry or glossy leaves, and breathe in their spicy scent, they seem like such old friends it is difficult to realize that only three years ago these aromatic herbs, except for the parsley, sage, and mint, were quite unknown to me.

Before writing a book about the herbs I decided to grow every plant to be described so that I could watch the seed unfurl into a leafy plant, the buds thicken and swell into flowers, and these drop their petals and in turn ripen their seeds. Since exceptionally wet, cold, dry, or hot spells affect the development of the plants, I grew them for three summers before I was sure I really knew them well enough to describe them.

During the first year, five of my friends sent me copies of Mrs. Bardswell's book, "The Herb Garden"; some, no doubt, in the hope that if I saw how excellent a book already existed on the subject I would desist from further efforts and behave as a normal, social being once more, instead of spending my days in the herb garden and my evenings in talking about it. Mrs. Bardswell, however, lives and grows her plants in England, the paradise of gardeners, and since the only literature on growing herbs in America consisted of one slender volume and some government pamphlets, I persisted in the attempt to write a book about how this group of aromatics smelt, tasted, and behaved in our quite different climate.

The first spade into the soil of herb lore was to consult two favorite catalogues, an English one which offered twenty-two herbs and a French one which under the heading of *Graines des Plantes Officinales* listed ninety-one herbs, many of them medicinal plants. I ordered all the herbs in both of these catalogues, although there were some duplicates, for I thought these would cover the mortalities, inevitable in all horticultural undertakings. After I had learned where to look for them I found that seeds of thirty different herbs are obtainable from commercial sources in America, and that plants of rosemary, lavender, wormwood, and sage as well as a few of the mints and thymes can be bought here. At present the seeds of all unusual varieties of basil, savory, or lavender have to be secured from Europe.

When the seeds arrived during the month of May, they were planted in a well-drained, sunny space which had been prepared for them. It was a warm season with almost no rain, and as many of the herbs are native to southern lands the little plants felt at home and grew lustily.

The first task was to find out which herbs to include and which to leave out of the book, and when the first crop matured I saw that a few of them like chicory, celandine poppy, and viper's bugloss were weeds, and others like melilot and tussilago were forage plants. After working over the problem for a long time I decided, with some exceptions, to choose the herbs some portion of which could be used as a condiment in cooking, or in the preparation of homemade sachets and perfumes, and which were easy for the amateur to grow in his garden.

To find out about the cultural requirements of the herbs, their background of history and legend, and which portion of each was the part used, when it was the seed, the leaves, stems, roots, or flowers which were to be dropped into the soup or minced into the chicken dressing, I first searched through all the old and modern books in my own library on the subject. Books were sent for from England, France, and Germany, and the collection of cook books in the Vassar College Library, and other sources, in the libraries of the Massachusetts Horticultural Society and the New York Public Library were consulted. In fact, for one year when not out in the garden I spent every spare hour in taking notes. The study finally culminated in two weeks at Washington in the Congressional Library and the Library of the Department of Agriculture where the librarian Miss Claribel Barnett and her assistants gave me help and suggestions.

Any available printed word which described the herbs was searched through, including cook books which down through the ages have mentioned the herbs used in flavoring foods and brewing drinks. The diaries of travelers, such as Kalm and Bartram, the journals of the Folk Lore Society, articles on ethnobotany, government pamphlets, and as with all research on gardening subjects, the horticultural journals in English, French, and

German and even some pamphlets in Spanish and Italian were read, although in these last only the high spots were understood. In order not to make the text too cumbersome with titles the authorities have not always been mentioned, but practically every author quoted is in the bibliography.

The books found most useful and which have spent the last two years on my study table were Piesse, "The Art of Perfumery"; Poucher, "Perfumes, Cosmetics and Soaps"; F. A. Hampton, "The Scent of Flowers and Leaves"; "The Toilet of Flora"; Pliny's "Natural History"; Eleanour Rohde, "A Garden of Herbs"; Sturtevant's "Notes on Edible Plants"; Fernie's "Herbal Simples"; Robinson's translation of Vilmorin's "The Vegetable Garden"; John Parkinson's "Herbal" and "Paradisi in Sole"; Gerard's "Herball"; and Culpeper's "De Candolle, Origin of Cultivated Plants"; Correvon, "Le Jardin de l'Herboriste"; Merck's "Index"; Rehder's "Manual of Cultivated Trees and Shrubs," and Bailey's "Manual of Cultivated Plants" was referred to so continuously that as soon as this manuscript goes to the publisher the poor, shabby book will have to be sent to the binder. As I read, I added or subtracted the names of plants from my list until I had it more or less as it is presented here.

Making out a list was simple enough, but locating the seeds and plants was quite another matter. Although most of them had been grown for thousands of years and had been described from Theophrastus' time in the fourth century B.C. down to Mrs. Grieve's in the twentieth, they were not listed in any seed catalogue and their whereabouts were unknown to horticulturists. In answer to my queries I was told repeatedly, "Seeds of this plant can be secured only from some country woman in a remote village," and for a time it seemed as if to obtain them I should have to embark upon an expedition of exploration through the cottage gardens of Europe.

One afternoon I told my troubles to the members of the Poughkeepsie Garden Club who had come to see my lilies, and to my great joy one of the members said her grandmother had grown costmary and that they still had plants of it, while another had ambrosia. With the generosity typical of all true gardeners they sent me a few of each. Friends sent me slips of fragrant geraniums, and the gardener of a famous herb garden in Connecticut drove seventy-five miles to bring me an unusual *Santolina* I had seen and admired when visiting him.

There were, however, still others to be garnered into the confines of my garden and having been unsuccessful in my appeals to the commercial people, except for Sutton's who have always been most helpful and this time got me a huge packet of *Nigella sativa* seeds. I turned to the authorities in cap and gown. Professor Hamblin sent me a few of the rare herbs and told me of the custom obtaining amongst the botanic gardens of the world of exchanging seed lists with one another in January of each year. Mr. Benjamin Yoe Morrison of the Department of Agriculture was helpful in every way. Not only has he gone over my proofs, but he assisted me in securing "a preferred amateur's permit" to enable me to import all the plants not to be grown from seeds. He sent me the precious lists from the botanic gardens and told me to mark the "herbs" I wanted with my initials, and as I wrote "H. M. F." in the margins opposite the thymes, or sages so rare that they had not even been described in any of the books I had come across, I felt as if I had been permitted to enter the innermost sanctum of the botanical élite under government auspices. Copies of my tentative list of herbs were sent to Dr. E. D. Merrill of the New York Botanic Gardens, and Dr. C. Stuart Gager of the Brooklyn Botanic Gardens who helped me secure many treasures. Regius Director Smith of the Royal Botanic Gardens in Edinburgh, besides giving me addresses of people to write to, sent me plants of mints, nepetas, and satureias. Other plants were obtained from English nurseries and some from far-away India. I collected many varieties of mints, thymes, tansies, and sages other than the ones used for flavor and fragrance, for I felt I could understand the individual better by knowing the whole family. I corresponded with horticulturists and botanists in China, India, and Europe as well as distant portions of America, all of whom were amazingly kind in answering letters and giving advice and information.

Either the seeds or plants of every herb on my list, and many more besides, were finally gathered together. In February, as the second spring was coming, seed packets arrived from Algiers, Portugal, Spain, India, France, England, and Scotland. By the end of March seedlings filled my little greenhouse to capacity.

The detective work, furthered by kind friends, had been perfect, but as the season advanced our brilliant beginning was somewhat dimmed by several horticultural disappointments and our pride, as usual, took a tumble. The sweet cicely sickened and died and our only angelica plant to grow up turned yellow and did not have the vigor to flower as it should have in its second season in the garden; a friend, however, sent me a flat full of little plants. Because of its place in the religious practices of the Hindus, I had particularly wanted to grow the holy basil, *Ocimum sanctum,* and compare it with the other basils used for flavoring. After much difficulty I had finally obtained three packets, but no matter how we treated the seeds, although we put some of them in the sun, others in the shade, and kept some of them indoors and a few outside, they would germinate and raise our hopes and then disappoint us by suddenly expiring. One packetful finally grew and flowered and smelt quite vilely and we thought, "this is it and perhaps the Hindus who like it and we differ about pleasantness in smells," but Dr. Merrill said these plants were a variety of *Ocimum basilicum* and not *Ocimum sanctum.*

In spite of the mishaps we managed to raise some three hundred different varieties of herbs. Planted at the top of the sloping cut-flower garden in three long terrace-like rows with little paths running between them and with a pink and white hedge of flowering cosmos behind them, they made an imposing array.

Every day with paper, pencil, and measuring tape I would sit on the ground beside the herbs, and measure, describe, taste, and smell them. Bailey's descriptions and those from other writers were carried with me on cards to compare with the growing plant and if there was any doubt about its identity a specimen was dried between blotters on a herbarium sheet and sent to Dr. Merrill, who had very generously offered to check up the nomenclature and happily for me kept his promise.

Miss Mansfield stayed with us while she was drawing the plates and in the cool evenings we would walk through the garden and look over the plants critically and discuss their beauty while deciding which she was to draw the next day. With her artistic training she would note the lines or ridges on a stem or a downward curve in the leaves which had often escaped me.

All this time I was cutting off the leaves and drying the seeds and roots to use in cooking. Recipes had been gathered during the months of research from such varying sources as the "Arabian Nights" (Mrs. Leyel's version), and from English, French, German, Jewish, Italian, and Spanish cook books dating from the sixteenth to the twentieth centuries. A great many of these were prepared. The first summer we had a fine cook from the south of France who like most of her race was an artist and delighted in creating new dishes. Every morning we had long culinary conferences in French, our voices growing louder and shriller as we became more and more excited over the custard or salad flavored with herbs. When a dish gave promise of not being too startling it was served to the whole family, but when we were not at all certain of its success it would be served in a little, separate dish to me alone. I would eat a spinach of borage or stewed mallow leaves with indications of intense pleasure in the hope of stirring a desire in the rest of the family to share them with me, but my blandishments either met with a smiling refusal or a gentle, "no, thank you," said in a tone such as might be employed to a person who is a bit "off." There were, however, some triumphal successes. The marigold pudding from John Evelyn's "Acetaria" came to the table in a creamy melon shape, with the golden marigold petals sticking out all over it like cloves on a baked ham and was greeted with acclaim while

Marie stood behind the pantry door to watch the effect of her masterpiece.

Marie could never tell me exactly how much of the herbs she used nor could she say at precisely what moment she dropped them in the liquids or mixed them into the solids. She would shrug her shoulders and say, "It is very simple, just a pinch at the last minute." Therefore, as I am an exceedingly poor cook, it was necessary to secure an experienced person to work out the exact methods of flavoring the food with herbs. Miss Bertha Shapleigh who lectured on "The Appreciation of Cookery" at Teachers College was recommended as "the expert on flavoring in the United States." She was known to be able to detect the ingredients which had gone into a dish as soon as she tasted it, and although she lived in California was to come East to give a course at the college that spring. Thereupon I wrote her a letter in which the flavoring with herbs was so enticingly portrayed that she succumbed and promised to come and help me out.

In anticipation of her arrival we fitted up a little house in the garden as a temporary kitchen, and jars of rose water and containers filled with saffron powder, sesame, cumin, anise, and other seeds, and the dried leaves of dozens of herbs were placed on the shelves ready for her use. She came for two weeks in September of the second summer, after the herbs had been harvested, and after reading over all the recipes I had collected, selected the ones she thought best for the modern menu and then tried them out. There were too many of these to include in the book, so a second selection was made from the ones we had liked best. They were rewritten to suit modern methods of cooking and are given under the recipes. As she cooked, Miss Shapleigh descanted fascinatingly on her subject and described how the different peoples flavored their food from Greek and Persian days to modern times.

All the information has been harvested and carefully gleaned and we hope this book will show the gardener and cook how to grow the herbs, pack them away for the winter, to flavor food and drink, and brew teas of them, and mix the dried leaves into sweetly smelling potpourris.

II

DEFINITION AND EXPLANATION

Digging and planting in the garden is one way man can engage in the satisfying experience of working hard with his body while planning the next move with his head. Perhaps the reason gardening is so healing to modern man who is speeded up almost beyond endurance by the pulsing beat of machinery is that it requires deliberate, loving hands, and cannot be done in a hurry. Seeds of cumin, anise, and coriander come up with the same gradual unfolding of stem and leaves in our present-day gardens as they did in Egypt and Mesopotamia five thousand years ago. Growing the herbs is an especially delightful form of gardening, for no other group of plants so strongly evokes our sense of smell. Although humble and modest in appearance, because of their potent aromatic, prophylactic, and medicinal qualities, they have been so important to man that he has woven legends and written books about them, and carried them with him in his migrations from India to Asia Minor, from Persia to China, and from Europe to America.

With few exceptions the herbs are not endowed with

conspicuous or brilliantly colored flowers. Theirs is a modest beauty, appreciated by gardeners long at their work who have learned to enjoy the less obvious and more subtle qualities in plants, such as the patterns formed by the leaves and stems of burnet and lavender, the wrinkled surfaces in the leaves of the sages, or the silvery color of some of the artemisias.

According to the dictionary a herb is a plant the stem of which dies down to the ground after flowering, in contrast to the trees and shrubs that have woody and persistent stems. Herbs may be annual, biennial, or perennial, but the word as used in this book is applied to the class of plants some portion of which because of aromatic or healing properties has been used for medicine, perfume, or flavor. A few of the aromatic plants, such as *Thymus vulgaris* and *Satureia montana*, have woody and persistent stems, and are not herbs according to the dictionary but most decidedly so in their characters. The word HERB may be pronounced HÛRB or ÛRB and the first is given preference in my dictionary.

In compiling the list of herbs there have undoubtedly been serious omissions as well as frivolous inclusions and I admit unashamedly that my selection is characterized by an inconsistency generally considered feminine. No two people would choose exactly the same plants and my only hope is that what appealed to me will appeal to the public. A friend said, "You will begin to learn about the herbs when the book has appeared and your readers write to tell you about the ones you have left out and the stories and recipes you have missed." I hope very much my readers will send me any facts they think should have been included, so that if there is a second edition

Salvia officinalis, sage

they can be added, for the subject is so vast it could not possibly be covered at a first attempt.

Herbs used for their medicinal qualities only were omitted because the subject of herbs in medicine requires far more specialized knowledge than could be expected of a mere gardener. Moreover almost every vegetable or fruit produces some effect on man and seems to have been employed for its healing properties at one time or another. The medicinal qualities as recognized in the pharmacopoeias of to-day have been included in the text, because it seemed advisable to tell as much about each of the plants as possible.

With every definition there are always some exceptions which, like the weeds along the edges, blur the clarity of the boundaries. In selecting certain herbs and discarding others therefore it was difficult to know when to exclude the vegetables. A vegetable, it seems to me, differs from a herb because it is eaten for itself, while a herb flavors other dishes. Unfortunately when it comes to classifying them many vegetables are herbs as well, such as fennel, onion, carrot, and celery. Portulaca and sorrel are sometimes classed as herbs, but I felt they belonged over the fence in the vegetable garden and left them out.

The weeds were the next problem in elimination, although many of them are valuable medicinally. In our gardens we cannot grow the ones which increase at such a rapid rate as to crowd out quickly the less vigorous plants.

The dandelion has been excluded in spite of its medicinal and culinary properties and the charm of its fuzzy yellow blossoms against the fresh green of the spring lawns. Pennyroyal, *Mentha pulegium,* is another herb long used medicinally and to flavor the cooking, but it is a pushing plant which creeps along relentlessly on its rootstocks, and has an unattractive smell, so it, too, has been omitted. The leaves of the *Malva rotundifolia* were formerly given as a cathartic because of their mucilaginous quality, but since the plant is weedy and untidy looking it has been left out. The mustards are weeds in this country, but have been described here on account of their importance as condiments. It was difficult to know which of the artemisias to include. All of them have been used medicinally and many in cooking. I left out *Artemisia vulgaris* in spite of its importance in herb lore, because it is no longer useful, and too coarse and spreading to be handsome in the garden.

With a few exceptions such as lemon verbena, rose geranium, and laurel, *Laurus nobilis,* the plants chosen are all hardy and can live through severe winters. We have never tried to grow the Oriental spice-bearing trees, such as nutmeg, *Myristica fragrans*, allspice, *Pimenta officinalis,* or cloves, *Eugenia aromaticus,* all native to the tropics, but they might be worth trying some time. A greenhouse or orangerie filled with them ought to be a most delightfully scented place.

Strawberries and roses are not really herbs, but enter into so many recipes that they have been included. The sweet cicely, burnet, lovage, and fennel flower are all useful, and I was particularly keen on growing and describing them because they seemed to have been forgotten by the present generation of gardeners and cooks. Wintergreen, fraxinella, and bee balm are described because their leaves make fragrant and unusual teas, and I am sorry I could not add the European linden and left it out, although we have the trees planted in many exposures on our place, because the blossoms are only faintly fragrant and like a sickly echo of the positively intoxicating perfume they exhale in France and England, and presumably in Germany, too.

Unless large quantities of violets, primulas, and clove carnations are grown there would not be enough flowers to make up the recipes, but they are included for their beauty, fragrance, and sentimental associations. Without the scent of violets or the presence of the golden cowslips, the herb garden in spring would be bereft of much of its poetry, as it would if the saffron crocus and Florentine iris were left out. Even if a sufficiently large crop of crocuses could be grown for practical purposes, it would not produce as fine a quality of saffron as comes from Asia Minor, nor is it likely that the iris would ever yield as fragrant and delicate an orris powder in most American gardens as it does in northern Italy.

When we go into the garden to gather leaves for the salad, or to give a flowery note to the soup, as we touch the rosemary or basil they give off a perfume so tempting that we put a leaf in our mouths, to taste them. At first we experience only a general sensation because our senses have become atrophied and dulled from disuse, but after a while we detect the fruity, camphoraceous, piny, or spicy elements, and notice that some pucker the tongue while others have a cooling effect. We find some of the leaves taste delightfully and others unpleasantly bitter, and that a few of them taste quite differently when fresh and when dried. As we chew a leaf or smell it, we wonder what it is that gives us these sensations, and when the taste stops and the smell begins. In the mouth, we are told, we can only experience the sensations of hot, and cold, sweet, sour, bitter, and salt and all other sensations come from our sense of smell.

It seems strange that so comparatively small a group of plants should be so fragrant while hundreds of others are not. F. A. Hampton in his book, "The Scent of Flowers and Leaves," thinks the perfume is a protection against the browsing animals who dislike the hot, burning taste of most leaf oils, and in proof of his theory says, "the goats who have denuded most of the vegetation in the Mediterranean basin spare the aromatic plants which compose the scrubby growth largely composed of lavender, rosemary, myrtle, bay, cistus, sage, thyme, and various small aromatic labiates, which give off an unforgetable scent under the hot sun."

In some plants the fragrance acts as a lure to attract the insects so they will carry the pollen from one flower to another and so effect cross-pollination. The fragrance is not always in the corolla, but in the leaves, stamens, or in the calyx as in the lavender. Often at the time of flowering there is a slight elaboration of the leaf oil which gives the general inflorescence a scent, as in the rose geranium, the leaves of which acquire a more flowery character as the buds open. This is also true of many of the labiates such as hyssop, mint, and thyme, which are most fragrant just as the flowers open. This is therefore the precise moment when the leaves should be harvested, for as Charabot says, at fecundation, when there is a slight slowing up of growth, a certain amount of this fragrant oil is used up.

Hampton says the scent of all flowers and most leaves is caused by an essential oil which is well distributed through the whole plant. In the flowers it is sometimes known as an attar, or otto, and this is generally a delicate, complex mixture of substances with a similar but not identical scent, whereas the oil in the leaves is much simpler, has a pungent, sharp, refreshing, and rougher character and contains substances which do not occur in the flowers.

III

THE WRITTEN WORD

In Exodus it is told how the Jews made burnt offerings of incense, and the priests anointed themselves and the sacred vessels with fragrant oils made from myrrh, cinnamon, sweet calamus, and cassia.

Exodus 31:

> This shall be an holy anointing oil unto me throughout your generations. Upon man's flesh shall it not be poured, neither shall ye make any other like it, after the composition of it; it is holy and it shall be holy unto you.

In Matthew, Chapter 23, verse 23, are the lines:

> Woe unto you, scribes and Pharisees, hypocrites! for ye pay tithe of mint and anise and cummin and have omitted the weightier matters of the law, judgment, mercy, and faith; these ought ye to have done and not to leave the other undone.

The first European to write on plants was the Greek Theophrastus, called the father of botany, who was born in 370 B.C. He was a pupil of Plato and later of Aristotle. His writings are fresh and unaffected and give glimpses of everyday life at the height of Greek glory. He describes how perfumes were compounded from thyme, bergamot, mint, saffron, lilies, sweet marjoram, and iris, and mentions the same fixatives and tropical spices as compose the perfumes of to-day. He gives a list of "coronary herbs" and says the garland makers' favorites are the gilliflowers and wallflowers. Speaking of savory, "Inquiry into Plants," he says:

> Savory and still more marjoram has a conspicuous fruitful seed, but in thyme it is not easy to find being somehow mixed up with the flower; for men sow the flower and plants come up from it. This plant is sought and obtained by those in Athens who wish to export such herbs . . . they say it can not be grown or become established where the breeze from the sea does not reach. This is why it does not grow in Arcadia while savory, marjoram and such plants are common in many parts.

He speaks of wild thyme:

> . . . which they bring from the mountains and plant at Sicyon, or from Hymettus and plant at Athens; and in other districts the mountains and hills are quite covered with it, for instance, in Thrace.

And of saffron he says, after describing the leaves:

> The root is large and fleshy and the whole plant vigorous; it loves ever to be trodden on and grows fairer when the root is crushed into the ground by the foot: wherefore it is fairest along the roads and in well-worn places.

Theophrastus must have had numerous followers, because Pliny speaks of having studied five hundred Greek and Roman authors, amongst whom there were surely some botanists and doctors. The three most important writers about plants in classical times are Galen, Dioscorides, and Pliny, because they are continuously quoted by later authors, both Christian and Mohammedan. Until the eighteenth century it was more admirable to be learned than to be original, and most books began with the Creation, even as I am doing now, and often did not travel beyond the Greek and Roman classics.

Claudius Galen, or Galen of Pergamus, lived from 130-200 A.D. and was a physician to Lucius Verus and Marcus Aurelius, and wrote many books. One of his lesser achievements is the invention of Cold Cream. The formula, known as Ceratum Galeni, is given by Piesse, in "The Art of Perfumery." I have had it made up and find it a delightful and most efficacious cream. It may be found on page 284.

Dioscorides Anazarbeus of the first and second century A.D. was another physician whose treatments and remedies were handed down through the centuries. His chief commentator and translator was Matthiolus, the first edition of whose works appeared in 1544.

Caius Plinius Secundus, known as Pliny, was born in A.D. 23. He was a traveler, soldier, administrator in Spain, and courtier, yet he found time to acquire the entire sum of human knowledge of his day. Much of his work was a compilation from his reading, but he also included his own observations. His easy, gossipy style is so amusing that it is not at all surprising his writings have delighted all scholars from his day to ours. It has been difficult to limit oneself to quoting only a few lines from "Natural History" translated by John Bostock, and H. T. Riley, 1856, Bohn Classical Library, Book XIX, Chapter 46:

Parsley is sown immediately after the vernal equinox, the seed being lightly beaten first in a mortar. It is thought that by doing this the parsley will be all the more crisped, or else by taking care to beat it down, when sown, with a roller or the feet. It is a peculiarity of this plant that it changes color; it has the honour in Achaia of forming the wreath of the victors in the sacred contests of the Nemean Games.

Chapter 53—The Poppy:

. . . That the poppy has always been held in high esteem among the Romans, we have proof in the story related of Tarquinius Superbus, who, by striking down the tallest poppies in his garden, surreptitiously conveyed his sanguinary message, unknown to them, through the envoys who had been sent by his son.

Chapter 57—The Maladies of Garden Plants:

The garden plants, too, like the rest of the vegetable productions, are subject to certain maladies. Thus, for instance, ocimum, when old, degenerates into wild thyme and sisymbrium into mint, while the seeds of old cabbage produce rape and vice versa. . . .

Out of the classical writers about herbs grew the herbals, which were generally ponderous tomes, containing a compilation of herb lore from previous writers with more or less contemporary material added. They are a mixed border in which medicinal remedies, cookery recipes, and botanical descriptions of plants are intermingled, and must have constituted valuable household encyclopedias for the castles and monasteries that possessed them.

The first herbals were manuscripts, and a very early one is that of Apuleius Platonicus, who lived in Africa in the fourth or fifth century, which is thought to be based on Dioscorides. It was repeatedly copied and one of these made in England in A.D. 1100 finally came to the Bodleian Library. This has been reproduced in modern days by the Oxford University Press. Gunther, who wrote the introduction, when speaking of the illustrations, says that although the original paintings which illustrated these early herbals may have been from nature, through repeated copying they became more and more conventionalized until they ceased to bear any likeness to the plants they were supposed to represent. Furthermore, the plants from which the first pictures were taken belonged to a southern flora and were not available to the artist who was doing the illustrations.

From the first, the plants were described in the herbals more or less as in Gerard's which appeared in 1597, where the headings were as follows: The Kindes, The Descriptions, The Place (where to "set" them), The Time (when they flower), The Names (names in many languages), The Temperature (it was thought all plants were either hot or cold in their effects), and The Vertues.

The printed herbals first appeared during the last quarter of the fifteenth century and from then until the end of the seventeenth a large crop of them grew in Germany, France, England, and Italy. The authors copied from each other, stole one another's plates, and behaved in general—shall we say—with medieval morality? The influence of the classical authorities was strong and the herbalist spent much time in commenting and wondering which plants growing in England or France would fit the descriptions of Galen or Pliny.

Arabic Spain contributed a share to herb lore, and although this has been translated into European languages only since the first half of the nineteenth century, the Arabic practices in agriculture had been carried wherever the Spaniards settled colonies. The writings of Ibn Baithar, a physician and botanist who lived in Malaga in the thirteenth century, have been translated into German. He, too, quotes from Galen and Dioscorides, but he also quotes from Arabic, Persian, Syrian, and Indian sources. Another writer was Ibn Al Awam, who called himself "The Illustrious Sheik," and lived and gardened near Seville. In his "The Book of Agriculture," written in 1158, which has come to us in a French translation, he described his own gardening experiences and those of his neighbors and also quotes from classical and Mesopotamian authorities. As with all Mohammedans, who are forbidden to drink wine, he stressed the distinctions between different waters, and when he speaks of the violet he says:

> The violet only likes soft light waters from rivers and fountains, heavy waters such as come from wells render it languishing and often kill it. . . . it should not come into contact with dust from a tomb nor with earth coming from cemeteries; that would cause it to weaken and a lengthy contact might cause complete destruction.

Of lavender, he says:

> The Persians are enthusiastic about the virtues of this plant; they consider it as an object of benediction; they say if one gazes upon it for a long while the soul experiences a joy, and that it dissipates sorrow, which comes from an unknown cause . . .

Slowly the roots of horticulture and botany were shaken free from their entanglements with medicine and magic, although they were still intertwined with cookery. By the end of the sixteenth century, books which combined gardening and cookery appeared in France and England.

"Les Délices de la Campagne," written by Louis XIV'S valet, Nicolas de Bonnefons, appeared in Paris in 1654. "The Delights of the Country" consisted in growing one's vegetables and then eating them as well as the birds and game from one's country estate. The details of the recipes are lingered over as if the author thoroughly enjoyed preparing a salad or a roast. I give one entitled "Little herbs of all kinds for salads" from Chapter XXIX:

> Tarragon, samphire, cress, *La Trippe Madame, La Corne du Bœuf, Herbe a l'Évêque* or corn salad, anise and a thousand others, flowers as well as herbs, serve to compose the little salad, dressed with oil or sugar which the more agreeable they are the more amusement they furnish: anise serves also to put into a glass to give to the wine of its taste and fragrance.

In England, Gervase Markham's books were a combination of gardening and cooking. In "The English Housewife, Containing the Inward and Outward Virtues Which Ought to be in a Compleat Woman," he gives recipes, some of which are so rich that it is no wonder gout, jaundice, and other results of luxurious eating were widespread.

Contemporary with these were treatises containing practical directions for farming and gardening, such as Jean de La Quintinye's "Instructions pour les Jardins, Fruitiers et Potagers," which went into many editions and was translated into English by John Evelyn in 1673. Quintinye had charge of the vegetable garden of Louis XIV, which still exists at Versailles, and he describes the herbs from the point of view of an experienced gardener.

John Parkinson, in his "Paradisi in Sole," London, 1629, which in my opinion is the finest garden book ever

Thymus vulgaris, common thyme

written, describes the plants he grew in his garden in Shakespeare's English. This was before the invention of botanical terminology, as the following quotations show:

> The ordinary Garden Thyme is a small woody plant with brittle branches, and small hard greene leaues, as every one knoweth hauing small white purplish flowers, standing round about the tops of the stalkes: the seed are small and browne, darker than Maieirome seed: the root is woody and abideth well diuers Winters.
>
> Dill doth much growe wilde, but because in many place it cannot be had, it is therefore sowne in Gardens, for the uses whereunto it serueth. It is a smaller herbe than Fennell, but very like, hauing fine cut leaves, not so large, but shorter, smaller and of a stronger, quicker taste: the stalke is smaller also, and with few joynts and leaues on them, bearing spoakie tufts of yellow flowers, which turne into thinne, small and flat seedes: the roote perished euery yeare, and riseth againe for the most part of its owne sowing.

At this time it was the custom for literary noblemen to collect recipes while they were making the Grand Tour. Sir Kenelm Digby did this and so did his contemporary, John Evelyn, the diarist. "The Closet" of Sir Kenelm Digby, which appeared in 1669, reads like the excerpts from the diary of a gallant, as for example his gossipy comment upon the recipe of "The White Metheglin of My Lady Hungerford":

> "Since my Lady Hungerford sent me this receipt, she sent me word that she now useth (and liketh better) to make the Decoction of Herbs before you put the honey into it."

John Evelyn was so much interested in gardening and farming that he translated several French books on the subject besides writing his own "Acetaria, A Discourse on Sallets," which appeared in 1699.

Evelyn presented the case of the vegetarian as follows:

> Certain it is, Almighty God ordaining Herbs and Fruits for the Food of Men speaks not a Word concerning Flesh for two thousand years. . . . And what if it was held undecent and unbecoming the Excellency of Man's Nature, before Sin entered, and grew enormously wicked, that any Creature should be put to Death and Pain for him, who had such infinite store of the most delicious and nourishing Fruit to delight, and the Tree of Life to sustain him?

He continues to say that man naturally went to the fruits for his food, and that the poets, recounting the happiness of the Golden Age, speak of "Their innocent and healthful lives in that delightful Garden."

In describing how to flavor a sallet, he says:

> Every plant should bear its part without being overpower'd by some Herb of stronger taste, so as to endanger the native Sapor and Vertue of the rest; but fall into their places like Notes in Music, in which should be nothing harsh or grating and tho admitting some discords (to distinguish and illustrate the next) striking in the more sprightly and sometimes gentler notes reconcile all dissonances and melt them into an agreeable composition.

However, no herbal with its meticulous descriptions of plants, nor even the cook book which causes our mouths to water when we read about the delicate flavors of the herbs, can compare with the poetic renderings we find in Shakespeare, as when Perdita in "The Winter's Tale," says:

. . . Here's flowers for you;
Hot lavender, mints, savory, marjoram;
The marigold, that goes to bed wi' the sun
And with him rises weeping: these are flowers
Of middle summer, and I think they are given
To men of middle age. . . .

and the verse from "A Midsummer Night's Dream":

I know a bank where the wild thyme blows,
Where oxlips and the nodding violet grows,
Quite over-canopied with luscious woodbine,
With sweet musk-roses and with eglantine: . . .

IV

THE WITCHES' CAULDRON

The cuttings and seeds of the herbs were carried from East to West by men in their wanderings, and with the plants came the myths and legends about them. The story about the laurel, said to be of Vedic origin, is here given in its Greek version. Apollo, it seems, fell in love with the nymph Daphne and she, not desiring his attentions, ran away from him. He pursued her and as he was gaining upon her, in her anguish she called upon the Gods to help her. They took pity on her and to protect her from him they changed her into a laurel tree. This transformation, however, did not lessen Apollo's love and ever afterwards he wore wreaths made of laurel leaves, and groves of this tree surrounded his temple.

When we read how the herbs have been employed from the earliest times down to the present, we learn what the people have eaten, of their illnesses and how they tried to cure them, of their wounds and infections, their fears and superstitions, and altogether we follow the intimate and personal side of history.

Through necessity primitive people had to know the

medicinal qualities of plants. Even to-day the American Indians heal the sick with herbs; for example, maidenhair fern, *Adiantum pedatum*, is taken as an emetic, black snakeroot, *Cimicifuga racemosa*, as an antidote for snake bite, and American pennyroyal, *Hedeoma pulegioides*, for colic and colds.

Much of the early herb lore was empiric, but a large portion of it had no other basis than superstition. A strange, but quite comprehensible, reason for attributing certain qualities to the herbs was their physical appearance. Rupturewort, *Herniaria*, was expected to cure ruptures because of its knot-like flowers, while throatwort, *Campanula trachelium*, with its throat-like corolla, was thought to be healing for diseases of the trachea. This was the "Doctrine of Signatures," and Mrs. Arber in her book, "Herbals," quotes an amusing example, relative to this, from a seventeenth century English translation of Paracelsus:

> I have ofttimes declared how by outward shapes and qualities of things we know their inward virtues which God put in them for the good of man. So in St. Johnswort, we may take notice of the form of the leaves. The Veins 1. The porosities of the holes in the leaves signify to us that this herb helps both inward and outward holes or cuts in the skin. . . . 2. The flowers of St. Johnswort when they are putrefied they are like blood which teacheth us that this herb is good for wounds, to close them and fill them up.

In the convents and monasteries, as well as within the castles' walls, herbs were grown and dried according to the directions of Pliny, Galen, and Dioscorides, but when the flowers in the woods and fields were in blossom the herb women, often considered witches, who knew where to find the plants went out from the villages to pick them. There were traditions as to which day was the best for gathering them, when, for one reason or another, they would be most efficacious. August 15th, the day of the Ascension of the Virgin Mary, was one, and St. John's Day, June 24th, the day of the summer solstice, was another.

There was a superstition that in order to be effective the bunch of herbs should consist of nine different kinds, and often the number, three or nine, was more important than the particular botanical specimen. Various combinations of plants were thought to be potent, and the following in which the initial letters of the herbs spell Johannes, John, or St. John is characteristic:

Jarum—possibly, *Carum Carvi, Caraway*
Origanum—marjoram
Herb benedictu—a valerian
Allium—onion or chives
Nigella—*Nigella sativa;* fennel flower
Nebelkraut—could not find
Extrementa diaboli—could not find
Succisa—a scabiosa

Some plants were thought to have a benign effect whilst others brought evil in their wake. The salutary plants were southernwood, rosemary (which was effective against witchcraft), lavender (against the evil eye), bracken, ground ivy, maidenhair fern, dill, hyssop, agrimony, and angelica which in Esthonia was rubbed on the body of the person affected by magic to cure him of his "possession." Yellow and green flowers growing in hedgerows were supposed to be especially repugnant to witches.

Other herbs had the opposite effect and were the means of invoking evil spirits. Mrs. Leyel in the "Magic of Herbs," says that the sinister herbs were vervain, betony, yarrow, mugwort, and St. Johns-Wort, this last, according to Paracelsus, used to exorcise them. She writes that it was thought that if coriander, parsley, hemlock, liquid of black poppy, fennel, sandalwood, and henbane were laid in a heap and burnt together they would call forth a whole army of demons.

Although in most garden books there is no sex interest, the herbals have recipes for love potions, and strangely enough most of the visitors to the herb garden ask about these. Southernwood, *Artemisia abrotanum*, was a favorite erotic herb and it was thought that if a girl put a sprig of it down her back she would marry the first boy she met, or if she placed a sprig of it under her pillow at night, the first man she met in the morning was the one she was to marry. Wagner in his opera "Tristan and Isolde," the story of which is taken from an old Germanic epic, has Isolde give a love potion to Tristan, after which the audience sits through three-quarters of an hour of passionate music until the drink takes effect.

In "A Midsummer Night's Dream," Oberon tells Puck to fetch love-in-idleness which was a name for the pansy, to bewitch Titania:

> And maidens call it love-in-idleness.
> Fetch me that flower; the herb I shew'd thee once:
> The juice of it on sleeping eyelids laid
> Will make or man or woman madly dote
> Upon the next live creature that it sees.

Other herbs are said to have aphrodisiac qualities. The water distilled from the leaves and flowers of myrtle has been used in every country as a love philter, as have the waters of dill and savory, while the essences and the distilled leaves of balm and mint are aphrodisiac, too, which last makes one a little fearful of mint sauce. Beside these, vervain, jasmine, coriander, wild poppy, anemone, purslane, crocus, malefern, periwinkle, lettuce, carrots, and endive are all considered to be of an erotic nature, and Mrs. Leyel says they were often combined with cantharides, a very poisonous aphrodisiac.

Sweet marjoram crowned the brows of young married couples; cumin and rosemary were more for remembrance than to stir the passions. When a swain went to the wars far from home his sweetheart would give him a loaf of bread, or a cup of wine seasoned with cumin to prevent his being untrue to her.

A quotation from "the Gudrunlied," the source of Wagner's "Ring," shows how herb drinks were given to induce forgetfulness, as when Gudrun, telling of her grief for Sigurd, says:

> Criemhild brachte
> das becher mir dar
> den Kalten herben
> dass des Grams vergesse.

This means that Criemhild brought Gudrun a cold drink concocted of herbs to cause her to forget her sorrow.

All this sounds remote and childish to us, but even to-day in our scientifically ordered world and in such a sophisticated city as New York, there are shops where powdered herbs are sold, not only for medicine but for "concentration work," love potions and the like.

Herbs were not used, however, entirely in fantastic and

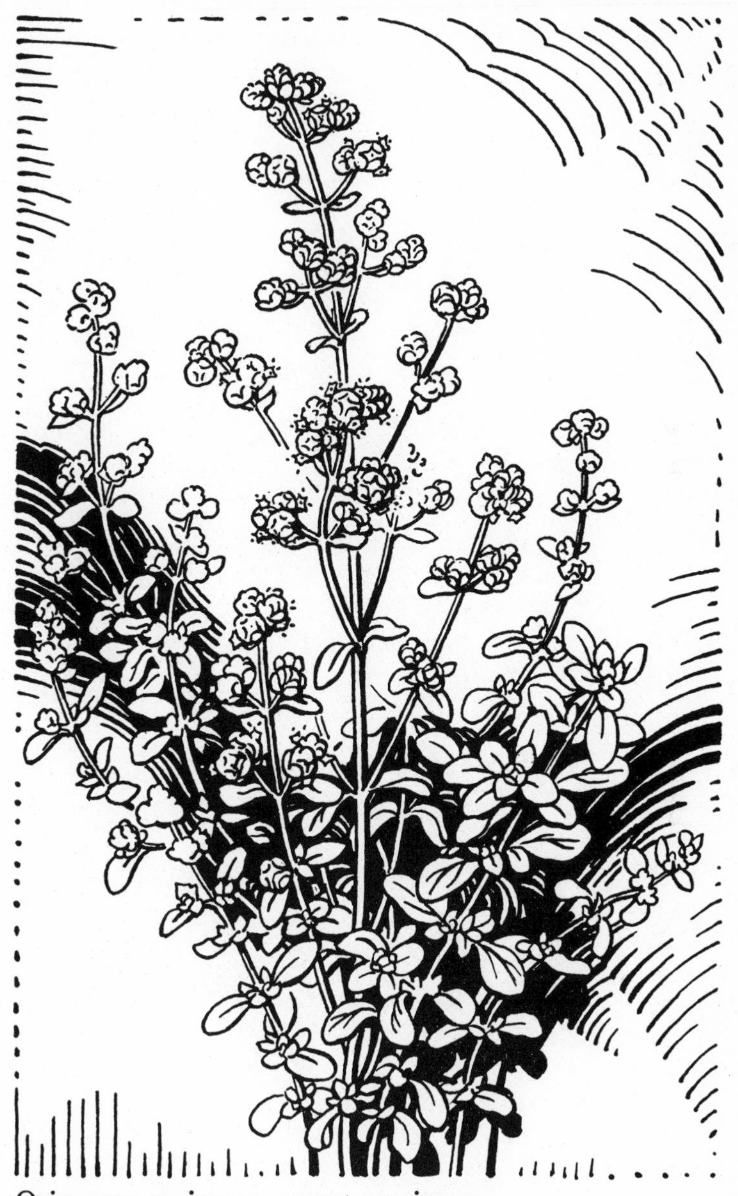

Origanum majorana, sweet marjoram

romantic ways. In northern countries, before they had rugs, some of them were strewn on the floors of churches and castles for warmth, and so provided a slightly refined version of the bedding of hay in the barn. Lavender, thyme, *Acorus calamus*, the mints, basils, balm, hyssop, and santolina were used for this, and were called Strewing Herbs. Marjoram was scattered over church floors at funerals for its supposed antiseptic qualities.

Northern people were not finicky about being overcome by the fumes of wine and the wassail was drunk to the sound of music, but the Greeks and Romans wore chaplets of saffron crocus, parsley, or rue to protect them from inebriation or perhaps to prolong their ability to soberly enjoy their drinking.

Unless we have sojourned in remote portions of Europe or the Orient, those of us who have grown up in cities with modern sewage and plumbing, cannot imagine what life under less hygienic conditions is like, and how important it was to have sweet-smelling plants and stimulating perfumes. In Roman times the theaters were sprinkled with saffron water, and at dinner parties the floors were strewn with rose petals, while rose-scented fountains perfumed the air. At the religious festivals of the Jews, Greeks, and Romans the sacrificial animals were filled with fragrant unguents to disguise the odor of burning flesh and also to keep the flies and vermin away. Incense is burned in all Oriental and many Occidental churches to-day during the litany partly for its stimulating and pleasant qualities.

When there were no ice boxes to keep the food fresh, the meats and fish were strongly spiced with herbs to disguise the taste of decomposition, and Pliny tells how the Roman cooks sprinkled coriander and mustard over the meats.

Herbs may not be disinfectants in a modern sense, yet in olden days they were thought to be, and extracts from them were mixed into vinegars as preventatives against infection from the plagues. The famous vinegar of the Four Thieves made during the plague at Marseilles in 1722 was used by the thieves to protect them from contagion when robbing the bodies of the dead. Piesse's "The Art of Perfumery" gives the recipe for it:

Take the tops of common wormwood, Roman wormwood, rosemary, sage, mint, and rue of each ¾ ounce, lavender flowers 1 ounce, garlic, calamus aromaticus, cinnamon, cloves and nutmeg each 1 drachm, camphor ½ ounce, alcohol or brandy 1 ounce, strong vinegar 4 pints. Digest all the materials except the camphor and spirit in a closely covered vessel for fourteen days at summer heat; then express and filter the vinegar produced and add camphor previously dissolved in brandy or spirit.

The dried petals and leaves of the herbs and other fragrant flowers were mixed with fixatives and placed in open jars in rooms where the warmth of the fires in winter caused them to give forth a flower-like fragrance reminiscent of summer, and no doubt were most grateful where plumbing was unknown and closed windows the rule. These potpourris are pleasant in any drawing-room in winter and are much used in England to-day.

Sometimes the essences from the herbs were diffused through hospitals or homes to dissipate unpleasant odors. One way of doing this is described in the "Toilet of Flora," published in 1775, as follows:

Take a root of angelica, dry it in the oven or before the fire, then bruise it well and infuse it four or five days in white wine vinegar. To make use of it heat a brick red hot and lay the angelica root upon the brick. The vapour that exhales therefrom is a powerful corrective of putrid air. The operation must be repeated several times.

The housewife made her own salves, powders, and cosmetics with herbs, and the recipes for homemade tooth washes, mustache dyes, and toilet waters in the old books sound quaint to us. The ingredients for the following aromatic baths for the feet, from the "Toilet of Flora," would probably all be growing in the herb garden, with the possible exception of juniper berries:

Take four handfuls of pennyroyal, sage, rosemary, three handfuls of angelica and four ounces of juniper berries; boil these ingredients in a sufficient quantity of water and strain off the liquor for use.

Take two pounds of barley, one pound of rice, three pounds of lupines all finely powdered, eight pounds of bran and ten handfuls of borage and violet leaves. Boil these ingredients in a sufficient quantity of water. Nothing cleanses and softens the skin as this bath.

Bees love the herbs and on a warm summer day the herb garden throbs with the sound of their humming. The thyme, lavender, bee balm, balm, marjoram, rosemary, sage, and savory were often planted near beehives to flavor the honey. In ancient days and even now Attic honey from Mount Hymettus is valued for its taste of wild thyme as is the Swiss honey which greets us at our first breakfast in the Spotless Republic.

The oils from the seeds of the herbs, such as those of sweet cicely, and the oil from the plants of sweet marjoram and of lavender were used to polish the oaken floors and the furniture which must have imparted a spicy scent to the rooms.

Last, and most important of all uses of herbs, is their function as condiments in food and drink. When we study the flavorings of our ancestors we find that we still prepare our meals much as they did and that our food has changed as little as human nature itself. The onion, garlic, chives, and shallot have flavored food from Egyptian days, and perhaps earlier; caraway seeds were found in the débris of the lake dwellings of Switzerland, and seeds of coriander in the Egyptian tombs of the Twenty-first Dynasty. Mustard has been a condiment from Brahman times, while mint has gone with lamb, dill with cucumbers, horseradish with beef, and sage with roast goose down through the ages.

Scattering poppy seeds on breads and cakes is so old a custom that the directions for making the seeds stick are found in Pliny, who says:

> The present-day country people sprinkle it on the upper crust of their bread making it adhere by the yolk of eggs, the under crust being seasoned with parsley to heighten the flavor of the flour.

And speaking of mint, he says it is a stimulant to the appetite and you will not see a husbandman's board in the country but all the meats from one end to the other are seasoned with mint, which sounds as if it might be a description of a present-day dinner in an English inn.

The seeds of fennel flowers, anise, sesame, caraway, and coriander have flavored bread and cake from the earliest days and for hundreds of years and even to-day the Europeans aromatize their beers, ales, and meads with the roots of elecampane and sweet cicely, the flowers and leaves of borage, and the leaves of costmary, wormwood, thyme, and mint to mention only a few. Rose petals and violet flowers may have been sugared first in Persia, but they can be bought in modern confectioners' shops to-day.

From time to time new plants were added to the menu, brought home by soldiers and merchants from distant lands. About the year 800 A.D. Charlemagne issued an order to his people to grow certain herbs and vegetables in their gardens, and this shows us what the European gardens contained then and for many centuries afterwards.

ORIGINAL ORDER OF CHARLES THE GREAT

We desire that they have in the garden all the herbs namely, the lily, roses, fenugreek, costmary, sage, rue, southernwood, cucumbers, pole beans, cumin, rosemary, caraway, chick pea, squill, iris, arum, anise, coloquinth, chicory, animi, laserwort, lettuce, black cumin, garden rocket, nasturtium, burdock, pennyroyal, alexander, parsley, celery, lovage, sabine tree, dill, fennel, endive, dittany, black mustard, savory, curly mint, water mint, horse mint, tansy, catnip, feverfew, poppy, beet sugar, marshmallows, high mallows, carrots, parsnips, oraches, amaranths, kohlrabis, cabbages, onions, chives, leeks, radishes, shallots, garlics, madder, artichokes or fulling thistles, big beans, field peas, coriander, chervil, capper spurge, clary.*

All through the Dark and Middle Ages the chatelaine in her garden, the monk in his tiny patch, and each villager in his front dooryard grew a large proportion of herbs amongst the plants. Every plant grown was made

*** From Pertz Monumenta Germania Historica, 1834, vol. 3, page 168, from Liek and Brendle, "Plant Names of the Pennsylvania Germans."**

to yield its utmost harvest. The seeds of cumin, coriander, fennel, and anise were crushed for their oil, and the juice was extracted from the wormwood leaves to flavor the fragrant liqueurs colored like emeralds or rubies which the monks brewed and sipped after a goodly repast as they sat in their spacious refectories.

With few roads, and those almost impassable, green vegetables could not be brought from warmer lands in the winter, nor were there any means for forcing them, so the dried herbs were most welcome and provided the vitamins absent from the winter diet, although they were, of course, not recognized as such. In spring, when the first leaves of tansy, sorrel, or sage showed green amongst the withered stems they were picked and either brewed in a tea or eaten as a "tansy"—that is an omelette into which the juice of the herbs has been stirred. The preparation of the first tansy of spring was almost a religious rite.

The superstitions, legends, and practices in regard to the herbs which existed in Europe were brought to the colonies by the settlers who continued many of the old ways of preparing medicines and flavoring their foods with them. In time they discarded some and when they came into contact with the Indians adopted new ones based on American plants and colored with Indian stories and beliefs.

V

HERBS IN THE UNITED STATES

As the settlers coming to the newly discovered land in North America sailed up the Hudson and the James rivers, how beautiful the shores must have looked to them after three months of cramped confinement in their tiny boats. Great trees, like the elms and oaks at home and yet slightly different, towered above them, while thick shrubs hung over the banks and dipped their branches in the water. When they went ashore they found familiar grasses and ferns carpeting the ground while strange flowers dotted the meadows and grew shyly under the trees. The roses, artemisias, strawberries, and garlic were so similar to the plants they had grown in their own forsaken gardens that they attributed the same qualities to these American herbs that had characterized their European relatives.

Many of the colonists had left their old homes because of an unwillingness or inability to accept the prevailing conditions, yet once they arrived in the new country they shaped their lives after the pattern of the ones they had led before. They sent to England for domestic animals and seeds, and along with the wheat, barley and clovers, and the straw beddings of the horses and pigs, came the seeds of daisies, dandelions, and buttercups which multiplied so quickly that they soon added a gold and white note to every landscape.

In the South, as early as 1495, Hernán Cortéz wrote to the King of Spain asking him to give orders at the Casa de Contracion at Seville that every ship leaving for "The Indies" was to bring seeds and plants in its cargo. These were distributed over the Spanish colonies in Mexico and our own Southwest.

Fortunately for the settlers, when their supply of provisions dwindled the Indians helped them out with food and gave them seeds to enable them to raise crops of their own. They taught the white men how to grow corn, Jerusalem artichoke, *Helianthus tuberosa*, lima beans, kidney beans, squashes, and ground nuts, *Apios tuberosa.*

As was to be expected of so primitive a civilization, the Indians used few flavorings in preparing their food. They ate wild onions and the roots of wild caraway, *Carvum Kellogii*, and cooked tubers of *Asclepias tuberosa* with buffalo meat, skunkweed with deer, and tubers of *Asclepias syriaca* and *Monarda menthaefolia* with other meats. It is said that the leaves of *Mentha canadensis* were placed *in the parflèches* to flavor dried meat, but one wonders whether this was a pre-Columbian or post-Mayflower custom. Roots of wild ginger, *Asarum canadense,* were gathered to season hominy grits and also to disguise the taste of mudfish and of animals long dead, for it was thought they eliminated the danger of poisoning.

Mrs. Earle tells us that in New England, until very

late, many of the herb gatherers were squaws who brought various roots and barks to market to serve as flavorings for the colonial beers.

The newcomers could not depend on native plants for flavoring and soon imported seeds and slips of the aromatic herbs. Besides these, the Reverend Francis Higginson says that amongst the New Englanders watercress was a garnish, potherb, and salad plant, and that *Sedum telephium,* potato tops, pepper grass, and smart weed, *Polygonum persicari,* were used with other potherbs to give them a better flavor. Adrian van der Donck in describing the plants he grew in his garden in Yonkers in 1653 mentioned herbs such as, "angelica, *calamus aromaticus, malva origaenum,* geranium, *altheae,* viola, iris, *indigo silvestris,* coriander, leeks, wild leeks—." According to John Josselyn of Kent, who wrote letters in 1673 and 1674 describing two visits to his brother who had settled in Maine, a great many herbs were being grown. Even though the mistakes have been corrected and the whole edited by Edward Tuckerman, these letters, I fear, are tinted with the rosy hue of imagination.

In South Carolina, where great plantations were owned by cultivated people, Mrs. Logan compiled a "Gardener's Chronicle" which appeared in 1756 and was the pioneer of feminine garden books in America. She tells when to plant the vegetables and flowers and groups all the herbs together under "Aromatick herbs" except parsley, red pepper, onions, and water and garden cresses, which she mentions separately.

Thomas Jefferson, besides his many talents and accomplishments, was a great farmer, and in his "Notes on Virginia" classified his plants as Medicinal, Esculent,

Ornamental, and Useful for Fabrication. The only herbs he mentions are *Malva rotundifolia, Angelica sylvestris* (a native), and the strawberries, but elsewhere in a letter he speaks of savory.

To find out what herbs were grown in the colonies I looked through the files of old newspapers but gleaned comparatively little. In the *South Carolina Gazette* in 1735 was the following:

> Just imported from London to be sold by John Watson . . . mustard seed,

and in the same paper, December 28, 1738:

> Just imported from London to be sold by Doctor Jacob Moon . . . anis seeds, carraway seeds, sweet fennel seeds.

In the *Virginia Gazette*, published at Williamsburg, Virginia, on September 9, 1675, was the item:

> To be sold at Mr. Miles Taylor's in the Town of Richmond, the following seeds, lately imported from Italy, viz. Sweet Basil, citron ditto, Chervil, Poppy, Sweet Fennil.

The catalogues of the Bartram nurseries in Philadelphia, published in 1807 and 1814, offered many herbs for sale, as did the catalogues of Prince's nursery at Flushing, Long Island, which first appeared in 1771. In 1801, at the threshold of the nineteenth century, Stearns wrote "The American Herbal," which told of the herbs used for medicine.

All this time, from the seventeenth to the nineteenth centuries, the colonial housewives had to supervise or do their own growing and harvesting of herbs. Living in a wilderness separated from any near-by source of supply, they were forced to provide as liberally as they could for food and medicine during the coming year. All through the growing season, as the fruits and vegetables ripened, everything that could be of any possible use was dried or preserved. Liquid extracts of herbs were done up for medicine or flavor, bunches of them were tied to the rafters to dry, while the dried leaves and flowers were mixed into potpourris or infused in vinegars.

We envy the colonial women their homy activities in their pleasant, pine-paneled kitchens opening onto gardens fragrant with thymes, sages, and mints. We picture the mistress in her crisp fichu and frilly cap, her sleeves rolled up and a big white apron protecting her flowered dress, busily at work with her sisters and perhaps the children to help and run last-minute errands. Perhaps, after the day's work was over, the mistress would sit in front of a wood fire and by candlelight write out the recipes in a book. There was no need to seek abroad for a career as an outlet for her creative instincts, for while she cooked and brewed she was inventing and creating at home.

In these manuscript cook books the herbs and other ingredients for making jams and jellies are mentioned as well as recipes for every variety of dish which was served to the colonial family. Sassafras flavored New Orleans gumbo; rose water exalted a wedding cake; the chicken dressing of Sally Washington had thyme in it. We can almost smell the fragrance which rises from "smothered veal" as the cover is lifted off the dish, for into this went parsley, thyme, carrots, turnips, roast chestnuts, potatoes, onions, and celery root. In Louisiana, the French flavored their foods with saffron, bay leaves, thyme, cloves, garlic, cayenne pepper, mustard, tomato, and parsley. Out West in countries settled by the Spaniards, marjoram gave a special note to chili peppers, and when a brown soup stock was made it had thyme, marjoram, and parsley chopped up and dropped into it. Other Spanish herb flavorings were coriander, saffron, cumin, anise, and sesame.

During the nineteenth century, cook books of American origin were published and the titles of some indicate the thrift and efficiency which was to become characteristic. Among these were Dalgairns, "Practice of Cookery Adapted to the Business of Everyday Life," Boston, 1830; Mrs. Mary Randolph, "The Virginia Housewife," Baltimore, 1823; Mrs. Eliza Leslie, "Directions for Cookery," Philadelphia, 1830; and Mrs. Child, "The American Frugal Housewife," the first edition of many, appearing in Boston in 1829. In these books, nasturtium, a South American plant, and peppers from New Mexico, were the new herbs mentioned.

With the introduction of steam transportation, spices like mace, cloves, and allspice could be bought cheaply at the grocer's and these, with tomatoes from the garden, gradually replaced the old-time herbs, which had been so popular during the preceding centuries. There was no longer the same leisurely savoring of food, nor were whole days spent in the preparation of a festive dinner. The decline in taste which showed itself in furniture, architecture, and gardens was also evident in cooking.

The Negroes and the newest arrivals to our shores still use the fragrant herbs and up to last year the Negro women brought their bunches of thyme and sage to sell in the market in Washington. In Italian districts one can buy fennel at the greengrocer's, and often a pot of basil stands on the window ledge of their homes to furnish the flavoring for their favorite bean soup. The Greeks grow sage for their cheeses and other dishes, and the Negroes use sesame seeds. The French and Swiss like chives as was once conspicuously demonstrated by a new gardener who, when he brought the crates and boxes of his household possessions, had a flat full of growing chives perched on top of them as the chief god of all.

From time to time herbs have been raised commercially in the United States. The Shakers are said to have been the first to grow medicinal plants for profit. Early in the nineteenth century this became an important industry with them, and by the fifties there were nearly two hundred acres under cultivation in the Shaker communities at Harvard, Massachusetts, and at Mount Lebanon, New York. The principal herb crops were *Hyoscyamus,* Belladonna, *Taraxacum,* aconite, poppy, lettuce, sage, summer savory, marjoram, dock, burdock, valerian, and horehound. Besides these, fifty others were grown as minor crops amongst which were rue, borage, plumeless thistle, *Carduus*, hyssop, marshmallow, feverfew, and pennyroyal.

Peppermint and spearmint have long been grown commercially in Michigan and New York to flavor the national vice, the graceless chewing gum. Since it is becoming increasingly difficult to collect plants of ginseng and golden seal which are used medicinally they are now grown under cultivation.

There have been attempts to grow perfume plants such as rose geranium in California and Florida in 1914–1917, so far unsuccessfully, but surely there must be some bit of littoral, or protected valley where clary, sage, rosemary, marjoram, or lavender could be raised satisfactorily in spite of our sharp changes in temperature, which are not as favorable to the storage of essential oil as is the more equable climate of Europe. However, growing herbs has not been profitable as yet in the United States, because too much high-priced hand labor is required in harvesting and curing them to compete with the much cheaper labor in Europe. Every now and then some one has the inspiration which he thinks is entirely original with him of growing or collecting herbs for profit, and forthwith shares this with the United States Government. To satisfy these people, the Department of Agriculture has grown many of the herbs and published bulletins about them.

There are drug gardens in the United States connected with colleges of pharmacy, or State universities, and one is on the grounds of a hospital. These show the students what the plants are like, and remind one of the numerous small botanical gardens connected with hospitals and universities in Europe which began as sources of supply for medicines.

Recently there has been a renaissance of interest in herbs for flavor and fragrance, and it is to be hoped that the patch given over to them will grow in dimensions and in the variety of plants, so that once again, this time in the most modern kitchens where electric appliances and aluminum pots stand side by side with peasant pottery, the housewife, trim and neat, will go back to preparing dishes redolent of the aromatic fragrances which characterized the food of her ancestors who first came to these shores.

VI

IN THE GARDEN

Herbs come readily from seed and are not finical or difficult to raise. Many of them are natives of the lands surrounding the Mediterranean, where they grow on dry, poor, and often rocky ground, and that is why they like a warm, sunny exposure, preferably facing south or east, and a well-drained, dry soil. As with all general statements, however, there are the usual exceptions; tarragon does well planted close to a wall or hedge where it is shaded for a portion of the day, while sweet woodruff grows in the woods, and most of the mints thrive in a moist soil. Except these, herbs will grow in any garden soil provided it is not too rich. Plants grown in too rich a soil are apt to be leggy and produce an essential oil poor in fragrant essences, while those raised in a comparatively lean soil will be compact and bushy and produce a more concentrated oil.

With the growing of herbs, as with all plants, the better the soil is prepared in advance of sowing the seed, the stronger and healthier the crop will be. The ground should be spaded to a depth of from eighteen inches to two feet, forked two or three times, and then finished off by a final patting and smoothing to give it a finely pulverized surface. When the soil is friable the roots do not stay near the surface where they dry out in periods of drouth, but grow deep down where they almost always find some moisture. Strong, deep roots anchor the plants against winds and heavy rains.

In the spring after the last killing frosts are over, generally from the end of April into early June in the northeastern states, it is safe to plant the herb seeds. Since almost every seed in the packet comes up, they are sown thinly and then lightly covered by sifting a little soil over them. The seeds are pressed down firmly with a board and if the ground is very dry they are watered. When they are about two or three inches high, if they are too thick, they are thinned out, to give those remaining room to grow and spread. They require almost no care except pulling out the weeds by hand from time to time and cultivating them after a rain. During three summers' experience with them the only pests have been a solitary attack of aphids on the wormwood and costmary. The other herbs have been perfectly healthy and clean and have grown lustily. In fact, as I write, during a long dry spell in July, the herbs look more cheerful and fresher than any other group of plants and not one of them is drooping or wan like some of the phloxes and roses. Watering is likely to cause the soil to bake, particularly if it is of a clayey consistency. I have raised seedlings during a season when it hardly rained at all without any watering, but I did keep a fine dust mulch around the plants to prevent the evaporation of the moisture which was already there. It is not necessary to shade the young seedlings.

Most of the annuals take from two to three months to flower, and, therefore if planted in May, will be ripe for harvesting early in August. A few, such as summer savory and borage, ripen quickly and then run to seed. If a continuous supply is desired, crops could be planted at intervals of two weeks until July, but we must admit that often our three crops, the planting of which has been spread so carefully over a period of six weeks, will all ripen at once as happens so frequently in the vegetable garden when an avalanche of string beans, peas, or corn descends upon us.

A few of the herbs are not raised from seeds. The tarragon sets no seed and is raised from cuttings, or divisions of the roots. The horseradish is propagated from pieces of the root, and the fragrant-leaved geraniums and lemon verbena are increased from cuttings. There are many kinds of fragrant-leaved geraniums with pretty flowers and gracefully curved branches which are attractive in pots or for a vacant space in the border. Pots filled with lemon verbena, and fragrant-leaved geraniums standing on the terrace or porch where we drink tea or after-dinner coffee give off their pleasant perfume as we walk past them and our clothes or hands touch their leaves. Dampness is said to bring out their scent, so they are placed along the margins of our garden pool as in Spain where the fragrance in flowers or leaves is as much valued as their form or color. Laurel, or sweet bay, is another plant which is increased from cuttings. When grown in tubs and trimmed into a pyramid or umbrella shape by a gardener who is also a topiarist, they make handsome and aristocratic-looking accents.

Most plants grow stronger and produce more of their essential oil when their roots are firmly anchored in the earth, where the breezes stir them, the sun shines down on them, and the sweet rains from heaven wash their leaves. In a pot a plant is cramped for space, and besides, has to be watered daily, often with artesian well water which may be cold, and may contain chemicals bad for the plant's digestion. People who have no gardens, however, and those who wish to keep on growing herbs during the winter, like to raise herbs to stand on the window sill. A few of them, like parsley and chives, do well when grown in this fashion. Flats of these two are often sold at the grocer's during the winter. It has been my experience that although they keep their flavor when grown this way they do not recover as quickly when their leaves are cut off as they do in the garden. Sweet marjoram is a decorative plant; its branches curve down prettily over the sides of the pot, but when I grew it indoors during the winter, it lost its fragrance. Summer savory, thyme, and rosemary might do well in window boxes. The sages, tarragon, and others would be too coarse, besides this seems unnecessary since their dried leaves are as fragrant as the fresh ones.

When one is a beginner at raising herbs and the plants are strange to the gardener, it is practical to plant them in long rows separated by walks, each row divided into tiny grave-like beds. Enough of most herbs can be grown in a space measuring two by four feet, but some of them, such as horseradish, balm, and pot marjoram, spread so riotously they must be given more room to follow their natural inclinations without interfering with the others. When each herb is in a little space to itself it can be studied or replaced and moved about without disturbing the other plants. For the cook's convenience, they should be conspicuously labeled, especially when she is new and as yet unacquainted with them.

If the beds are kept clean and tidy they will be attractive, for the beauty of any garden is in its order. By keeping back the weeds and pests and having each plant healthy and exactly where he wishes it to be, man shows he has been able to impose his will upon nature and conquer it. This is the root from which all garden art has grown and flowered, whether it is exhibited in a field of forage crops, a planting of vegetables, or an elaborate design by Le Nôtre.

Once the herbs are well known and their idiosyncrasies understood, we can begin to play with them and move them about. Since most of them are not strikingly beautiful it would seem difficult to fashion a pretty effect with them; but, as with all plants, when they are given a setting in harmony with their colors and in scale with their size, their charms are set forth to the best advantage.

If there is plenty of space, a collection of herbs is attractive in a little garden by itself shut away from the other flowers and vegetables by an enclosing wall or hedge. This enclosure keeps the plants warm and sheltered and protects them from the winds which scatter their perfume. When the gate into the garden is opened a rich odor of spice, anise, and resinous oils greets the visitor. In such a garden the beds could be laid out in a geometric or, as some prefer to call it, a formal design. The gray-leaved plants perhaps could be in beds to themselves and balancing these, or next to them for contrast, beds filled with dark green ones. The red basils could border beds of gray-leaved plants; in fact this was such a stunning combination that my own herb garden was hedged in by bushes of a rose with dark red leaves, the *Rosa rubrifolia*, Vill.

Herbs can also be grown in a double border on either side of a path of grass, or of bricks laid in an old-fashioned pattern. The low basils, savories, and *Thymus vulgaris* will furnish the edging as they do around beds of vegetables or of other herbs in European gardens. Winter savory is charming as a border and if left undisturbed it forms a thick, undulating ribbon and when sheared makes a stiff little hedge, a good substitute for the box if this is too expensive or not hardy. Behind the low edging plants can be grouped the *Umbelliferae*, the white-flowered anise, and pinkish coriander in the foreground, backed by tall fennels and dill with their yellow-green, wheel-like flowers and alternating with these clumps of pink, white- and blue-flowered hyssop. At the back of the border, *Inula helenium* lifts its daisy-like yellow flowers, and the tall spires of *Salvia sclarea* send forth their sagy scent. A damask rose or two stands at some pivotal point, and tucked in where their colors harmonize, are red- and pink-flowered bee balms, golden calendulas, violets, nasturtiums, and both the blue and the white varieties of borage, so pretty one wonders why they are not grown more in the flower garden. There are clumps of Florentine iris, and the spear-like leaves of *Acorus calamus*, while here and there an artemisia gives a silvery note with its gray leaves. Varieties of artemisias such as *abrotanum, absinthium, stellariana*, and *dracuncu-*

Carvum carvi, caraway; Pimpinella anisum, anise: Anethum graveolens, dill

lus rightly belong in the herb garden, and besides these one might include the feathery-leaved *pontica* and *albula*, called artemisia Silver King, a handsome native of our Southwest with entirely gray foliage; and another native, *filifolia*, called silver sage, or white rabbit bush with very finely cut leaves. *A. lactiflora* has green leaves and is grown in many nurseries, but is so large and spreading it is best off in a corner of the shrubbery.

In the old gardens in Europe, the fragrant herbs, clipped like box edgings, have long been arranged in designs like interlacing ribbons and are called knots. Lavender cotton, *Santolina chamaecyperus,* with its leaves like stiff branches of gray coral, is often chosen for the gray ribbon, while hyssop, winter savory, or rosemary furnish the dark green ones, and feverfew, *Pyrethrum parthenium*, provides the yellow note. Mazes were made of sheared hyssop, but shearing deprives one of the flowers which are too pretty to be dispensed with, especially since they come in late summer.

Lavender, when grown in Spain or in favored places in England, makes perhaps the handsomest of hedges. When varieties with light and dark blossoms are planted together and placed beside Nankeen lilies or bushes of yellow roses the effect is like a song in color. In my own fragrant garden the lavender bushes grow behind an edging of lavender cotton, and close beside them are the silvery artemisias and in the wall behind misty tufts of pale pink gypsophila, the *Gypsophila muralis.* Although the rosemary grows beside the lavender in southern France and Spain, where it is so common that the dried bushes are used for kindling, it is not nearly so hardy here, perhaps because it lacks the protection of furry hairs on its leaves.

Where it thrives, it, too, makes a handsome hedge, and a garden bed hedged with either of these two gives off a heady, almost intoxicating, fragrance during the heat of the day. In the south, where the geraniums grow to shrubs, the less spready ones also make deliciously scented hedges.

Herbs, besides making hedges and edgings, serve as good ground covers, where grass cannot be grown, on dry slopes, over rocky soil, or between shrubs. Bacon described walks paved with burnet, wild thyme, and water mints. I agree about the wild thymes, which creep and snuggle caressingly over the stones on walks or between steps, and when in flower look as if a purple or magenta-colored cushion had been dropped down on the ground. I also like the purple patches they make when they have seeded themselves into the green lawns, although most gardeners consider this a pest. I do not approve, however, of burnet or water mints on walks. Perhaps the Elizabethans lifted their feet higher than we do, or maybe they ruthlessly stepped on the plants, because the flowers of burnet and the branches of mint grow so high that present-day people would have to jump to avoid them and not stumble over them. Bacon also speaks of chamomile as a ground cover, and Shakespeare, in "Henry IV," has Falstaff say, "For though the chamomile, the more it is trodden on the faster it grows, yet youth, the more it is wasted the sooner it wears." It is a low creeping plant and makes a satisfactory covering, especially on banks and between shrubberies.

When a plant with glossy evergreen foliage is desirable as a ground cover, the winter savory as well as some of its close relatives are most satisfactory. I grow several which resemble the winter savory, *Satureia montana,* such as *S. alpina, S. croatica, S. cuneifolia,* and *S. kitaebelii.* Only *alpina* and *montana* are at present obtainable in our country.

Why we do not grow more of the fragrant violets in our gardens is a mystery. The leaves are lush and green and even if the flowers hide behind them, their fragrance is so pervasive one can smell it from afar. Planted under yellow or pink roses or under white tulips they are the most poetic of ground covers. In Spain, flower beds are carpeted with them to act as a mulch.

All through the summer the branches and flowers of herbs make delightful nosegays, in jars, indoors. The borage is handsome alone or with other flowers and lasts well in water after it has been cut, as do the calendulas, bee balms, artemisias, and sages. Branches of rose, nutmeg, or ivy-leaved geraniums give a green note and a perfume to arrangements of scentless flowers like the gladioli and dahlias. The gray branches of southernwood or wormwood go well with white phlox or delphinium; while lavender is handsome with yellow thermopsis; and rue is stunning with orange lilies; *Lilium elegans,* and clary, *Salvia sclarea,* makes an effective ensemble with *anthemis tinctoria* and yellow foxgloves. On a hot day a vase filled with the branches of gray-leaved mints, and the crisped ones, costmary, balm, and marjoram, is cool looking as well as fragrant and unusual.

When we see the flowers prepare to open their corollas, it is time to harvest the thyme, hyssop, and others of the *Labiatae,* for this is the precise moment when the plants are richest in essential oils. Early on a clear summer morning, while the dew is still on them, I pick the leaves and flowering tops into large baskets and carry them into a little garden house near by which has windows on three sides, and a door on the fourth. The flowering tops are cut off and the older leaves further down are stripped from the stems, which, with all imperfect leaves, are discarded. The leaves and tops are washed and the moisture shaken off them. They are spread out on trays, over which a clean piece of cheesecloth has been laid, and dried indoors. The trays are made of wire screening and are propped up so that the air circulates under as well as over them. Every morning the trays are shaken about to make sure the leaves have all been exposed to the air. In hot weather they dry quickly and are ready for storing the second or third day. The quicker they dry the less chance there is of their becoming mouldy. We have tried heating them over a stove to dry them but do not find this necessary. When dried indoors they generally keep their color quite well, but when dried out-of-doors the sun darkens the leaves, the wind is likely to blow them away, and there is always the fear of a dog or cat playing havoc with them, or of an annoyingly tidy person busying himself with stacking the trays and perhaps mixing up the different herbs.

The dried leaves can be crumbled between the fingers before packing, and as far as I know this does not affect their taste. It is more attractive, however, to keep whole the leaves to be used for the teas.

As soon as they are dry the crisp green leaves are placed in close-stopped containers. For storing the herbs one can have Mason jars, or paper bags, cardboard or japanned boxes such as contain the expensive teas. One of my friends has Italian pottery jars with pewter covers and beautifully lettered labels for them, and when standing in the herb cabinet made expressly for them, they are a sight to stir envy in even the most sweet-natured of herb gardeners.

In olden days the bunches of herbs were hung picturesquely from the rafters, where the heat from the kitchen slowly dried them, and where they collected dust which might or might not add to the delicacy of the food. Much of the fragrance must also have been dissipated.

Leaves and seeds grown and dried at home are far more fragrant than the ones bought at the druggist's or grocer's. Perhaps this is because they are fresher, but it may be due to keeping them shut up in a container and not having to open them for the numerous customers coming into a shop.

Seeds of anise, coriander, fennel, and the like are harvested as they ripen and before they fall to the ground. Dr. Stockberger recommends picking them "a little before they are open in order that they may retain their bright, fresh appearance." They are picked into baskets lined with clean paper, cleaned of their stems, and then washed and the water strained off. Then they, too, are spread out on a clean cloth laid over the trays of wire screening and turned about daily until they are quite dry and ready to be packed into jars.

The roots of horseradish, iris, calamus, and others are generally harvested in the fall, but sometimes in early spring. They are washed and dried. The large fleshy ones are sometimes split and sliced and then spread on clean trays and often turned. The roots can also be dried on racks in fruit dryers hung over the stove. They are dry when they break open upon being bent.

VII

HERB TEAS

There is a story that Confucius, in order to induce the Chinese to boil their drinking water, invented the tea made from the leaves of the *Thea bohea* or *Thea viridis*. Whatever the origin of the practice, all drinks made from brewing fragrant leaves or flowers in hot water are known as teas.

One of the pleasures of a herb garden is the harvest of leaves and flowers which can be infused into such teas. Originating teas by using new combinations of leaves and blossoms is a field open to a modern Confucius; and to assist the would-be conjurer of fragrant drinks, I am mentioning a few of the plants which, in the past, have been steeped in hot water to metamorphose an otherwise dull and tepid drink into one of jewel-like colors and poetic fragrances.

At present most of us cannot differentiate between black and green teas, nor do we know them by name. When we are asked, "Do you wish India or China tea,

Oolong, White Rose, or Jasmine," as likely as not we mention a name we know rather than a flavor we prefer.

Herb teas are healthful, delightful to the senses, and will increase our scale of appreciation, for when we imbibe drinks of new ingredients, we are more conscious of the variations in flavors and fragrances than when taking the habitual China tea, cocoa, or coffee every morning upon arising.

When we see what subtle means the Chinese employ to flavor their teas, we realize how sensitive they must be to shadings in taste and smell. They flavor certain of their teas with jasmine and others with orange blossoms, or the petals of roses, or peonies. We, too, can put the petals of the damask or Provence roses in with the leaves of sage, bee balm, or costmary for a day or two to flavor them and then sift them out, or if we live in the South, mix jasmine flowers or orange blossoms in with the dried leaves of the herbs to flavor our homemade teas, as the Chinese do in their more intricate and expert way.

Robert Fortune, who wrote a book about his visit to the tea districts of China, says that black or green teas can be made from the same plants and that it is the method of drying and not the plant which makes the difference. The black teas are left to lie on the flat bamboo trays much longer than the green ones and undergo "a species of heating or fermentation" during their exposure to the air which turns them black, while the green teas are dried off quickly and do not ferment and consequently keep their color. Black teas are supposed to be more healthful than the green ones. The leaves for the herb teas are dried as quickly as possible indoors, and, like the green teas of China, they are not permitted to ferment.

People all over the world from the most primitive to the highest stages of civilization have steeped herbs in hot water. Infusions of sage leaves have been given for colds, chamomile flowers or peppermint leaves for indigestion, and balm to bring out perspiration, and countless others for their soothing or stimulating qualities. At one end of the scale are the American Indians, who drink herbs steeped in hot water as medicine, and in the middle are the Europeans from south to north who drink teas for health as well as pleasure, while at the furthermost peak of civilization are the Chinese who, before the Japanese had made a religious rite of drinking tea, had laid the foundation for the tea ceremony of the latter country.

Chinese teas played a dramatic rôle in American history, because the tax on the fragrant leaves, without the consent of the people, was the last straw which precipitated the War of Independence with Great Britain. Since it was politically expedient to refrain from drinking the China teas, a propaganda against their healthfulness was promulgated as an added inducement to keep the people from "bootlegging" tea when their patriotism was not sufficiently strong to prevent their indulging in the fashionable drink of the day. An article in the *Virginia Gazette*, Williamsburg, Virginia, January 13, 1774, signed by Philo-Aletheias, is an amusing example of the lengths to which an ardent propagandist can go. It begins as follows:

> Can posterity believe that the constitutional liberties of North America were on the Point of being given up for Tea? Is this exotic Plant necessary to Life? . . . But if we must through Custom have some warm Tea once or twice a day, why may we not exchange this slow poison which not only destroys our Con-

stitutions but endangers our Liberties and drains our Country of so many thousands of Pounds a Year for Teas of our own American Plants, many of which may be found pleasant to the taste, and very salutary, according to our various constitutions . . . Here permit me to propose a list of several kinds of Teas with a hint of their Uses; any of which would be more pleasant than Bohea, etc., provided we used them as long.

Then follow seventeen different kinds of teas such as "sassafras root sliced thin and dried with raspings of lignum vitae" and the following:

Sweet marjoram and a little mint; mother of thyme, a little hyssop; sage and balm leaves, joined with a little lemon juice; rosemary and lavender; a very few small twigs of White Oak well dried in the Sun with two leaves and a Half of Sweet Myrtle; Clover with a Little Chamomile; Twigs of Black Currant Bushes; Red Rose Bush leaves and Cinquefoil; Mistletoe and English Wild Valerian; Pine Buds and Lesser Valerian; Ground Ivy with a little Lavender Cotton or Roman Wormwood, or Southernwood (sounds quite horribly bitter); Strawberry Leaves and the Leaves of Sweet Briar, or Dog's Rose; Golden Rod and Betony, drunk with Honey; Twigs of liquid Amber Tree (commonly called Sweet Gum) with or without the flowers of Elder; Peppermint and Yarrow.

All these have their medicinal values appended, to which is added a footnote:

Every sort of tea is rendered disagreeable by being too strong.

The colonial housewife made drinks from the herbs in her garden, and undoubtedly long before the Revolution had found substitutes for the expensive imported teas. Whenever she came upon a plant with fragrant leaves, she would probably ask a trapper, or perhaps a squaw, whether the bush was poisonous, and if she found it was innocuous would steep the leaves in hot water to concoct an aromatic drink. Although these drinks antedated the Revolution, many of them were called "Liberty Teas."

Besides the ones mentioned by Philo-Aletheias, the following were used: the scented leaves of spice bush, *Benzoin aestivale;* of wintergreen, *Gaultheria procumbens;* bee balm, *Monarda didyma;* ambrosia, *Chenopodium ambrosoides;* and sweet fern, *Myrica asplenifolium.* The leaves of march tea, *Ledum palustre*, and of Labrador tea, *Ledum groenlandicum*, are said to be less palatable; while the dried leaves of a variety of goldenrod called *Solidago odorata* are said to make a pleasant tea, as are the leaves of New Jersey tea, *Ceanothus americanus,* and those of raspberry bushes. The leaves of the American pennyroyal, *Hedeoma pulegioides*, made "grateful beverages" we are told, sweetened with honey, molasses, or sugar. The Swedish traveler, Peter Kalm, says he noticed that people took an infusion of this for colds and pains in the head.

In the South, sassafras tea, made from the bark of the root, as a substitute for tea, was a favorite drink during the Civil War, and the extract from the root now furnishes the flavoring for root beer. During another war, a drink was made from the flowering tops of encenilla or chaparral, *Croton corymbosus.* In western Texas this was much liked by the Mexicans and Indians as well as the Negro United States soldiers, who are said to have preferred it to coffee.

Okakura Kakuza, in his "Book of the Tea," says:

> Like art, Tea has its periods and its schools, its evolution may be roughly divided into three main stages; The Boiled Tea, The

Whipped Tea and The Steeped Tea. We moderns belong to the last school. These several methods of appreciating the beverage are indicative of the spirit of the age in which they prevailed.

When teas are made from herbs which give readily of their essence, the ceremony is exactly like that which accompanies the preparation of China tea. The leaves are portioned out into a porcelain pot, boiling water is poured over them, and they are allowed to steep for a few minutes. The liquid is then strained off into another porcelain pot which has been previously heated. Certain of the herbs, however, do not yield quickly of their savor and have to be boiled in the water for a few minutes. All herb teas, except peppermint and spearmint, are improved when flavored with sugar and lemon. To serve them they should be poured boiling hot into translucent cups, already flavored with the right amount of sugar and with a thin slice of lemon floating on the amber or jade-colored liquid to mingle its fruity scent with the spicy fragrance of the teas. Naturally no milk is added to cloud their color or flatten their taste. The color of green tea does not indicate its strength. The herb teas are green teas and never become as dark as the black teas, but always maintain a light green or pale gold color.

Upon trial I found the dried leaves of the following herbs yielded pleasant teas. The young leaves of costmary, *Chrysanthemum balsamita*, make a tea which when strong is very bitter, but when weak and flavored with sugar and lemon is good. It does not have to be steeped long. A good handful of the leaves of balm, *Melissa citriodora*, to a cup should be boiled in water to bring out the flavor. The tea is good but mild in taste, at any rate from plants grown in our climate. The leaves of wild bergamot, *Monarda fistulosa*, have to be boiled in the water too, and the tea has an aromatic and delightful taste, whereas the tea of *Monarda citriodora* has a pleasant peppery taste. Although a large pinch of leaves is taken of *Mentha citrata* for one cup, the tea does not have much flavor. The leaves of *Salvia officinalis* when steeped in hot water have a warm, pleasant flavor. Those of gas plant, *Dictamnus fraxinella*, taste of lemon, mint, fresh greens, and a little bitter. The leaves and flowering tops of hyssop are also brewed into teas. The flowering tops of peppermint and spearmint are stimulating and refreshing. I like a cup of mint tea in the middle of the afternoon with a few gingersnaps, as I rest between hours at the typewriter.

Teas of jasmine, linden, and chamomile flowers and of the leaves of sage and peppermint can be bought, but they are not as fragrant as the ones cured and grown in one's own garden.

A tea is made from the flowers of the linden tree called *tilleul* in French, and tastes somewhat as the blossoms smell. In July all along the roads of France, wherever the lindens are growing, one sees ladders placed against the trees for gathering the flowers. One summer in Tours I saw the gardener cut down branches of the trees and bring them into the convent where a group of little children under the supervision of a nun picked off the flowers, while all of them were singing a song for this special occasion.

In France, where the people have made a fine art of living perhaps second only to the Chinese, and know how to derive the utmost pleasure from each of their five senses, it is the custom to partake of a herb tea before retiring. These teas are said to insure sweet dreams and a quiet sleep, and how could it be otherwise when the last waking sensations are of a warm golden liquid exhaling a delicious aroma.

DRAMATIS PERSONAE

My observations will be drawn from a threefold source: from personal experience on my own farms; from my own reading, and from what I have heard from experts.

Varro, "Rerum Rusticarum," written in 36 B.C. and translated with an Introduction, Commentary, and Excursus by Lloyd Storr-Best, London, 1912.

DRAMATIS PERSONAE

ACORUS CALAMUS, L.

SWEET FLAG

Acorus aromaticus, Calamus, Sweet Cane, Sweet Grass

Araceae Perennial

The sweet flag, thought to have come originally from India, grows along streams and lakes throughout the Northern Hemisphere.

Root. The roots are a thickened rhizome from which numerous fleshy rootlets grow in parallel lines. The inside is smooth and white and smells like the leaves of lemon, and is more powerful when dried than when it is fresh.

Leaf. The leaves rise from a sheaf and are yellow-green, linear, smooth, shiny, terminate in a point, and somewhat resemble those of *Iris versicolor.* In my garden they grow to two feet or more high, but Bailey says they rise to six feet. They are one-third to three-quarters of an inch broad and have a prominent midrib a little to one side, which is raised on both under and upper surfaces. Their lemony scent is given off without touching them, and when they are crushed there is more of the lemon peel and sweetness in the fragrance. Some say it is like the scent of bay leaves; others, like violets, lemon, or apple.

Flower. The inflorescence is a green, cone-shaped spathe about three inches long, at first incrusted with little golden dots around tiny green nobs, later forming a spiral pattern as in a textile. These are the flowers, which are too small to see without a microscope. They are bisexual, come early in June, and last a long while.

Variety. A variegated form is spoken of which might be a good garden plant.

HISTORY AND LEGEND

The sweet flag is mentioned in the Bible and by Theophrastus. In Parkinson's day it was used medicinally and the leaves and roots when tied to a hive of bees were thought both to prevent them from wandering away and to attract other bees. It was in Adrian van der Donck's garden at Yonkers in 1653. Bartram listed it in 1814. In India it has been used medicinally, especially for bowel complaint in children, and there is a severe penalty upon the druggist who refuses to open his shop door at night to sell it.

In China, the rushes are hung up at the Dragon boat festival, its property of killing insects is known, and the leaves are woven into mats.

USES

The roots are laid amongst furs to protect them from moths, and also amongst books and stuffs as a protection against other insects. The rushes were strewn on the floors in olden days.

Medicine. It is a pleasant aromatic and stomachic, and is official in most pharmacopoeias, but not much employed in modern medicines. The candied roots are used medicinally in Turkey and India.

Perfumery. The essential oil from the bark of the

roots is used in perfumery. The roots are pulverized and made into toilet and sachet powders.

Food. The leaves flavor custards and creams, and are said to be particularly delicious in a creamy rice pudding. The Tartars put a piece of the root in their mouths before drinking water to purify it. In New England the roots are cut into rings and preserved in sugar. It is used by country people throughout the United States as an ingredient in wine bitters. The Swedes make a spirit from the corn, and the English use the oil from the bark of the root to flavor gin and certain kinds of beer.

CULTURE

It grows wild in moist situations, yet under cultivation it will grow in fairly dry upland soil, and seems to like the sun.

Propagation is by divisions of old roots, which should be set out in the fall, one foot apart, and well covered.

Harvest. The roots are harvested in the fall, after the plant is dried. The small rootlets are removed before marketing. The roots should not be peeled, for it is the bark of the root which yields the essential oil. The annual importation of calamus root is from five to ten tons, and it comes principally from South Russia.

ALLIUM SCHOENOPHRASUM, L.

CHIVES

Liliaceae Perennial

Chives, called *ciboulette* by the French, grow wild throughout Europe, in Siberia, and in North America along the shores of Lakes Huron and Superior, and further north. The variety now used probably comes from the European Alps. Many writers think the flowers are pretty and that the plant belongs in the flower garden. They do not appeal to me, personally, but the delicate flavor of the chives is so delightful that these plants should be in every collection of herbs. The whole plant forms a little bush of spreading, slender, tubular leaves from which rise dun-colored flowers about ten inches or more high, scented decidedly of onion.

Bulb. The bulb is three-quarters of an inch long, narrow, and white, with many white rootlets.

Leaf. The leaves are round, slender hollow tubes of a yellowish green terminating in a point, and are about twelve inches long.

Flower. The flower stems are slender, round, and a blue-green. The flowers form clusters of dusty, lavender blossoms. Each little perianth is six-parted and each segment has a pointed, whitish tip and a dark rib down the center of it on the outside. The anthers are whitish, and the filaments the same color as the flowers.

Seed. The seeds are longish, shiny black, and three-angled.

HISTORY AND LEGEND

Chives were planted in European gardens in the sixteenth century and were in American gardens before 1806. Bartram had them on his list in 1814.

USES

Medicine. Chives are not in the official pharmacopoeia.

Food. The leaves, finely chopped, give a delicious

Allium schoenophrasum, chives

flavor to salads, omelettes, and certain sauces, and go well with cheeses and with sweet herbs. They are even used by the Ainus of northern Japan.

CULTURE

They are not at all difficult to grow. The plants are propagated by dividing the clumps, and planting the little bulbs, and can also be grown from seeds. Vilmorin advises digging them up and replanting them every two or three years, and says they do well as edgings to beds of other plants, better in fact this way than when grown in a bed to themselves. In my garden they have to be fed at intervals, for the constant cutting weakens them, although this does not seem to be true in France, where Vilmorin says the more they are cut the more vigorously they grow.

ANETHUM GRAVEOLENS, L.

DILL

Umbelliferae Annual

Dill is native to Asia Minor and Europe. The gray-green stems, feathery leaves, and lacy umbels of greenish yellow florets compose a handsome, fragrant plant.

Root. It has a single, slender taproot from which tiny rootlets grow.

Stem. The stems are gray-green, smooth, hollow with a bloom on them, and little lines along them. They grow two and one-half to three feet or more high.

Leaf. The leaves are compounded into thread-like divisions, and are six inches long, diminishing in size as they ascend the stem. When fresh they taste a little bitter, penetrating, and stimulating like a combination of orange peel and onion.

Flower. The greenish yellow flowers are arranged in a large, circular, very open umbel as much as six inches across composed of smaller circles. The tiny petals roll inwards and have no bracts.

Seed. The strongly fragrant seeds are shaped like a brown leaf with cream-colored veins and margins, concave on one side and convex on the other, and are about one-quarter of an inch long. They taste sharply like camphor, or anise, and a little bitter.

HISTORY AND LEGEND

The East Indians use it medicinally and for flavoring, and it is said to be on sale in every bazaar. In their festivals the Romans crowned themselves with the flowering branches of dill. Pliny wrote of its medicinal functions, as did Ibn Baithar, who also mentions it as a flavoring. It was on Charlemagne's list. Magicians used it in their spells and as a charm against witchcraft. It was an old German custom for the bride to carry it and new-born calves were rubbed with salt and dill. John Josselyn mentioned it in 1674.

USES

Medicine. The herb boiled in broth has been used with great success in preventing obesity according to Poucher's "Medical Botany," 1869, which, if true, ought to insure its popularity.

Perfume. The oil distilled from the seeds is fragrant, and is mixed with other essences for perfuming soaps.

Dill water is more of a druggist's than a perfumer's article, according to Piesse, who says that some ladies use a mixture of half dill water and half rose water as a simple cosmetic to clear the complexion.

Food. Dill is famous because its partnership with cucumbers has produced the dill pickle, which is not a recent affair but a long-established relationship. Parkinson, in his "Paradisi in Sole," says, "It is also put among pickled cucumber where it doth very well agree, giving to the cold fruit a pretty spicie taste or relish."

The young tops and leaves of the plants are used to aromatize vinegars, and are also mixed into fish sauces to which they lend a piquant taste.

CULTURE

Since dill is an annual, it is sown every spring after danger from frost is over. It comes readily from seed, and takes two and a half months from seed time to harvest. It should be sown thinly, and when the plants are two or three inches high, if it is necessary, they should be thinned, for dill does not like transplanting. It is a good plan to time the planting so that it will ripen with the cucumbers, for the fresh leaves are used as well as the seed in making the pickle.

Harvest. The fresh leaves are picked when the flowers begin to open, and the seeds are harvested when ripe.

ANGELICA ARCHANGELICA, L.

ANGELICA

Umbelliferae Biennial

The angelica is native to Europe and Asia, mostly in

cool northern climates. It is a large, handsome plant with spreading, tropical-looking leaves, and a dome-shaped inflorescence borne on tall stems and is most decorative as an accent or background to other herbs. It is said to remain in the garden for several years if the flowers are cut back, otherwise it dies after bearing seeds.

Root. The roots are white, firm, and fleshy inside, and are sometimes called the "roots of the Holy Ghost."

Stem. The stems are fleshy and strong, with many raised veins. The leaf stem begins as a sheathe and then rounds into a compound leaf. From within the sheathes rise the flower stems. When raw they taste intensely bitter and have no scent and after cooking they taste pleasantly aromatic and a bit like parsley.

Leaf. The leaves rising from these strangely formed stems are divided into five very much compounded leaflets. Each of the five has a stem from which grow toothed leaves, some of them deeply cut and yellow-green in color, smooth above and dull gray-green below. There is no scent to the leaves, even when crushed, and they taste piny and pleasant when raw. They die down at the first autumn frost, but if the plant has not flowered, come up again the following spring.

Flower. The flowers blossom the middle of June and last a long while. The topmost inflorescence is at the tip of a stem four feet high, the largest measuring six inches across, and is made up of stems two and a quarter inches long, each having three-quarter inch long greenish clumps of nobby-looking florets. Others are at the terminations of long stalks rising from where the sheaf of the leaf surrounds them. As they ripen they grow bigger and spread further apart.

Seed. The seeds are brown, long, leaf-shaped, concave on one side and convex on the other with one prominent rib. They are covered with an oblong, flat, straw-colored envelope which looks as if it had been pleated, and are one-quarter of an inch long.

HISTORY AND LEGEND

Angelica was considered a preventive against evil spirits and witchcraft. In Courland and Livonia, and the low lands of Pomerania and East Prussia, where it grows abundantly, when the peasants carry the flowering stems of angelica to market they chant a verse they learnt in childhood, which is so old that it is unintelligible to the singers themselves and is most likely of pre-Christian origin.

The herbalists recommend, "to bite and chaw a root of angelica against the plague."

Angelica was mentioned as being in Adrian van der Donck's garden at Yonkers in 1653. Perhaps he meant the native *Angelica atropurpurea* which was much used medicinally. It is a smaller and less handsome plant with a purplish tinge and is said to be more fragrant than any other indigenous plant. Angelica seed listed as *Angelica purpurea* was offered for sale in the advertisement of the *Boston Evening Post* in 1771, and by Bartram in 1814.

USES

Medicine. The root was used medicinally as a stimulant or tonic and given in an infusion.

Perfume. The oil distilled from the root, leaves, and seeds is an ingredient in the manufacture of perfumes when a special note is desired. Angelica water made from the leaves was formerly highly regarded.

Food. The leaves and stalks were eaten as a salad either roasted or boiled, and the stems were at one time a popular vegetable, blanched as celery is. The roots were eaten by the Lapps and Norwegians, and in England the roots were preserved and the leaves candied.

The oil is a flavoring for liqueurs like Benedictine and Chartreuse, Ratafia d'Angelique, and Vermuth. It is said to give a muscatel flavor to wines and is a flavoring for creams and custards.

The stems of angelica can be purchased already candied. This product is a specialty of Niort and Chateaubriand in France.

CULTURE

Angelica seems to like a fairly moist soil and a cool climate. The seeds do not keep their vitality long and should therefore be sown as they ripen in July and August. The plants can be transplanted in the autumn or the following spring, three feet or more apart. It is quite difficult to procure angelica seed in the United States, but once the plants have been started they are quite hardy.

Harvest. The roots are washed and dried in the open air for a few days before storing. The leaves are harvested in the spring of the second or third season; the seeds in August.

ANTHEMIS NOBILIS, L.

CHAMOMILE

Compositae Perennial

There seem to be three plants which are called chamomile: the German chamomile, *Matricaria chamomilla*, the Roman chamomile, *Anthemis nobilis*, which comes with a single crown of white ray florets, and another which has a double row.

Anthemis nobilis as we grow it from seed has a single wheel of white ray florets around a circle of yellow disk flowers. The double-wheeled variety does not come from seed and was not procurable in the United States. *Anthemis nobilis* is native to the south and west of Europe, and in the United States has escaped a little into the wild. The whole plant is pleasantly scented and forms flat mats of leaves which, with their many divisions, look like a kind of moss.

Root. The roots are small and soft.

Stem. The stems creep along the ground, rooting as they go, and from the mats the flower stems rise about twelve to fourteen inches high bearing daisy-like blossoms. The authorities say there should be hairs along the stems, but to the naked eye none were visible either in my own plants or in the herbarium specimens.

Leaf. The leaves are slightly gray-green, compounded and much cut, and look like wiry little ferns.

Flower. The sparse white ray florets, with chaffy scales between, encircle the yellow disk ones. The whole apartment house (for the *compositae* always remind me of apartment houses, so many flowers being tucked into so small a space), measures about three-quarters of an inch across. As the flowers age, the yellow center rises up into a little mound.

Seed. The seed is an achene; that is, a small, closed fruit. It is obtusely three-angled, says Bailey, and has no pappus; that is, thistledown.

HISTORY AND LEGEND

The plant has been cultivated for centuries in Europe and was introduced into Germany from Spain at the close of the Middle Ages. In old gardens, seats made of raised earth, more like little mounds, were covered with the mossy-looking chamomile. Bacon suggested it as a covering for paths in his famous "Essay on Gardens," and we find his idea a good one. There is an old belief that if chamomile is dispersed about the garden it will keep the plants healthy.

USE

Medicine. Chamomile tea, made by pouring boiling water over the dried yellow disk flowers and steeping them for a little while, is said to be good for the complexion, to have tonic properties, and to be strengthening for a weak stomach. It is the plants with single rays which should be used for this and not the ones with the double rays. In France and Germany this tea is given for indigestion, and in Germany blond girls rinse their hair with chamomile tea, and in almost every beauty parlor in the United States chamomile rinses are given to soften the hair after a shampoo.

CULTURE

Chamomile seems to like a sunny, dry situation.

The plants of the single-rayed flowers can be grown from seed and from bits of the rooting stems. Sown indoors in February at Foxden, it was transplanted to the garden in April, and flowered late in August. I have sown it out-of-doors with success, too.

ANTHRISCUS CEREFOLIUM, HOFFM.

CHERVIL

Salad Chervil

Umbelliferae Annual

The seed of my chervil plants came from France, where it is a favorite seasoning. It looks and tastes like refined parsley. The *chervil frisé* of the French catalogues is identical with curled chervil and is the variety to choose in preference to the type, for with its curled and frilled leaves it is prettier. It is sparingly naturalized in the eastern United States.

Root. It has a white and single tapering root.

Stem. The stem grows to four inches in my garden although Bailey says it reaches a height of one to two feet. It is squarish, much branched, light green and hairy, with lines on it.

Leaf. The leaves are not flat but in several planes and are much compounded and divided.

Flower. The white florets are arranged in tiny umbels. The whole plant smells of anise, and tastes a little peppery and of anise.

Seed. The seeds are long, pointed, with a conspicuous furrow from end to end.

HISTORY AND LEGEND

Pliny says that the seed in vinegar stops hiccough. Parkinson says the leaves put in with "a sallet gives a marvelous relish to the rest" and that "some recommend the green seeds sliced and put in a sallet of herbs and eaten with vinegar and oil, to comfort a cold stomach of the aged . . ." The roots, which take a long time to boil, were eaten in time of plague and should be washed but never scraped, says one authority. It was mentioned by Josselyn.

USES

Medicine. The dried plant is applied externally to bruises and local tumors.

Food. In France to-day it is often in the combination of "*fines herbes*" and is delicious in salads, particularly potato salad, and as a condiment in soups.

CULTURE

The chervil is an annual, and comes readily from seed. When the leaves are cut off they are said to shoot up again, but in our hot summers the plants seemed not at all robust and soon withered and died. Perhaps, as one grower suggests, they need a little shade.

Vilmorin says its chief merit is that it cannot be confounded with any other plant, and that is indeed a virtue, because when one goes to pick the leaves of the *Um-*

belliferae for the salad, one is apt to mistake the coriander for the leaves of the cumin, or anise, a fatal dampening of ardor for the eating of herbs.

ARMORACIA RUSTICANA, GAERTN., MEY. AND SCHERB.

HORSERADISH

Cruciferae Perennial

Horseradish, also called *Radicula armoracia,* comes from southeastern Europe and is naturalized in America. It is so rampant, once it has been planted in the garden, that it seems foolish to grow it, but as it is such an important flavoring I have included it. The plant is coarse, with large leaves and inconspicuous flowers.

Root. The root is deep below the surface, branching, long, and cylindrical with a slightly wrinkled white skin. The flesh is white, somewhat fibrous and tastes like hot mustard.

Leaf. The leaves are most unusual. The first ones to appear look like big green combs, they are so cut. They are nine inches long and four inches across at their widest point. Later come the radical leaves which are fourteen inches long and five to six across, shiny, green, oval to oblong, with margins having rounded, uneven scallops. The tip is scalloped and the midrib prominent. The stems of the radical leaves are four to six inches long and are rounded on one side and concave on the other, as if a sharp groove had been cut out of them. Above these grow narrow leaves five inches long, opposite, and with no stems. The leaves taste of fresh herbs, a little bitter, and leave a biting sensation behind.

Flower. The flowers bloom in May and are greenish white, borne in loose, irregular panicles, on a stalk two feet or less high; they have four petals, are not fragrant, and do not produce fertile seed.

HISTORY AND LEGEND

Horseradish has been cultivated in Oriental Europe for over a thousand years, but not in western Europe. It is the *armoracia* of the Romans. The German name *meerrettich*, which means sea radish, is said to have been given to the plant either because it came from the Black Sea or because it was grown in Brittany, the land of the sea. During the Middle Ages it was grown for medicine, and in 1542 Fuchsius mentioned it as a condiment. It is grown in almost every German garden to-day, and was in American gardens before 1806.

USES

Medicine. It is said to stimulate the appetite, and can also be applied externally as a counter-irritant wherever mustard is appropriate.

Food. It is a favorite condiment either hot or cold with meat or oysters. With oily fish or fatty viands it acts as a corrective and helps the digestion. The French soak it in olive oil or carnation oil to lessen the sharpness of the taste. In Alsace it is present at all meals. It can be bought conveniently bottled ready for use.

CULTURE

One can buy pieces of the root which should be planted

two feet deep and about three feet apart in well-prepared soil. The difficulty with horseradish is not in coaxing it to grow, but in keeping it from spreading. It is absolutely hardy.

Harvest. The roots are dug up in the autumn and stored in sand or earth to protect them from withering until they are needed.

ARTEMISIA ABROTANUM, L.

SOUTHERNWOOD

Old Man, Old Man's Love, Lad's Love, Maiden's Ruin
Garderobe

Compositae Perennial

The gray, much threaded foliage suggests the name "Old Man." Bailey says the name *Abrotanum* means "elegant" in Greek, descriptive of the form of the leaves and their aromatic odor. This artemisia is a feathery gray-green plant and the leaves smell, without crushing, of daisies mixed with spice.

Root. The root is fibrous and brown.

Stem. The stems are gray marked with brown, round, glaucous, and a little furry. In my garden they grow about two feet high, but they are said to reach up to five feet.

Leaf. The gray-green leaves are pinnately divided into from one to three thread-like divisions.

Flower. The yellowish-white flowers are in a loose panicle. They are bisexual, and the receptacle is not hairy.

HISTORY AND LEGEND

Parkinson says the seeds and dried herb were given to

children to kill worms, and that the ashes of the dried herb mixed with oil causes the hair to grow back on the head and beard after it has fallen out.

For one who spoke in his sleep it was thought southernwood tempered with wine, and partaken of in the morning, and before going to bed at night would cure him. It was well known as a love charm.

USES

The names are suggestive of its association with the God of Love and the consequences thereof, such as Lad's Love and Maiden's Ruin. The French name, *Garderobe,* which means guardian of clothes, that is, a closet, was derived from the fact that the dried stems of the southernwood were supposed to keep the moths away, and so stand guard over the dresses.

The Pennsylvania Germans laid branches of it in the cupboards and pantries to keep out the ants.

Medicine. According to "Merck's Index" of 1907, it is used as a tonic, as a deobstruent and anthelmintic, and in aromatic baths and for poultices.

CULTURE

According to Miller's "Gardener's Dictionary," it is a popular plant in English cities for window boxes, for it endures the smoke of the city better than most plants and is fragrant besides.

The plants can be bought in America and are hardy. In my garden they thrive in a sunny situation in clay soil.

I raised mine from divisions of the roots.

ARTEMISIA ABSINTHIUM, L.

WORMWOOD

Absinth

Compositae Perennial

The wormwood is a handsome, furry, gray-leaved plant, almost shrub-like, growing to three feet in height. It is native to Europe whence it was brought to America and has escaped into the wild. The plants die down to the ground every winter but come up again in the spring and are hardy. As summer advances they become somewhat straggly and spready. It is a good plan, therefore, to cut them back to keep them within bounds.

Root. The root is deep below the ground, spreading and fibrous.

Stem. The main stems are strong, firm, ridged, and of a gray-green, tinted with a little brownish purple.

Leaf. The leaves are a soft, thin, silky texture, and irregularly cut and divided, grayer on the under surface.

Flower. The flowers are very small, about one-eighth of an inch across, numerous, and inconspicuous. As Parkinson says, "The stems are much branched at the top whereon grow small Buttons with pale yellow flowers on them."

Seed. The seeds are gray and very small.

HISTORY AND LEGEND

Wormwood was always known for its bitter taste, and next to rue it is said to be the bitterest of all the herbs. Ibn Baithar quotes Dioscorides as prescribing a wine made of the herb for sickness, when there is no fever, and advises drinking it the summer before one's illness to keep well! If cows browse upon it the bitterness is said to enter into their milk as it does into the milk of mothers who drink it. In the Middle Ages in France the midwives rubbed the babies with the juice so that they would never be cold or hot as long as they lived. This had to be done before the thirteenth day or it would not be of any value.

At one time there was much agitation about restricting the sale of the liqueur absinth in France, made from the juice of the plant, for it was said to make the drinkers irritable, nervous, and to destroy the digestive organs.

USES

Medicine. It was the principal ingredient in "Portland Powder" given for gout.

Food. The dried leaves infused enter into the manufacture of the liqueur absinth. Brewers add the fruit to their hops to make the beer healthful; it acts as a rectifier in spirits.

CULTURE

Wormwood is very easy to grow. It seems to like a sunny situation and thrives in my clay soil.

Wormwood was grown in the United States commercially before prohibition was enacted.

When a strong gray accent is desirable in the garden, wormwood is a satisfactory subject. The branches cut and brought into the house are attractive with summer annuals, or with white phlox, gladioli, and pink or yellow lilies.

The seeds germinate readily. Plants can be bought in American nurseries.

ARTEMISIA DRACUNCULUS, L.

TARRAGON

Estragon

Compositae Perennial

Tarragon comes from eastern Europe, Siberia, Tartary, and Chinese Mongolia. It is a small, shrubby plant about two feet high, the branches of which are so leafy and twisted they look like a maiden's long hair being blown in the wind.

Root. The root is twisted, brownish, and not woody.

Stem. The stems are yellow-green, woody, rounded, and slightly ridged.

Leaf. The leaves are alternate, slender, and pointed at the tips, with entire margins. They taste of a combination of anise, camphor, and are a little bitter and leave a tang and puckering in the mouth for quite a while. When the leaves are rubbed between the fingers the scent has something of anise in it.

Flower. The tiny round flowers are whitish-green and measure one-sixteenth to one-eighth of an inch across. They are carried in panicles and bloom in July or August. There are two kinds, the pistillate and bisexual flowers, and they produce no viable seed, only chaff.

HISTORY AND LEGEND

The name, meaning little dragon, is said to be derived from the fact that the roots coil in a serpent-like fashion.

Ibn Baithar was the first European to write about it, and he says it was known to the Syrians who cooked the tender tops with other vegetables, and also that the juice of tarragon combined with the juice of fennel was one of the precious drinks of the kings of India and of Chorasan, by whom it was taken for its medicinal effects. He said it was soporific and sweetened the breath, and was good to chew before taking medicine, for it dulled the taste.

Parkinson wrote of a legend about tarragon, " . . . that it was first produced by putting the seede of Lin or Flaxe into the roote of an Onion, being opened and so set into the ground, which absurd and idle opinion, Matthiolus by certain experience saith has been found false."

It was known in the United States before 1806.

USES

Perfume. A volatile oil extracted from the green portions of the plant is known as estragon and has an odor similar to anise. This flavors confectionery, and is mixed into perfumes to obtain a special effect in fancy bouquets, and in the fern and new-mown hay types of perfumes.

Food. The tops and leaves are the portions used for flavoring. Alexandre Dumas in his famous cook book says that no vinegar is good without estragon. Along the Corniche, in France, the leaves are put into preserves. Tarragon leaves also flavor brown stock, mayonnaise, and fish sauces. *Sauce Bearnaise* is something else without the tarragon to give its peculiarly delightful taste. The leaves chopped and scattered over the lettuce leaves give an unusual flavor to a salad. It is not good in soups according to my taste, nor should it be added to the *"fines herbes,"* for it does not blend well, but is apt to dominate any dish it enters.

CULTURE

When one buys seed labeled "tarragon" from certain German nurseries it is likely to be *Artemisia redowski*, which is quite different in taste from true tarragon and is a more vigorous plant.

True tarragon produces no seed and has to be propagated by cuttings from the roots. It is best to plant out the roots in spring, for it is a somewhat finicky plant and I find it will winter better after the plants have made a summer's growth. The stems are cut back and the plants protected either with straw or, as is done with roses, by hilling up the soil around them. Tarragon likes a little shade. In Europe it is cultivated in frames to have the fresh leaves during the winter. The commercial growers say it should be renewed every three or four years.

ARTEMISIA STELLERIANA, BESS.

OLD WOMAN

Beach Wormwood, Dusty Miller

Compositae Perennial

Like most of the artemisias this is a handsome plant for the gray garden.

Root. The roots are fibrous.

Stem. The stems are woody, and creep flatly along the ground spreading from two to three feet.

Leaf. The leaves are not fragrant. The older ones

have a tinge of jade green, the new ones are quite gray. They are woolly, soft, floppy, compounded and divided, roundly toothed, almost white underneath, and two to three inches across.

Flower. The little flowers are subtended by bracts and hang down like gray tassels with many yellow fringes. Although they are not showy, the yellow with the gray is a charming color combination.

USES

The Chinese are said to use it medicinally, and as a charm.

CULTURE

This plant seems to like average garden soil and a sunny situation. It dies back in the winter, but spreads widely over the surface again the following year. In Spain it is frequently planted in pots, and was an edging plant around the stiff flower beds of the Victorian era.

ASPERULA ODORATA, L.

SWEET WOODRUFF

Waldmeister, Sweet White Star (from the French), *Thé Suisse, Belle-Etoile, Hépatique Etoile, Etoile Blanche, Blanche Croix*

Rubiaceae Perennial

The little plant flowers in May. Its stems, with their whorls of leaves, form an attractive ground cover for shady places. Sweet woodruff is native to Europe and the Orient, and has naturalized itself in the North American woods. The clumps measure fifteen inches across and the plants are about eight inches high.

Root. The roots grow from shallow reddish underground creeping rootstocks.

Stems. The stems are grooved, angular and smooth, arising from the rootstocks.

Leaf. The leaves are oval-lanceolate, yellow-green, slender, and in starry whorls of six to eight, growing longer as they ascend the stem. The margins are entire, and have tiny hairs along them, and underneath on the central rib. When the fingers rub against the hairs, the leaves feel rough. When crushed, and especially when dried, the leaves smell of sweet young hay and a little of vanilla.

Flower. The flowers measure one-eighth of an inch across, are scentless, starry, tiny, and white. They grow in a loose umbel. The four white petals are joined into a tube and then open out. The anthers form dark tips to the four stamens and placed in the angles between the little petals look like the tiniest of punctuation marks. The calyx is green, rounded, and furry like a tiny button.

Seed. The seed is almost spherical, dark brown, covered with bristly golden-brown hairs, and looks like a wee ball of chenille.

HISTORY AND LEGEND

Parkinson speaks of the Germans using it "very familiarly in wine" and says, "It is held good versus the plague." Mrs. Bardswell says in olden times woodruff and lavender were woven into garlands to decorate churches, and that, when bruised, sweet woodruff was laid against cuts and wounds.

USES

Correvon in "Fleur des Champs" says the peasants put it in their closets to perfume their garments and linen.

Food. In Germany the sweet woodruff is picked to flavor a white wine cup drunk on May Day.

To bring out the hay scent of the leaves they should be crushed or dried. One could flavor other drinks with sweet woodruff as well as the wine.

CULTURE

Asperula odorata likes half shade, and I have noticed that it grows in damp soil in the woods, but in my own garden it does very well in a fairly dry soil. As a ground cover in the shade under taller plants, such as lilies, or *Meconopsis*, it is charming. The scent is strongest when the stems first grow up in the spring. The dried plants are more fragrant than the fresh ones and remain sweet for a long while.

BORAGO OFFICINALIS, L.

BORAGE

Beebread, Star Flower

Boraginaceae Annual

This unusually pretty annual is native to Europe and North Africa and, like its relatives, the anchusas and mertensias, has flowers which reflect the deep blue of the southern skies with an underglow of pink, which, in the white borage, appears as a blush under the creamy surface. The whole plant is covered with bristly hairs.

Root. The root is single, like a taproot with rootlets growing out from it.

Borago officinalis, borage

Stem. The stems rise up eighteen inches to two feet.

Leaf. The leaves are oval, rough, and hairy, with somewhat fluted margins. Ibn Baithar says they are shaped like ox tongues. The longest ones measure from four to six inches, and they grow smaller as they ascend the stems.

Flower. The flowers are borne in leafy clusters at the tips of the stems which bend way over so that their faces are hidden unless the plants are high on a bank, or hanging over a wall. They have a starry look; the five-pointed petals alternate with five slenderly tipped green sepals. The petals rise into a whitish-lavender crown in the center. Inside of this raised circle are purple filaments with white anthers, and within this circle is another set of stamens with black anthers. The two sets of stamens form a cone and the whole face of the flower makes a pretty pattern. The corolla lifts, whole, right out of the calyx.

Seed. The seeds are large, rough, ridged, blackish, and their base is like the base of a cone.

Variety. The blue-flowered borage is the type. There is a white-flowered variety with lighter green stems and leaves, and dark brown filaments. There are red- and violet-flowered ones, too, but so far these have eluded my diligent searching. The several plants together must make a lovely combination of color.

HISTORY AND LEGEND

The Crusaders are said to have introduced borage into Europe. Its Arabic name is *abu-raj*, which means, "father of sweet." The old verse, "I, borage, bring courage" comes from the Latin saying, *"Ego borago gaudia semper ago."*

Ibn Baithar said that borage drunk in wine made one

jolly, and cooked with honey it cured hoarseness of the windpipe and larynx, and that the burnt leaves of borage were good for the sore mouths of children.

As a medicine some said it was cooling, and others that it was hot. It was given in slow fevers, presumably for its cooling properties, and on the other hand administered in cold wine as a cordial and bracer to the spirits, and above all to stimulate courage.

Quintinye grew it in Louis IV's garden and it is one of the plants mentioned by Peter Martyr as planted on Isabella Island by the companions of Columbus. It came to the American colonies quite early, but is not on John Josselyn's list.

USES

It was grown as a bee forage.

Food. In olden days the flowers were candied as a sweetmeat and flavored cordials. The leaves have a certain mucilaginous quality and when cooked lose their bristliness and become like a dark green spinach. Most of us, however, will not get too excited over the prospect of a new spinach. The flower sprays and leafy tops were, and still are, steeped in cold drinks such as claret cup, negus, and cool tankards to which they impart a cucumbery flavor.

Separated from their calyces the corollas can be floated in cold drinks as one would maraschino cherries, and also can be used to garnish salads.

CULTURE

Borage flowers quickly after sowing and likes a dry, sunny exposure. It might be sown at intervals during the summer to keep a succession of bloom. It should not be sown too closely, and when the plants are up a few inches, if they are too thick, they can be thinned out. Borage can be transplanted. If the flowers are cut off the plants continue to bloom, although the stems become coarser.

It is so pretty it rightly belongs in the flower garden, and it possesses the virtue of being a good cut flower, keeping well indoors in water.

Borage is grown from seed, which keeps its vitality a long time.

BRASSICA ALBA, RABENH.

WHITE MUSTARD

AND

BRASSICA NIGRA, KOCH

BLACK MUSTARD

Cruciferae Annual

The black and white mustards are native to Europe and Asia and widely naturalized in the United States and Europe. It is difficult to tell the two apart, but when dead, dried, and spread out on herbarium sheets their differences stand out. They are pretty plants and, as with the dandelion, if they had not multiplied so obtrusively but instead had thrown out a challenge to the gardener's skill, they would be admired and valued for their pale yellow flowers. As it is, one hesitates to advise any one to grow them, for they are a weed.

Root. The root is a taproot, light colored and stiff.

Stem. The stems are light green, ridged, branching, and with rough hairs on them. Bailey says *alba* grows to four feet high and *nigra* to ten.

Leaf. The leaves are yellow-green, roughly hairy below, deeply and irregularly cut, shaped somewhat like a lyre, with margins irregularly lobed. The lower ones are eight inches long, growing smaller as they ascend the stem.

Flower. The four-petaled pale yellow flowers are in clusters and along the stems. The blossoms of *Brassica nigra* in their twig-like racemes do not overtop the central unopened buds, while the flowers of *Brassica alba* do overtop them. They have a delicate fruity fragrance with a bit of heaviness underlying it, and the whole plant tastes pungent.

Seed. The principal difference is in the seed capsules and seeds. The seed capsule of *Brassica nigra* is one-half inch long, narrow, ribbed, and has a projecting end with a little nob at its tip. It generally contains about twenty small spherical red-brown seeds; whereas the seed capsule of *Brassica alba* is one and one-half inches long, curves up and out, has a hairy receptacle, and looks like the top of a fool's cap. The seeds are white, spherical, and their smallness has become proverbial. The seeds only smell when crushed and some say they have sulphur in them; they taste piquant and bitter.

HISTORY AND LEGEND

Skinner, in the "Myths and Legends of Flowers," tells this parable about the mustard seed, from one of the Buddha stories: A baby had died and its distracted mother carrying the cold body in her arms implored the wise man to heal it, and he looked at the little dead face and said, "It can only be healed if you can get some mustard seed from a house where no child, husband, parent, or servant has died." So the mother hurried from house to house, but wherever she went she found that some one had died, and at last she understood, and realized that death at some time had visited every house.

Mustard has been a condiment since the earliest days, and in Europe during the Middle Ages was eaten with salted meats.

USES

In France, the oil extracted from the seeds enters into the manufacture of a yellow soap. In Japan and Bengal it is used for illuminating.

Medicine. Both the white and the black mustard are in the United States Pharmacopoeia, and are used as an emetic when taken internally, and as a poultice in the guise of the famous mustard plaster when applied externally as a counter-irritant. White mustard is said to have the same qualities as black only to a lesser degree.

Food. The young leaves are good and peppery in a salad of lettuce or endive leaves, or as "greens."

Mustard seed is bruised and made into a spicy condiment to serve with meats, and it flavors many sauces.

Mustard can be purchased as a powder or made up into a sauce according to the English or the French way.

CULTURE

The plants flower quickly from seed and should be sown several times to continue the supply of young leaves. The seeds lie dormant on the ground for a long time and suddenly germinate. Around our place it is a rampant weed. If the young leaves are to be picked, it is best to grow it, and not depend on collecting from the fields. The plant grows very quickly and by cutting it back one keeps it from flowering.

CALENDULA OFFICINALIS, L.

POT MARIGOLD

Marybud, Gold Bloom

Compositae Annual

This handsome and popular annual of the flower garden is native to Asia, southern Europe, and the Levant. The Latin name, calendula, comes from *calends* or *calendae*, and means, "through the months," and truly the round yellow or orange blossoms keep on opening all summer and have the great advantage of coming forth in greatest abundance toward the fall long after the first frosts have blighted the garden. The plant feels sticky and furry to the touch and has a warm, sweet, spicy scent.

Root. It has a small root.

Stem. The stems are somewhat prostrate, ridged, furry, and of a darkish green. They branch from the base and have many leaves.

Leaf. The leaves are soft and longish, about one and one-quarter to two and one-half inches across and four to six inches long and clustered. They are rounded, with a prominent midrib, and the base partially envelops the stem. On some of them little thorn-like sharp jags are sparsely placed along the margins, and one of these is at the tip of the leaf.

Flower. The flower buds are round, the flowers flat and velvety, generally with many rows of ray florets surrounding the center disk ones, and in color some are pale yellow and others deep orange, while a few are in several tones. The flowers measure about two inches across. The calyx is composed of numerous furry, narrow sepals of dark green tipped reddish.

Seed. The seeds are curved and ridged, something like tiny dried worms, and are about one-quarter of an inch long. Vilmorin says their germinating power lasts three years.

HISTORY AND LEGEND

Katherine Neals, who has written at length of the history of this flower, says that in India the Buddhists hold it sacred to the goddess Mahadevi, whose trident emblem is adorned with the flowers, while her devotees crowned themselves with marigolds at her festivals. The Greeks liked it and made decorations of it. To dream of a marigold foretold marriage, riches, and success. There is a superstition in Brittany that if a maiden touches a marigold with her bare foot she will be able ever afterwards to understand the language of birds. It was the appropriate flower for Lady Day, the 25th of March. During the reign of Henry VII, baskets filled with marigold flowers were sent to ladies by their admirers. In Mexico, however, this sunny flower is strangely the emblem of death, and is used to decorate churches, but not on festive occasions. According to an old German account, it was called *Todtenblume,* and no one would accept it as a present.

USES

Marigold petals give their golden color to butter, and are also an adulterant for saffron.

Medicine. During the Middle Ages a decoction of the petals was taken for different ailments. The petals in a tincture were used by the surgeons during the Civil War. It is in the British Pharmacopoeia.

Food. The petals have no taste before they are cooked and after cooking taste a little bitter, but when mixed with almond paste and other ingredients they have an unusual and savory flavor. The deepest orange flowers are said to have the strongest taste.

CULTURE

The marigold comes readily from seed. They can either be planted in flats indoors and transplanted later, or seeded where they are to stay and flower. Nowadays the marigolds are often forced for winter blooming and for this should be planted in the early fall.

Harvest. Cut the flower heads in full bloom, and then remove the ray florets by hand and dry these indoors in the shade so that none of their warm color will be lost.

CAPSICUM ANNUUM, L.

PEPPER

Red Pepper, Chili Peppers, Cayenne Peppers, Bell Pepper, Cherry Pepper, Cluster Pepper, Squash Pepper, Tomato Pepper

Annual (in the North)

Solanaceae Perennial (in the South)

The modifying adjectives of the names indicate the

Capsicum annuum, pimento

variety of shapes and colors of the peppers. Only a few were given, for, according to one writer who has counted them, there are "fifty mild and edible ones, for those who have acquired the taste; twelve hot ones for pickles and sauces; and six ornamental kinds." The *Capsicum annuum* is native to Central and South America, where it is a perennial woody plant, but in northern countries it is grown as an annual. The whole plant is smooth and somewhat shiny, and with its colorful fruits and neat habit of growth makes a decorative pot plant for the house in winter.

Stem. The stem is woody, much branched, and grows up to eighteen inches or two feet.

Leaf. The leaves are pointed, slender, with margins curling in and somewhat fluted.

Flower. The creamy white flowers have a short calyx and often face downwards, and like their relatives, the deadly nightshade, they have five flat-pointed petals and measure about three-quarters of an inch across. The stamens are greenish, shorter than the pistil, and all are bunched together in the center of the blossom. The fruits and flowers appear simultaneously on the plant.

Fruit. The fruits are podlike, hollow, generally pendant with a thick covering and contain the white kidney-shaped seeds. The larger the fruit the milder the flavor. The seed catalogues give a long list of peppers, the fruits of which vary in length from two to six inches, and in form from those like clustered cherries to huge bell shapes, and in color some begin green and turn red as they ripen, while others are yellow or dark violet when ripe. The variety pictured in this book bears shiny twisted tubular fruits with pointed tips which at first are bright green and later turn a brilliant scarlet. According to the catalogue, a variety called "Rainbow" begins green, then turns white, then golden yellow, and finally ends its chameleon-like career under a brilliant scarlet cloak.

HISTORY AND LEGEND

Peppers were said to have been brought to Spain by the physician in Columbus' fleet in 1494. In South America numerous varieties had been cultivated. The Spaniards brought the chilis to the Southwest along with melons, watermelons, and onions.

In Jamaica, during the early colonial days, the juice of a pepper was put into the eyes of the slaves as a punishment. Some of the Indians were said to have injected the juice into their own eyes before going out to strike fish to help them to see better. There is a superstition that peppers grow better if planted by a red-headed or a high-tempered person, and in line with this is the following, from the *Journal of American Folklore*, as told by an American Negro. "My old woman and me," said he, "had a spat and I went right out and planted my peppers and they came right up."

USES

The flesh of the fruit is the portion used.

Medicine. The dried flesh of the peppers is eaten by the people of the Southwest as a stimulant to a sluggish digestion. It is also thought to be effective in curing a sore throat, for malaria, colic, and alcoholism.

Food. The southern people around the world seem to flavor their dishes with peppers. The sweet peppers are filled with cream cheese, sliced, and laid on lettuce leaves.

They are stuffed with meat, cut up into salads, *pilaffs*, and other rice dishes, and mixed with pickles. Tabasco sauce is flavored with peppers. The long pointed type of fruit grown in Hungary is dried to make "paprika." The dried fruits of pepper are powdered and mixed with turmeric and other spices to prepare curry powder. They are very important in Southwestern cooking where the chilis are ground to a powder on a *metate* and cooked with meat, and eaten as a sauce with *tortillas*. In the fall when the cottonwoods turn a golden yellow, the scarlet peppers strung on yucca slips hang down in long waving garlands from the flat roofs of the native salmon-colored adobe houses.

CULTURE

In the North, in February or March, the seed is sown either in a flat indoors, in a hotbed, cold frame, or greenhouse. As soon as the plants are up a little they are transplanted into paper pots, so they will make a good clump of roots and not receive a setback from their next move, which is into the vegetable garden, after all danger from frost is over.

Harvest. The fruits are picked when they are ripe and dried. For the average cook, however, fresh peppers can be purchased all winter, and there is not much point in troubling to dry them unless a particular variety with a special flavor is desired.

CARVUM CARVI, L.

CARAWAY

Umbelliferae Biennial

Caraway is native to Europe and has become naturalized a little in the United States. Its feathery leaves are similar to those of its close relative, the carrot, which it resembles, except that it is a taller and more leafy plant.

Root. It has a long and tapering root, yellowish-white, fine grained, and with a flavor not unlike the carrot.

Stem. The stems are glaucous, marked with horizontal lines, and over two feet high.

Leaf. The bluish-green leaves are much cut into thread-like segments. Their taste has something of the carrot and the parsley, a little bitter, yet pleasant.

Flower. The flowers come the second season, in May, and are borne in flat umbels and from a distance look greenish-yellow. Upon close examination they prove to be a creamy yellow with the tiny petals curled in at the edges, greenish-yellow centers, and thread-like stamens which give the whole inflorescence a lacy look.

Seed. The seeds ripen in June and early July. They are about one-quarter of an inch long, concave on one side and convex on the other. They are dark brown with ridges much lighter in color and have a little button at one end. They smell of caraway, camphor, and anise; their taste is sharp, of camphor, warm, and pleasant, all composed into a distinct caraway flavor. The fresh home-grown seeds taste much stronger than the bought ones. They keep their vitality a long while.

HISTORY AND LEGEND

The name is said to come from the former province, Caria, in Asia Minor. The seeds of caraway were found in the débris of the lake dwellings of Switzerland. Pliny and Apicius mentioned it, and Dioscorides prescribed it for pale-faced girls. The roots mixed with milk made a sort of bread, called *chara* by Julius Caesar, was eaten by the soldiers of Valerius. Ibn Baithar speaks of caraway, and Charlemagne had it on his list. It was customary for the farmers of England to give caraway seed cakes to their laborers at the end of the wheat sowing.

USES

Medicine. The oil extracted from the seeds is given internally for colic, digestive disturbances, to correct griping cathartics, and also to improve the taste of bitter remedies.

Perfume. Small quantities of the oil distilled from the seeds in combination with other oils flavor mouth washes, cheap perfumes, and, in England, soap as well. The ground seed is good with other ingredients in sachet powders.

Food. On the Continent the oil has been used for centuries in brewing liqueurs, such as *kümmel,* in Germany and Russia, and *l'Huile de Venus,* in France. The Germans are especially fond of the taste of caraway and flavor their sauerkraut, bread, biscuits, cakes, and cheeses with the seed. The Dutch cultivate it extensively and put it into their cheeses, too. Roast apples, or other baked fruits flavored with caraway seeds, are good. Caraway comfits, which consist of the seeds encased in white sugar, decorate and flavor cookies and cakes.

CULTURE

Caraway is grown from seed and likes a sunny, dry situation. It is hardy, and fruits well in this country, especially in the North. The end of the first season the leaves will be up about eight inches. During the winter, I have protected my plants with a light covering as I do the other perennials and biennials, but am not sure that this is necessary.

Most of the seed used in the United States is imported from Europe.

CHRYSANTHEMUM BALSAMITA, L.

COSTMARY

Alecost, Mint Geranium, Sage o' Bedlam, Goose Tongue, Bible Leaf

Compositae Perennial

The costmary, a native of western Asia and escaped a little in North America, is a hardy, weedy-looking plant growing three feet high in my garden and increasing rapidly from the side shoots until it is almost as thick as a shrub.

Root. The roots are shallow, wiry, slender, and branching.

Stem. The shrubby stems are ridged, one-quarter of an inch across, and the side shoots branch out from them, one growing out from the next.

Leaf. The leaves are long, narrow, rounded at the tip, gray-green and downy. The margins are "snipped about the edges," to quote Parkinson, and somewhat frilled. The stalks are as much as three inches long, and the lower leaves up to six inches in length, and about one and one-half inches across. They are very fragrant at the first sniff, smelling, without crushing, pleasantly of lemon, chrysanthemum, and a bit of mint.

Flower. The flowers come in August in terminal

clusters of twelve or more. They are round, flat, daisy-like, and have a yellow center with short white ray florets, and are about three-quarters of an inch across. Bailey says when the white rays are absent the plant is known as var. *tanacetoides*.

HISTORY AND LEGEND

The name *balsamita* comes from its balsamic odor; costmary from *costus*, a violet-scented plant from the Himalayas, the roots of which made an expensive perfume; and from the Virgin Mary to whom the plant seems to have been dedicated in most European countries; alecost, because of its function of aromatizing ale and beer. Al Makkari, a historian of Arabic Spain, who wrote in the fifteenth century, says the plants were a well-known product of Spain and were exported to all parts of the world for the sweetness of their scent. In Elizabethan England the leaves were put amongst the sweet herbs to make a "sweet washing water." Parkinson says the leaves were brewed "to comfort both stomache and heart and to warm a *moist, dry brain.*" (The italics are mine.) The leaves were formerly used in salads but are too bitter for most modern palates. Samuel Stearns mentions it in "The American Herbal" in 1801.

USES

Medicine. The volatile oil is used, and it appears in the "National Standard Dispensary" of 1916, but is not important medicinally.

Food. In France the leaves are sometimes used as a condiment and it has entered into veal stuffing. The dried leaves make a good tea.

CULTURE

Costmary is perfectly hardy, but dies down to the ground every winter, coming up again the following spring. It seems to like a dry, sunny situation and average garden soil.

I increased mine from cuttings of the root.

Harvest. The leaves are cut off before the plant flowers. The young leaves seem more tender than the old ones.

CORIANDUM SATIVUM, L.

CORIANDER

Umbelliferae Annual

Coriander is a dainty and attractive little plant, native to Europe.

Root. It has a slender taproot.

Stem. The stems are cylindrical, smooth, and spreading, growing to fifteen inches in height in my garden, and elsewhere to two or three feet.

Leaf. The leaves are a yellowish-green. The radical ones are rounded, not much divided, and are incised and toothed. The stem leaves, however, are very much divided into thin linear segments. The leaves taste horribly, and since they look very like those of anise, one should be careful not to pick them by mistake for the salads.

Flower. The grayish-white, or slightly rose-tinted florets are borne in sparse umbels of six to nine florets and three or four little umbels combine into one large one at the termination of the stem. The florets are irregular and remind one of the enameled flowers decorating the brooches which adorned the bosoms of our Victorian grandmothers.

Seed. The seeds at first are a shiny yellow-green and striped, and are like hard little balls about one-eighth of an inch long. When they ripen, they are still round, fairly large balls with a point at the tip, ridged, straw-colored and hollow. The unripe seed and foliage have an unpleasant odor. In fact the name of the plant comes from the Greek word *koris*, which means bedbug because of the resemblance of the scent to that of the beetle. The ripe seed tastes of orange, sharply and pleasantly, with a characteristic quality of its own. It smells as it tastes.

HISTORY AND LEGEND

Seeds of coriander were found in the Egyptian tombs of the Twenty-first Dynasty, and it is one of the bitter herbs ordained to be eaten at Passover. Pliny quotes Varro as authority for sprinkling coriander, lightly powdered with cumin, and vinegar over all kinds of meat to keep it from spoiling in summer.

Ibn Baithar says there was much discussion by the classical and Arabic herbalists as to the medicinal effects of the juice, and that it was cooked with fat hens.

Two German couplets from the Pfalz in which coriander figures are as follows:

"Kimmel un Korjaner
's is' ener wie de anner!"

"Annis, Fenchel, Koriander
's is der E wie der ander!"

Which means "cumin and coriander all taste alike"; "Anise, fennel, and coriander all taste alike."

It has been grown in China since the fifth century where the seeds are said to confer immortality, and it is now grown in India. It was mentioned by John Josselyn, and appeared in the advertisement of the *Boston Evening Post* of 1771.

USES

Medicine. It is not important medicinally, according to the "National Standard Dispensary," except to render other drugs more agreeable to the taste.

Perfume. Small quantities of the oil distilled from the seeds enters into *eau de cologne* and *eau des carmes,* but not in perfumes. Before distilling, the seeds should be crushed.

Food. In Egypt, the seeds flavor bread, and elsewhere, sausage. They enter into curry powder, mixed spices, and certain liqueurs. The oil distilled from the dried ripe seeds is a condiment in confectionery, bread, cake, and cordials. Under the name of theobromine it improves the taste of inferior grades of cocoa. The seeds coated with sugar make little sugared balls called coriander comfits which are beloved by the children. In Yucatan, coriander seeds with lemon juice are served with deer steak.

CULTURE

Coriander grows in almost any good garden soil but prefers a warm, rather light one. Planted in May in my garden the fruit ripened the end of July. A second self-sown crop came up early in September. The plants should be sown thinly and if necessary thinned later to four or five inches apart in the rows.

It is cultivated on a large scale in Russia, Germany, and

North Africa. One million and a half pounds of coriander seeds were imported into the United States in 1927.

Harvest. The seeds should be picked before they begin to drop off.

CROCUS SATIVUS, L.

SAFFRON CROCUS

Iridaceae Perennial

This is a fall-flowering crocus distinguished from all others of its kind by the fact that the three-parted, orange-scarlet stigmas hang down outside the perianth as if falling through by their own weight. In late October, at Peekskill, when the frosts have blighted the dahlias, it is a delight to come upon the delicate grayish-purple blossoms, so like the first crocuses of spring, in the otherwise devastated garden.

Corm. The crocus is a bulbous plant, having a small satiny brown corm with a dimple at its base, covered with lengthwise straw-colored fibers, as if to protect it. From each corm rise three to six scapes with as many flowers and several leaves.

Stem. The stem and flower are about three to four inches high.

Leaf. The leaves are grass-like, have a white midrib, and are twelve to seventeen inches long, so long that they fall over. They come in the spring without the flowers and then die down.

Flower. A tuft of leaves and one single flower rises from a pale whitish spathe with two bract-like envelopes. The flowers, as Ibn Al Awam says, are shaped "like a long nut" or goblet not much opened at the mouth. The margins are wavy at the tips and are lavender striated a deeper color. There are three yellow stamens, and the yellow anthers are borne on flat, broad, lavender filaments. The pistil has an orange-scarlet stigma divided deeply into three parts, which is the saffron of commerce. The little flower has a sweet scent, faintly like that of a lily, with a little heliotrope, and something of violet. All writers agree that it smells less strongly in northern climates.

HISTORY AND LEGEND

The saffron crocus has a famous past, and was valued for its color, flavor, and fragrance by the Mediterranean people probably even before the Phoenicians carried it over their trade routes. It is mentioned in the "Iliad" and by Theocritus and Theophrastus, who noticed that it grew best along the roadsides and in well-worn places, and presumed this was because it liked to be trodden upon. At Egyptian banquets, lotus and saffron flowers were strewn on the floors and in Roman days it was customary to sprinkle the theaters with saffron water. Ibn Baithar said it was a stimulant, and that when mixed with wine it caused people to gesticulate like animals. I wonder if this was the drink given to Ulysses's men by Circe. In Nürnberg, in 1444 and 1456, people went to the stake for adulterating saffron. In Ireland the women are said to wash their sheets in saffron water to strengthen the limbs.

USES

Medicine. It is mentioned in the "National Dispensary" and is official in most pharmacopoeias but not in the

United States'. It is occasionally used for flatulent dyspepsia. The Pennsylvania Germans make a tea of it to bring out the measles. Elsewhere in the United States it is made into a mouth rinse for cases of thrush.

Perfume. Saffron oil is strong in the odor of saffron, of a somewhat culinary tone, says Poucher, and is attractive when mixed with the Oriental type of perfumes. It is now too expensive for coloring, and is replaced by tetrazine yellow.

Food. The dried saffron, to my palate, tastes like a disinfectant. When blended, however, with other condiments, it gives a definitely agreeable tone to the food which Southerners like, and it colors everything a brilliant yellow. John Evelyn in his "Acetaria" says, "Those of Spain and Italy we know generally make use of this flower, mingling its golden tincture with almost everything they eat . . ." And this is still true to-day. The Germans are said to flavor potpie and noodle soup with it. In Cornwall, England, "saffron cakes" are made with it. In Spain many dishes are gilded with saffron.

CULTURE

The saffron crocus is now grown from Spain to Kashmir, but mostly in Spain, according to Bowles, the authority on the crocus. It was formerly a small garden crop in Lancaster and Laban counties in Pennsylvania. Bowles says it is sterile and should be increased by the corms, as does Vilmorin, who says it sometimes sets seed. I planted the seed and it did not germinate, but that may be my fault. Bowles says it does best in a sunny, sheltered bed and should be divided every three or four years or it will produce nothing but leaves, and the corms will dwindle in size. For us it does very well and increases rapidly in the flower bed and is not planted in the grass. As with all bulbs, the leaves should be allowed to ripen before cutting them off. The corms can be bought at almost every bulb house in America.

Harvest. The flowers are picked as soon as they open and the stigmas are cut off with the finger nails and then dried in the sun or over a fire. Since this is tedious work and since 500,000 flowers are required for one pound of saffron, which, in the United States in January, 1927, cost nineteen to twenty dollars a pound, it is hardly profitable to grow the saffron crocus commercially.

CUMINUM CYMINUM, L.

CUMIN

Umbelliferae Annual

The cumin is native to the Mediterranean and is said to have been native to Egypt. Cumin is a low, untidy-looking plant with its flowers so dully colored one can hardly see them.

Root. It has a taproot.

Stem. The branching stems with their thread-like foliage spread out a little like spider's legs, and grow from four to eight inches high.

Leaf. The leaves are sparse and compounded into thread-like divisions. They taste bitter and balsamic.

Flower. The tiny flowers are not numerous. They are borne in umbels of from ten to twenty flowers at the extremities of the branches and are a dull magenta-pink.

Seed. The fragrant seeds are light yellow-brown, flat

on one side, one-quarter of an inch long, ribbed, and with a bit of the stem adhering to them. When unripe they taste like a disinfectant to me, but when ripe taste hot, and balsamic.

HISTORY AND LEGEND

Cumin is mentioned in Isaiah and in Matthew as a portion of the tithe paid by the Pharisees in Judea. Pliny in his usual chatty fashion tells us it produces paleness in those who drink the oil from the seeds in water, and that the disciples of Porcius Patro, a celebrated professor of eloquence, used to partake of this drink to acquire the paleness of their teacher and so look as if they, too, had spent long hours in study. Other writers, however, claim it cures pallor caused by illness!

It has been used in India, China, and Europe, is on Charlemagne's list, and appeared in American literature, but is probably not grown very much here. Amongst the Greeks, cumin symbolized cupidity, and misers were said to have eaten of it. Fernie says, "The herb was thought to confer specially the gift of retention, preventing the theft of any object which contained it, and . . . also keeping the fowls and pigeons from straying and lovers from proving fickle." In the Middle Ages, in Germany, the bride and groom carried cumin with dill and salt in their pockets during the marriage ceremony.

There is a Thuringen story about cumin. A wood nymph lived near to a peasant family and her airy presence brought them good luck. But the peasant wife wanted to make sure that the nymph would not leave them, so she cunningly baked some *kümmel* (cumin) in the bread, carried it to the grove of trees, and gave it to the nymph.

The fairy tasted the *kümmel* as soon as she bit into it and realized that the woman had not had faith in her. She was very angry and left immediately, and thenceforth good fortune no longer abided with this family.

USES

Medicine. An oil distilled from the seeds is carminative, and a stimulant.

Perfume. The oil from the seeds is very fragrant and enters into a synthetic cassia.

Food. The seeds flavor liqueurs, principally *kümmel* and *crême de menthe.* The Dutch and Swiss aromatize their cheeses with it. In Germany it flavors the bread, and with juniper berries and fennel, it flavors the sauerkraut. In combination with saffron and cinnamon it gives an unusual character to certain Spanish dishes. In Egypt, Turkey, and India it is a condiment and is one of the herbs mixed into curry powder.

CULTURE

Cumin is grown to-day in Sicily, Egypt, Asia Minor, India, Malabar, Persia, and Denmark.

According to Vilmorin, the seed, which retains its germinating power for two years, should be sown in the open ground as soon as it is warm enough. It is not at all difficult to raise. Planted the end of May at Foxden it bore fruit the end of July; that is, in about eight weeks after sowing.

Harvest. The ripe seeds are picked and dried.

DIANTHUS CARYOPHYLLUS, L.

CARNATION

Clove Pink, Picotee, Grenadine, Sops in Wine, Clove July Flower

Caryophyllaceae Perennial

This carnation is native to South Europe and India and is said by a German writer to be "The father of the garden pink." It has been difficult to obtain the seeds, and now I have grown it the plant seems to vary from Bailey's and other descriptions, so I checked up by having a herbarium specimen with which to compare it.

The plant is smooth and bushy, eighteen inches or more tall, with many leaves, leafier than *Dianthus plumarius*, and the stems rise up straighter, making a handsome subject for the border.

Root. The root is rather woody and branched, with many fibers.

Stem. The stems are angled, have prominent nodes, are gray-green with a bloom on them, as on the leaves, and rise to two feet and more.

Leaf. In the herbarium specimen the long, narrow linear leaves terminated in an obtuse end; in the garden now and then there is a leaf with an obtuse tip, the rest being pointed. In the garden the leaves are numerous, linear, channeled, acute, entire, and glaucous. The midrib is prominent on the under side. At the base they are three and one-half inches long, and grow shorter as they ascend the stem. They are in opposite pairs along the stem but form clusters at the base.

Flower. The flowers bloom in late June and early July

when the *Dianthus plumarius* is over. They are solitary on their own stems, five or more rising from a principal stem. The four short bracts outside the calyx come to a sharp point. The calyx is tubular, terminating in five sharply pointed tips. The corolla is of five broad, very dark red petals said to be sometimes flesh-colored. They are irregularly fringed, sometimes overlapping, and the claws are white, not bearded. The stamens, ten in number, are white, tipped red, and curve out at the tips to surround the ovary which is shaped like a bright green top and has a two-parted style beginning rose and terminating deep scarlet, each half curving out beyond the calyx like a graceful flourish to the letter V. The flowers are sweetly and spicily fragrant with a permeating quality.

HISTORY AND LEGEND

This is one of the flowers called "gilliflower" stock, *Matthiola incana*, and wallflower being others.

At Bologna the carnation is associated with the cult of Saint Peter, and the 29th of June is Carnation Day.

This carnation was listed in Prince's catalogues in 1790, and Bartram had it in 1814. Stearns' "The American Herbal" speaks of clove gilliflowers.

USES

Perfume. Piesse and Poucher, two writers on perfumes, both say the carnation is not used in perfumery but that a synthetic reproduction of its scent bears the name "carnation."

Food. Formerly a syrup was made from the flowers and they were conserved in sugar, pickled, and used to flavor wine and vinegar. The petals were picked out of their calyces, and the white heels cut off. Hill, in "Useful Family Herbal," 1770, says a tea was made of them which was a "cordial and good for disorders of the head," as follows: Over three pounds of flowers, as prepared above, five pounds of boiling water were poured. This was allowed to stand twelve hours and then the clear liquor strained off without pressing, and dissolved in two pounds of the finest sugar to every pint of liquid.

CULTURE

These plants come readily from seed sown in June or July in cold frames. At Foxden they are transplanted to the garden the following spring because I find so many carnations die out during the winter, but elsewhere they could no doubt be safely placed in their permanent positions in the fall. This dianthus will not flower the first year even if it is started in the greenhouse in January. It can be increased from cuttings and is perfectly hardy out-of-doors. Several plants died out in the rock garden with me, but liked the soil in the border.

DICTAMNUS ALBUS, L.

FRAXINELLA

Dittany, Bastard Dittany, Gas Plant, Burning Bush

Rutaceae Perennial

This plant is so fragrant in every portion that its perfume permeates the whole garden and even greets us over the hedges on our way in. Some of its names come from the fact that it will give forth a flash of light on a still evening, when a burning match is held under the flower cluster near the stem. It comes from South Europe and North China, and is a handsome and popular hardy garden plant. The white-flowered kind is the type and smells of lemon, lemon peel, and other fragrant elements. The pink-flowered variety is more fragrant and smells less of lemon and has an undertone of almond and vanilla. The plant is about three feet tall.

Root. It is shallow and fibrous, and falls to pieces easily.

Stem. The stems are round, the upper portions are incrusted with yellowish hairs, and are sticky to the touch. Each of the many branches rise from the roots and curve out a little.

Leaf. The leaves are compounded into from nine to eleven opposite leaflets. The central portion of the leaflets is convex on the back, concave on the upper surface, and grooved. The leaves are pointed at the tip and grow wider at the base and are shiny, finely toothed on the margins, dark green above, lighter and shiny below.

Flower. The flowers are in a loose, terminal spike on hairy pedicels, opposite, showy, like open butterflies, and two inches across. The calyx of the white variety has small greenish-white, five-parted, pointed sepals. The corolla is five-parted into white, pointed, slender petals, broader at the tip and then terminating in a slender foot. It faces sideways, and the lower petal is depressed. The stamens curving out beyond the petals are the most conspicuous part of the flower. They have four-parted yellow anthers on white filaments. The pistil is globular, and the ovary is five-parted, green and furry, and becomes a hard, divided capsule. The style and stigma are greenish in color.

In the pink variety the upper portion of the stem is marked with red and the calyx is also green, marked with red. The petals are of a pale pink with crimson lines on them. The anthers are also pink with red hairs at their tips. The pistil is pinkish. The ovary is reddish and hairy. The flower panicle is twelve inches high and six inches across at the base.

HISTORY AND LEGEND

Parkinson says it is profitable against the stinging of serpents, and a protection against contagious and pestilent diseases. The root is the most effective portion, yet the seed is also sometimes used. It grew in Gerard's garden, and he quotes Dioscorides as saying that the wild goats being stricken with darts, or arrows, would cause them to fall out of their bodies by eating dittany.

USES

Since the leaves, when dried, make a delicious tea, it is included in this book.

CULTURE

According to Bailey it is increased by seeds sown as soon as they are ripe in the open ground and covered one inch. They will germinate the next spring and when two years old the seedlings can be moved to the garden. It seems to thrive in a clay soil and to like sunshine, but will grow in partial shade. The older the plant the higher the flowering stems. It lives for years and is a perennial in the true sense of the word. I bought my plants from a nursery.

FOENICULUM DULCE, D.C.

FLORENCE FENNEL

Finnocchio

Umbelliferae Annual

This annual fennel is a low-growing, thick-set plant with a short stem. The stems are bushier, dwarfier, and spread out at the base and overlap each other only at the base, not all the way up the stem as in *F. vulgare*. The joints set very close together towards the base, which in time forms a bulbous thickening, firm and white. When cooked this makes a pleasant anise-tasting vegetable. It is a darker green than the others and the thread-like divisions of the leaves are shorter. It is very fragrant of anise.

Vilmorin says the plant never grows over two to two and one-half feet high. He describes the leafstalk as of a light green.

Seed. The seeds are oblong, very broad in proportion to their length, flat on one side and convex on the other, with five prominent ribs between which the gray color of the seed shows through.

USE

The Italians use the stem bases to aromatize wine, and eat the stem as a vegetable. The seeds of this variety are said to have the most agreeable taste of all and are used by the English as a condiment. The plant is grown extensively in California and sold as a vegetable in the Eastern markets.

CULTURE

For summer crops the seed is sown in spring and, where winters are not early, towards the end of summer for an autumn crop. It should be thinned to from eight to twelve inches apart and watered fairly frequently. When the head of the enlarged leafstalk is about as big as a hen's egg, says Vilmorin, it may be slightly earthed up so as to cover half of it and about ten days later the most forward plants can be cut. So far I have not succeeded in getting the leaf bases to swell up to a sufficient size, nor did the plant flower for me the first summer, but that may be the fault of insufficient skill and experience, for a neighbor of mine has been successful.

HISTORY AND LEGEND

The old writers did not always specify which of the fennels they were describing, so I have selected the history which may have been applied either to *F. vulgare, officinalis*, or *dulce*, and brought it under one general heading. Fennel is mentioned by Theophrastus, Hippocrates, and Dioscorides, and by Pliny, who said that before serpents cast off their old skins they ate fennel, and that the juice of the plant sharpened the sight, while the roots boiled in wine and applied to the eyes were thought to have cured cataract. It was thought if too many stalks of boiled fennel pickled in brine and honey were eaten they gave one a headache. It is said that female deer purge themselves with fennel before their young are born.

Ibn Baithar mentions it, and it is on Charlemagne's list.

John Josselyn said, "fennel must be taken up and kept in a warm cellar all winter." To-day it is grown commercially in southern France at Nîmes and near-by places, in Italy, Germany, and in California.

FOENICULUM OFFICINALIS, L.

SWEET FENNEL

Common Garden Fennel, Long Sweet Fennel

Umbelliferae Annual

Foeniculum officinalis comes from South Europe. The whole plant is stiffer and does not wilt as quickly when picked, nor is it as tall as *F. vulgare.*

Root. The roots are strong and thick.

Stem. The stems are blue-green, hollow, stiff and much branched, and grow to three feet high.

Leaf. The leaf bases are thickened and slightly surround the stem, but not nearly as much as in the other varieties. The leaves are divided into thin thread-like segments, are sparse at the tip and full at the base, and taste like anise.

Flower. The yellowish-green flowers are borne in broad terminal clusters and blossom all summer. The pedicels are sturdier than in the other fennels.

Seed. The seeds are almost one-half an inch long, ridged, grooved, the tip is divided into two, and the end often has the stem adhering to it. When crushed, they smell of anise and taste very sweet and like liquorice.

Use. When the plant is running to bloom the fresh, tender stems, still enclosed in their expanded leafstalks, are cut off and stood in water until it is time to serve them raw, as an *hors d'œuvres*. The seeds are used as a condiment. The leaves flavor sauces.

The var. *piperitum,* DC. called Carosella is beloved by Neapolitans, who eat the stems raw as one does young onions or celery. It is on every table from Naples to Rome from January to June, says one traveler.

FOENICULUM VULGARE, MILL

BITTER FENNEL

Common Wild Fennel

Umbelliferae Perennial

This fennel is also native to South Europe. It flowered the first summer in my garden, but was killed at the first "black frost." The whole plant is smooth, fragrant of anise, and tastes of anise.

Stem. The stems are tender, hollow, glaucous, gray-green, ridged, not the least woody, but of a quite herbaceous consistency and grow up to five feet high.

Leaf. The striking characteristic of this plant is the broad leaf bases which half surround the stems. Each base overlaps the preceding one and bends outward, and the effect is as if one had been braided in and under the next. These leaf bases are striated and light in color, especially at the margins, and where they join the stem. When the broad part ceases, the leaf continues as a central stem from which others branch off, and each in turn is divided into branching thread-like segments many of them one and one-half inches long. These leaflets are a bit droopy.

Flower. The flowers are borne in terminal umbels which are not flat, but made up of about twenty smaller umbels carried on stems of varying lengths. There are about fifteen yellowish-green florets to each of the little umbels.

Seed. The seeds are dark gray, round at both ends, and retain the remains of the withered stigmas. They have five ribs, three of them on the back, and one on each side. According to Vilmorin they keep their germinating power for four years.

USES

Food. Fennel seeds flavor liqueurs such as *L'anisette* of Strasbourg; in England they flavor soups; in Germany, bread. The leaves flavor the famous Polish soup, *bortsch,* and are also put in with boiled mackerel. They were a garnish to fish and in sauces as early as Parkinson's day. They are supposed to help digest the fat of the fish, whence perhaps the idea that to eat fennel was thinning.

Medicine. The dried ripe seeds are used. Culpeper said this fennel was the best for medicinal uses, and it is now in all pharmacopoeias. The action is carminative and it stimulates the secretion of sweat. Sometimes it is given hot in infusions such as barley water. The oil distilled from the fruits is also applied externally in eye lotions, and internally to cover the taste of unpleasant remedies, and to quiet babies.

Perfume. The oil from the seeds of *F. dulce* and *F. sativum* is not used much in perfumery, but occasionally in soaps.

CULTURE

It comes readily from seed and flowered the first summer for me in light, well-drained soil, and did not seem to need watering. The seeds should be sown as early as possible in the spring and thinned, if they are too thick, to about twelve inches apart in the rows. The plants can be transplanted if started indoors, but this sometimes proves fatal.

Harvest. The seeds should be gathered before they are fully ripe, according to Dr. Stockberger, who also writes that during recent years 275,000 pounds of seed have been imported annually.

FRAGARIA VESCA, L.

WOOD STRAWBERRY

Alpine Strawberry, Perpetual Strawberry

Rosacea Perennial

There are many strawberries, varying in the size and shape of the fruit, the facility with which the runners are produced, and the earliness and frequency of fruiting, as well as the delicacy of the flavor. From hundreds of horticultural varieties, and between twenty and thirty species, I have selected the following for their historical interest.

The strawberry longest known in Europe is the *Fragaria vesca,* the Wood Strawberry, a native throughout the whole Northern Hemisphere. It grows in woods, especially in mountainous districts where, because of the variations in altitudes, the fruits continue to ripen from June to September.

The plants are small, from six to twelve inches high, with leaves divided into three.

Stem. The stems are pinkish and woolly.

Leaf. The almost palmate leaves are divided into three, and have sharply and coarsely dentated margins. The surface is uneven, swelling up between the veinings, shiny green above, dull below, and hairy on all the ribs below.

Flower. The white blossoms, and later the fruits, are borne on erect branching, hairy stems standing higher than the leaves.

Fruit. The fruit is rounded, or conical and pendant. It is a delicious berry, a little tart, tasting of roses, and pleasantly. Its smell is characteristic.

HISTORY AND LEGEND

This species, according to Sturtevant's Notes, was mentioned as a wild plant by Virgil, Ovid, and Pliny. De Candolle says it was cultivated in the mediaeval period. Shakespeare mentions it, and in his day the doctors ordered a tea from the leaves to provoke urine, and used the roots for their astringent qualities. The leaves of this plant decorate the coronets of the English nobility, and hence the expression, "strawberry leaves," has come to mean a dukedom.

Prince in 1790 lists the "wood strawberry," and John Bartram lists the *F. vesca, virginiana*, and *elatior*.

FRAGARIA VIRGINIANA, DUSCHENE

VIRGINIA STRAWBERRY

Scarlet Strawberry

This strawberry is native to eastern North America. Sturtevant says the New England Indians called it *Wutta-*

shimneash. It grows on dry, sunny slopes, and flowers the end of May and early June. The plant makes runners early in the season.

Leaf. The leaves are about three inches long, quite broad, and stand four to six inches high, and are shiny green above and gray-green below, and only hairy on the midrib below.

Flower. The flowers are white, in clusters, and three-quarters of an inch across, and appear at the end of a longish hairy stem.

Fruit and Seed. The fruits are ovoid, plump, and borne on slender stalks, and the seed is deeply sunk, small, and brown.

HISTORY AND LEGEND

The American Indians bruised this strawberry with meal in a mortar to make bread. It is mentioned by Edward Winslow in Massachusetts in 1621, and Hutchinson describes how the settlers on the ship *Arabella* went ashore at Salem on June 12, 1630, and ate of the fragrant strawberries. Roger Williams says of this berry, "It is the wonder of all fruits growing naturally in these parts. It is of itself so excellent; so that one of the chiefest doctors of England was wont to say, that, 'God could have made, but God never did make, a better berry'." It was first mentioned in England by Parkinson in 1629. Sturtevant says that the modern varieties in America seem to belong mostly to the species represented in nature by the *F. virginiana*, although they are supposed to be a hybridization with *F. chiloensis* (a variety native to Chile), and the higher-flavored class with *F. elatior*. Furthermore he says the strawberry is so variable that if careful search were made almost all the cultivated types could probably be found growing wild. There is a white-fruited variety.

USES

The juice of the berry has long been used to clear the skin of spots.

In olden days strawberry leaves were added to cooling drinks and used in baths. According to Eleanour Rohde, strawberry wine was a favorite of Sir Walter Raleigh. But best of all uses is to eat the berries with sugar and the thick, clotted cream of Devonshire, called *crême renversée* in France. The wood strawberries served with white wine are luscious too.

Strawberry juice is used to color and flavor drinks of other fruits. Jams and conserves of the fruit are very popular, and in the United States strawberries laid between the layers of a cake or short biscuit are a national dish, the strawberry short cake.

GAULTHERIA PROCUMBENS, L.

WINTERGREEN

Checkerberry, Deerberry, Aromatic Wintergreen, Mountain Tea, Boxberry, Tea Party

Ericaceae Perennial

The checkerberry is a low-growing, shrubby plant with evergreen leaves. It is native from Newfoundland to Manitoba and south to Georgia and Michigan. The shiny yellow-green young leaves, tinted red, attract one's attention in the shade of the woods.

Root. The roots are little, fine, and hair-like coming from the underground stems.

Stem. The stems creep under the ground, and have a brown, scaly bark. From these grow the upright woody stems three to six inches high, smooth below, downy and crowned with leaves above.

Leaf. The leaves are evergreen, oval, and the largest measure one and one-half inches in length and one inch across. The smaller and younger ones are about one-half an inch long and one-quarter of an inch across. All the leaves are smooth and have tiny thorns growing out from the margins. The old ones are dark green above and yellow-green below. The young leaves are shiny, a fresh yellow-green, tinted reddish and are borne on new stems. When crushed they smell like peppermint candy.

Flower. The flowers come in June and July and are waxy white, slightly tinted pink, drooping, produced mostly singly in the axils of the leaves and borne on red stems.

Berry. The berries are crimson-red, subglobular, aromatic, and taste pleasantly. They have a five-celled capsule.

HISTORY AND LEGEND

Barton in his "Vegetable Materia Medica" says it was so abundant in the pine barrens of New Jersey that bunches of it were brought to the Jersey market of Philadelphia in November and December and sold for one cent each, and that deer and partridges fed on this and the *Mitchella repens* in late autumn. The country people thought that the peculiarly delicate flavor of venison came from the berries of the *Gaultheria procumbens*—hence one of its names, deerberry. These berries were also eaten by the Indians of Michigan and Wisconsin.

USES

The oil from the bark of sweet birch, *Betula lenta*, is nearly identical with the oil of wintergreen and is frequently sold as such.

Medicine. It is no longer in the United States Pharmacopoeia, nevertheless the volatile oil distilled from the leaves is much used to rub on joints for rheumatic pains, for lumbago, sciatica, and similar complaints. It is also administered internally in the treatment of rheumatic fevers. In America, oil of wintergreen was widely known because it was an ingredient in the quack medicine called the Panacea of Swain. It was introduced into England in 1762.

Perfume. The oil can be used in the preparation of synthetic cassia oil and in compounding new-mown hay perfumes, also in soaps.

Food. The berries infused in brandy or spirit make a beverage like bitters. Because the leaves were used for tea during the American Revolution, it is included in this book.

CULTURE

The *Gaultheria procumbens* grows in shady woods and likes a sandy or loose soil. When the plant is cultivated the soil should be mixed with leaf mold to a depth of four inches or so. The divisions of wild plants can be obtained and set out in the spring or fall six inches apart.

Harvest. The plants are usually gathered at the end of the growing season, and then are dried and packed for the market. For extracting the volatile oil the plants are first soaked in water for twenty-four hours, and then distilled in steam. Over 2,200 pounds of wintergreen oil were produced in the United States in 1909, and 6,000 in 1915. The production has gradually declined and the price advanced. In the past, collectors earned five cents a pound for the herb. It is difficult, however, to find quantities of it now, and not practical to grow it for profit.

HYSSOPUS OFFICINALIS, L.

HYSSOP

Labiatae Perennial

Hyssop is a perennial subshrub native to Europe and temperate Asia, and it has escaped and become naturalized in Michigan. It is a most attractive, fragrant plant, with its dark, sturdy-looking foliage, and flowering spikes of either pink, white, or blue, which bloom over a long period. In my garden it grows from fifteen to eighteen inches high, but in Europe it grows much taller.

Root. The roots are woody and spreading.

Stem. The stems are much branched from a woody base, angular and covered with a bloom.

Leaf. The leaves are dull, dark, and glisten with the dots of the fragrant oil. They are opposite, each pair at right angles to the one above, slender, entire, rounder at the tips and curve up from the stem in a happy fashion. They taste sharp, resinous, and camphory, and smell sagy and sweet, while the flowers smell more spicy and balsamic.

Flower. The tiny flowers, one-half an inch or less long,

are in loose terminal spikes about five inches long, made up of whorls of three flowers opposite to another group of three. The three upper petals and the two lower ones in the type are a dark blue with deep blue stamens topped with bronze anthers, which extend beyond the corolla. The five-parted calyx is purplish-green and the sepals are united almost to the tips, which are pointed. The flowers open at the end of June and keep on into September. The plants smell strongest just before flowering, of an aromatic, musty, slightly animal smell, which improves when the plant is dried. At Peekskill, however, they are less fragrant than they must be abroad.

Variety. Hyssopus officinalis var. *alba* has white flowers which look cool with the dark green foliage. *Hyssopus officinalis* var. *ruber* is a good shade of rose-pink without blue in it, and is grown in quantities at a nursery in Maine. *Hyssopus officinalis* var. *cristata* has the leaves notched at the margins, rounded at the tips, and turning up straight instead of in a curve as in the type. The surface of the leaves is dull underneath, shiny above, and a very dark green. It died over the winter in my garden. Parkinson speaks of a "yellow or golden hyssop" which is so handsome that the ladies wore it "on their heads and on their arms with as much delight as any fine flowers can give." This must be a variegated kind.

HISTORY AND LEGEND

Hyssop was so frequently mentioned in the Bible that Sturtevant thinks it must have grown wild in Syria and Egypt. In Leviticus, Chapter XIV, hyssop is mentioned as a purifying plant used by the priests to cleanse lepers. At the Passover, Moses commanded the Israelites to take a bunch of hyssop and dip it in the blood of the lamb to sprinkle the lintel and doorposts, after which none were to pass out until morning. David mentions it in a prayer, "Purge me with Hyssop and I shall be clean," Psalm LI, 7. Saint John wrote in Chapter XIX, 29, at the Crucifixion, "There was set a vessel full of vinegar: and they filled a sponge with vinegar and put it upon Hyssop and put it in His mouth . . ." It was known to the East Indians, and both the Arabs and Jews venerated the plant. Dioscorides recommended boiling it with rue and honey for a cough. It is said to keep off the evil eye and evil magic in Sicily.

USES

Hyssop is said to give a fine scent and taste to honey and should be planted near beehives.

Medicine. It is in the "National Standard Dispensary" as aromatic, stimulant, and diaphoretic, and is taken as an infusion. A tea made from the leaves and flowering tops is given for troubles of the chest, and to help expectoration of the phlegm, and in France it is used in a preparation for healing wounds.

Perfume. An essential oil extracted from the green portions is fragrant, and used in making melissa water, and in English *eau de cologne,* and, like clary sage, gives a note to perfumes to-day.

Food. The leaves and tips have been a condiment to supply a bitter taste. Hyssop has gone into the preparation of the liqueurs of the monks of Chartreux and the Trappist Fathers. It is a favorite tea in France. Eleanour Rohde says it enters in French and Italian cookery, and that sometimes the flowers were used in soups and strewn on salads.

CULTURE

Hyssop comes readily from seed, either indoors or right out in the garden. Once started the plants grow well and are hardy through the winter. In Europe one is advised to renew the plants every three or four years. Most growers say hyssop prefers a chalky soil, but any well prepared and not too fertile soil seems agreeable.

INULA HELENIUM, L.

ELECAMPANE

Elfwort, Elf Dock, *Enula campana*

Compositae Perennial

Elecampane is not a potherb or a perfume plant, but is included because of sentiment, and because, with its somewhat coarse, daisy-like golden flowers, it is a handsome plant for a background to the other herbs. It is native to Europe and northern Asia and naturalized in the United States.

Root. The root is thick and branched, blackish outside and white within; very bitter-tasting when fresh; and is said to have an aromatic, camphory scent which improves when dried.

Stem. The stem is over four feet high, brownish-green, round, and roughly hairy.

Leaf. The huge, coarse basal leaves have a petiole of seven inches and the leaf is fifteen inches long. The bottom stem-leaves clasp the stem and measure sixteen inches in length and decrease in size as they rise. The tips are yellowish-green, soft to the touch, very downy on the under side, with rough hairs on the upper surface. The margins are scalloped, a long one alternating with a short one.

Flower. The flowers are either solitary, or a few are borne at the tips of the stems. They have a golden-brown disk surrounded by a wheel-like circle of golden yellow, thinly spaced, ray florets, the tips of which are fringed. They measure three and one-half inches across.

HISTORY AND LEGEND

Inula helenium was described by Dioscorides, and Horace told how, when the Romans were surfeited with rich food, they craved turnips and "the appetizing enulas from Campana." Saint Isidor of Seville in the seventh century mentioned it as did Ibn Baithar. Parkinson and Culpeper spoke of using the roots "beaten" in a new ale, or beer which when drunk daily was said to strengthen and clear the eyesight, a superstition dating back to Pliny, who probably got it from earlier writers. It is a very old German custom when gathering a bunch of herbs to have the *Inula helenium* in the center of the nosegay, for the flower resembles the sun and so symbolizes Odin's or Baldur's head (later Saint John's), Josselyn mentions it, and it is in Claytonius' "Flora Virginica" of 1762. It is on the list of seeds for sale in the *Boston Evening Post* of 1771, and Bartram advertised it in his catalogue of 1814.

USES

Medicine. The roots are candied for a cough medicine.

It is supposed to have tonic and stimulating properties. It is in most official pharmacopoeias, but not in that of the United States. The dried roots are used internally as an expectorant. Elecampane roots and juniper berries are the two main bases in domestic veterinary practice, being given to horses for coughing and to sleek their coats.

Food. Even when sugared the roots are exceedingly bitter, and seem to grow more so after they have been in the mouth some time. It is also used to flavor absinth.

CULTURE

Elecampane is said to thrive best in a deep clay loam which has been well prepared and supplied with moisture. The plants should be three or four feet apart.

It is best propagated by division of the roots, but grows readily from seed sown out-of-doors. It does not flower the first year from seed.

Harvest. The fresh roots are gathered in the autumn from two-year-old plants, and are dried in the shade. Fifty thousand pounds of elecampane roots a year were imported into the United States before 1914.

IRIS FLORENTINA, L.

FLORENTINE IRIS

Fleur-de-lis

Iridaceae Perennial

This exquisite iris is a hardy plant native to central and southern Europe, and in our own South it is almost a weed. It flowers about the third week in May and rises eighteen inches or more high. In spite of the fact that it is not new or in the least expensive its pearly iridescent color and delicate iris-like fragrance make it one of the most desirable irises.

Rhizome. The root is a rhizome, shiny white and smooth outside, and inside creamy white, and of a smooth, solid, chalky-looking consistency when fresh. For the odor to develop the root has to be dried.

Stem. The stems are round with a bloom on them and gray-green.

Leaf. The leaves are fifteen to eighteen inches high, light green, in sheaves at the base. They are fairly wide and terminate in a point, sometimes curving a little.

Flower. About five flowers are borne on a stem. They are the palest of blues marked with chartreuse green on either side of the deep golden beard. A rosy glow is over the three caps to the stamens, which have a blue line down their center. The standards are ice blue.

HISTORY AND LEGEND

Iris is the name of the Greek Goddess of the Rainbow, who, with Hermes, was the messenger of the Gods. The iris was the emblem of the kings of France, was conventionalized in the royal coat of arms, and was called fleur-de-lis. The rulers often wore pale blue velvet trains embroidered with white or golden fleur-de-lis. In the seventeenth century, calamus roots and orris roots were used to make washing balls. Prince's catalogue of 1790 lists twelve varieties of iris and Bartram listed the *Iris florentina* in 1814.

USES

Babies use beads of orris root to teethe on; Leghorn

and Paris export twenty million of these beads a year. Orris thrown on open fires gives a pleasant smell, and counteracts the smell of liquor, garlic, and tobacco from the breath.

Perfume. Poucher says that the orris comes from *Iris pallida, Iris florentina,* and *Iris germanica,* but that the best roots come from the *Iris pallida* in Tuscany. Powdered orris root is used in violet powder because of its delicate violet scent, and also in dental preparations. It is the basis of sachet powders and much employed in violet soap. It enters into *Frangipani,* the most lasting perfume made, according to Piesse, and into a tooth powder. Orris oil is distilled from the rhizomes, and is used as a blend in perfumes, and a base for violet compositions.

CULTURE

It does not require a rich soil, but needs a warm, sunny situation.

It is propagated from divisions of the root.

Harvest. The root is collected in the summer and then peeled and dried in the sun.

LAURUS NOBILIS, L.

LAUREL

Sweet Bay

Lauraceae Tree

The laurel is native to the Mediterranean region where it grows to a tree up to forty feet high. Its glossy, evergreen, scented foliage is famous as composing the wreaths of victory and the tree has played an important rôle in Greek and Roman mythology. No one could call the laurel a "herb," but the leaves are so constantly mentioned in recipes, and it is such a handsome plant, either growing in the ground or, where it is not hardy, in tubs, that we recommend every herb gardener to have at least two of them, for in a garden scheme pairs are so much more attractively disposed of than single specimens.

Stem. The stems are woody, sometimes reddish or olive green.

Leaf. The evergreen leaves are alternate, smooth, shiny, and dark green, of a stiff texture and three inches or more in length and one across at the widest parts. They terminate in points both at the base and tip, and are lighter and yellowish on the under side where they show a network of veins, the side veins branching out from the central one. The margins are slightly rippled, and there is a prominent midrib. When crushed they smell deliciously of lemon and resin.

Flower. The flowers are yellowish, inconspicuous, and are unisexual or dioecious (the male and female flowers being on separate plants). They measure one-eighth of an inch across and bloom in early spring in clusters of three or more to a stem, which rises directly from the woody main stem.

Fruit. The berries are dark purple or black. The wrinkled skin covers two seeds and they taste balsamic, bitter, and fatty.

Variety. There are several varieties of the laurel, differing in stature and the form of the leaves; one having curled and another variegated foliage; some of the varieties are named according to the shapes of the leaves such as var. *angustifolia*, var. *latifolia*, and var. *salicifolia.*

HISTORY AND LEGEND

The laurel was sacred to Apollo, who preferred it to all other trees, and his temple stood in a laurel grove. It was the augury of victory, and hence of good news.

De Gubernatis says the God of the Sun wears the laurel which is supposed to be luminous, and, like the God, to bestow light, fame, and glory, and that this light-giving quality is why it was used in connection with the oracles. The tripods of the Pythonesses were decorated with it, and they also ate the leaves to help them prophesy, and those who came to ask their advice were crowned with the leaves.

In Roman days the letter announcing a victory was fastened with laurel leaves, while victors in battle, and, in Greece, in athletic and poetic contests, were crowned with it. The statues of the Gods Apollo, Bacchus, Libertas, Salus, Esculapius, and Hercules were decorated with the branches of it. To-day in Italy, Sicily, and Corsica, the laurel plays a part in religious and other festivals. In Corsica the house is decorated with it at weddings, and near Bologna there is a custom which seems like a debased descendant of the oracles, consisting of burning the laurel leaves to predict the quality of the harvests. If they crackle it will be good, but if not it will be poor.

Ibn Baithar mentioned its medicinal uses and said if a single leaf is picked, not allowed to fall to the ground, and then laid behind the ear, it will prevent one's being affected by wine. There is a modern Andalusian song which prefers the laurel to all other trees, Ana above all other women, and the carnation to all other flowers:

Entre los arboles todos
Se señorea el laurel
Entre las mujeres Ana
Entre flores el clavel.

USES

Medicine. It is used for insect stings.

Perfume. An oil expressed from the fruit is called oil of bay and enters into toilet preparations.

Food. It is indispensable in a number of bouquets and is used for flavoring soups, certain sauces, and the preparations of pickled beef. There is always a bay leaf in the preparation of game, duck, chicken, and it flavors custards and milk puddings.

CULTURE

The laurel thrives in rich, peaty soil with plenty of moisture. It is much grown in European gardens for its fragrance and evergreen foliage, and is generally but not always clipped. It is grown in the South and in Mexico, but in the United States to-day it is scarce and exceedingly expensive, a clipped plant of any size bringing five hundred dollars in 1931.

It is propagated by cuttings of ripened wood three to four inches long, put in sharp sand under glass. As soon as they are ripened they are moved to small pots in fairly rich, sandy loam. According to Bailey they grow best in rich, sandy loam with perfect drainage. If grown in the North, in pots, they have to be wintered indoors where the temperature does not reach the freezing mark.

LAVANDULA VERA, DC.

TRUE LAVENDER

Labiatae Shrub

There seems to have been some confusion about naming these plants, and this lavender is also called *L. officinalis, Chaix., L. angustifolia, Moench,* and *L. spica, L.* All the lavenders are native to the Mediterranean region and grow wild in southern France, Spain, Italy, Corsica, and Sicily. The true lavender is distinguished from the spike lavender by having narrower leaves; by the character of the branches which are more numerous, compact, and erect and with only one spike and one pair of opposite leaves to each flowering stem. The whole plant has a woolly, grayish tinge, and when in flower the numerous, straight stems bent outwards by the weight of their spike-like inflorescence resemble a many sprayed silvery fountain. It is a beautiful plant and especially endearing because of its fragrance.

Root. The roots are woody, fibrous, and matted.

Stem. My plants did not rise above thirty inches in height, but they are said to grow to four feet. The furry stems are square, deeply furrowed, and sharply ridged.

Leaf. The leaves are linear with a strongly marked central rib, and curve down a little, being concave on the under side. They are in whorls of two or three at the end of the stem, forming a spike of from five to seven whorls.

The leaves have, to me, a slight tang. They combine the scents of turpentine, spice, and camphor.

Flower. The flowers which come in July are a true lavender color, are labiate and shaded darker at the edge of the petals. The two upper petals stand back and the three lower ones form a lip. They are one-quarter of an inch across. At the base of the corolla is the calyx, one-eighth of an inch long, a roundish, lavender-greenish, furry cup which contains the fragrance, the corolla being scentless. The calyx is subtended by a green bract which does service for two or three flowers. Some think it smells of bergamot, rose, and eucalyptol, hot and harsh. To me it smells sweetly of heliotrope, sharp, refreshing, and stimulating.

Seed. The seed is brown, oblong, and with a well marked white spot at the end where it is attached to the calyx. Its germinating power, according to Vilmorin, lasts five years.

Variety. L. vera Munstead, dwarf, twelve inches tall.

Lavendula vera alba is listed in the catalogues, but when grown from seed had lavender flowers. It probably has to be increased from cuttings. This one is said to have been popular in olden days, and in Queen Henrietta Maria's garden at Wimbledon, according to Eleanour Rohde, there were "great and large borders of rosemary and white lavender." Lamotte places *L. delphinensis* under this variety. According to the French, who are interested in the lavenders because of the oil used in perfumery, the ones growing wild are natural crosses, and hence the many different varieties.

There is a charming annual lavender called *L. abrotanoides, Lam.*, the seed of which came to me from Portugal as *Lavandula dentata.* It has much cut leaves and branches widely, is fragrant, but not of lavender. *Lavandula latifolia,* Vill. or *L. spica,* spike lavender, is more spreading than the true lavender and less shrubby. It also has larger leaves. According to Vilmorin, the flower stems are less numerous, more vigorous, less erect, and bear more developed branches than the true lavender. The flowers are also smaller and the fragrance not so delicate. *L. Stoechas* is a tall shrub growing up to three feet high. The leaves are thin and small and many of them grow together on little stems, which in turn grow out from all along the main stem, more like the rosemary's leaves. The flower clusters are club-shaped. It is sometimes cultivated in gardens, but is less fragrant than either the spike or true lavender.

HISTORY AND LEGEND

The Romans perfumed their baths with lavender, and hence the name, for the Latin word *lavare* means "to wash." The spikenard of the Bible is lavender, the name being composed of Nardus, a town in Syria, and spike. In Chapter IV of Saint Mark, 3, 4, 5, when Christ was in the home of the leper, "There came a woman having an alabaster box of ointment of spikenard very precious and she brake the box and poured it on His head . . . and there were some that had indignation within themselves and said 'Why was this waste of ointment made?' For it might have been sold for more than three hundred talents and given to the poor."

In Tuscany lavender is said to protect little children from the evil eye, and the Kabyle women of North Africa think it protects them from maltreatment by their husbands.

Josselyn mentioned it, and it was in Prince's catalogue and in Bartram's as *Lavandula spica.*

USES

Oil of aspic from lavender is used to dilute delicate colors for painting on porcelain and it also enters into the composition of varnishes.

Medicine. The "National Standard Dispensary" says it is practically never employed in medicine, but Merck says of true lavender that it is stimulant, tonic, and used internally and externally in hysteria, headaches, fainting, nervous palpitation, and giddiness. In olden days a decoction of the flowers was much used as a mouth gargle and for the above ailments. The oil cured old sprains and stiff joints and was put on wounds. The famous Palsy drops, which sound as if the heroines of Jane Austen, ever ready to faint and languish, might have taken them, were made of lavender flowers, the tops of rosemary and other ingredients.

Perfume. The deeper the color of the calyx the stronger the scent. In some dark flowers there is said to be a suggestion of jasmine. *Lavandula vera* produces the best oil. In France the oil is distilled from the wild plants, and in England, where the best of all lavender perfumes are obtained, the oil is extracted from cultivated plants. The oil, which improves with age, is distilled from the young tops and flowering spikes, and is used, blended in with other ingredients, in perfume, *eau de cologne,* lavender water, and soaps. Lavender flowers are dried and laid in with the linen to scent it, whence the expression, "laid up in lavender." It is said to keep the moths away from the clothes, and is an important ingredient in potpourris.

Food. The leaves are sometimes used in flavoring, and sweets are made of lavender flowers. In England, according to Eleanour Rohde, it was the custom to serve small desserts, fruits, or sweets on lavender.

CULTURE

The lavenders grow wild on dry, stony lands, and in cultivation seem to like a sunny situation in a light, chalky soil, overlaid with loam. Dr. Stockberger says low, moist land is fatal to them. At Peekskill it grows in the rocks and in dry, sunny places, and lives through the very severe winters with only a slight protection, which may not be necessary. If one desires to perpetuate certain bushes it is quite simple to increase them from slips put into sandy soil. It can also be grown from seed, started indoors and transplanted later. For commercial purposes it is said the plants should be renewed every six or seven years, and that the best yields are in the third and fourth years. It has never been grown much commercially in the United States. One can buy plants of *L. officinalis* and its variety, the dwarf Munstead, also of *L. spica* from nurseries.

Harvest. The stems and flowering branches are cut in sunny weather in the afternoon, as close to the woody stock as possible. This is done when the whole spike is in flower and the lowest blossom has begun to darken. The yield of oil from sixty flowering spikes is one ounce. In England in Surrey, Hertfordshire, and Lincoln, where the best oil is produced, according to Sawyer, twenty-five pounds of oil can be expected from one acre of plants.

LEVISTICUM OFFICINALIS, KOCH.

LOVAGE

Umbelliferae Perennial

Lovage is native to Europe, and according to Vilmorin the whole plant has a sweetish aromatic odor, which it did not have in my garden.

Root. It has a taproot.

Stem. The stems are very tall, rigid, and fleshy. They taste pleasant, a little bitter and of camphor, and resin when raw.

Leaf. The leaves are large, dark green, shiny, similar to those of celery and are divided in two or three divisions, and toothed. Each leaf division is two inches long, and one and one-quarter inches broad, sometimes much larger. The stems of the leaves are broader at the base, where they start and envelop the base of the stem.

Flower. The yellow flowers are in umbels.

Seed. The seeds are highly aromatic, hollowed and with three prominent ribs.

HISTORY AND LEGEND

It is mentioned by Pliny, and is in Stearns' "The American Herbal," 1801.

USES

Medicine. The roots are used as a drug. The seeds were formerly used medicinally. In cases of sore mouth or throat, the Pennsylvania Germans use the hollow stems as a tube through which to drink water or milk.

Perfume. The flowering tops yield a volatile oil which Poucher says has a limited use, in a few tobacco flavors.

Food. The young stems are treated like those of angelica. The leafstalks and bases of the stems are blanched like celery and eaten as a salad. The seeds flavor confectionery.

CULTURE

It is propagated by seeds. Some say to plant them immediately upon ripening, and others that they are fresh until they are three years old. They are usually sown late in summer and the seedlings transplanted in the fall or early spring. Until germination, the ground for the seedlings should be kept moist. The plants like a rich, moist soil, and last for several years if cultivated, like angelica.

LIPPIA CITRIODORA, HBK.

LEMON VERBENA

Verbenaceae Perennial

The lemon verbena is a subshrub from Chile and Peru, and was imported into Europe in 1784, where it has become naturalized in Italy and other portions of Europe, and is popular in gardens. It is also grown in India, Martinique, and Réunion (South Africa). Where the winters are severe, the lemon verbena is not hardy. It is a leafy shrub, growing, some say, to five feet and others to ten feet in height. In pots we have seen them reach four feet.

Root. The roots are stringy and white.

Stem. The stems are woody and branching, a little grooved, slightly downy, and marked with red.

Leaf. The leaves are somewhat verticillate, of a crisp texture, light yellow-green, oblong, but terminating in a point. They are slender, entire, shiny above, and dull below, rough to touch, with one central vein, and are two to three inches long. When brushed against by the clothing or the hands they give off a pleasant lemon scent with something of the lemon rind in it.

Flower. The flowers, blooming in summer and autumn, are very small and arranged in spikes, or terminal panicles, often six to seven inches long, made up of smaller opposite spikes three inches long. They are white with purplish tubes, and are not especially decorative.

USES

The leaves are used for flavor and perfume. Infused in a cold fruit drink such as barley water, lemon squash, and iced tea, they are said to enhance the flavor of the lemon in the drinks, and make it taste like fresh limes. The dried leaves are said by some to be good as teas, but we found them tasteless. Perhaps this is owing to the climate. We float a few of the leaves in the finger bowls, flavor our jellies with them, and place a leaf on a piece of honeydew melon instead of a slice of lemon.

CULTURE

In northern countries they must be grown either as

bedding plants, or in pots, and set out after all danger from frost is past, for they blacken and shrivel at the very first breath of winter which leaves geraniums and dahlias quite unharmed. A friend, however, kept hers in the cold cellar of an unheated house during the winter and did not water them. When stored in a heated cellar they should be watered about once a week.

This is through cuttings of half-ripened wood which strike readily in summer or early spring under glass.

Harvest. The leaves are picked as needed all through the summer.

MARRUBIUM VULGARE, L.

HOREHOUND

Labiatae Perennial

Horehound is native to the Old World and widely naturalized in the United States. It is rather weedy looking, but the roundish wrinkled leaves curving out and down form an attractive pattern. At Foxden the whole plant had no scent, although elsewhere it is considered an aromatic. It tastes frightfully bitter.

Root. The roots are woody and deep.

Stem. The stems are gray-green, angular, and with a white bloom on them.

Leaf. The leaves all along the stems are downy, much crinkled, almost square, but with rounded angles. They branch out and then turn down in opposite pairs, and are toothed. Their surface is covered with a fine network.

Flower. The flowers are inconspicuous and in compact

whorls in the axils of the leaves, growing in tiers to the top of the stems. They are tiny, cream-colored, and greenish. They blossom from June 15th to September.

Seed. The seed is small, oblong, brown, pointed at one end and rounded at the other, and the germinating power lasts two to three years.

HISTORY AND LEGEND

Pliny mentions it as a highly esteemed medicinal plant, and Strabo recommended it against magical poisons. It was thought that if the horehound plant were put in milk and set in a place pestered with flies it would speedily kill them all. In the "Toilet of Flora," a recipe is given for making a powder of the leaves in the same manner as snuff. Claytonius in "Flora Virginica," 1762, mentioned it as *Marrubium album vulgare.* Prince had it in his catalogues in 1790, and Bartram in his in 1814, and it was mentioned in Stearns' "The American Herbal," in 1801.

USES

Medicine. The leaves and flowering tops were used for medicine. The juice, or a sweetened tea of the leaves was given for a cold and for coughs.

To make horehound candy, a popular domestic medicine, the fresh plants are boiled down until the juice is extracted, and then sugar is added and the whole boiled until it candies. It tastes bitter, but has a definite flavor of its own.

The "National Standard Dispensary," 1916, said it is not used medicinally although it is said to be an expectorant and a diaphoretic.

Food. In Norfolk, England, a beer called horehound beer was made from it.

CULTURE

We grew ours from seed bought in America. It thrives in poor, light soil, and can be increased by cuttings or divisions. I saw it spreading over a deserted pueblo in New Mexico in the blazing sun, on the dryest of soils.

Harvest. Just before flowering, the plants are cut close to the ground. By planting them close together the plants will have smaller stems and yield a finer quality of crop. The annual importation is from sixty to seventy tons.

MATRICARIA CHAMOMILLA, L.

GERMAN CHAMOMILE

Wild Chamomile, Sweet False Chamomile

Compositae Annual

The plant is an annual, and is much smaller and has coarser leaves than those of the *Anthemis nobilis.* The flower stems are glabrous, rising to seven or eight inches high, and bearing flowers three-quarters of an inch across. The receptacle is without scales, elongated and becoming hollow as the flower ripens. The plant is cultivated in Hungary where the oil distilled from it is an ingredient in a platinum coating put on glass and porcelain, and it is also blended with perfumes.

MELISSA OFFICINALIS, L.

BALM

Lemon Balm, Garden Balm

Labiatae Perennial

Balm is native to the Mediterranean and has escaped sparingly in the United States. It is a weedy plant which spreads over the ground, with inconspicuous flowers. For me it dies down during the winter. The charm of balm as a garden plant, aside from its interesting history, is the delicious lemony, minty scent from its leaves. If grown on a bank where one can stroke it in passing, it is always a delight to sniff its fragrance on one's fingers.

Root. There are numerous thin fibrous and shallow roots.

Stem. It grows up to three feet high, but my plants have not grown beyond fourteen inches, perhaps because they are in an exposed position. The stems are much branched, tall, straight, ridged, and hairy.

Leaf. The leaves are numerous, larger at the base and growing smaller as they ascend the stem; they are a deep green, of a thin texture, notched at the margins in round scallops; are covered with stiff little hairs above but only on the veins below; are opposite; and each pair is at right angles to the one above.

Flower. The flowers are in whorls in the leaf axils, not too numerous, more or less all the way up the stem. They are yellowish-white, and appear in August. The corolla is two-lipped, the upper one three-toothed, and the lower one with two longer, pointed spiny teeth. When bruised or touched the plant smells of lemon and mint, and it tastes like lemon peel. In my garden the flavor or scent is not very strong, possibly owing to the climate.

Variety. There is a variety of *Melissa officinalis* with variegated, yellowish leaves.

HISTORY AND LEGEND

Balm was known to Theophrastus and from this beginning was constantly mentioned by the Latin and Greek poets and the herbalists. The name melissa comes from the Greek word bee, and the plant has always been known as a bee plant. It was grown in Spain, and Ibn Al Awam advised mixing balm with honey or sugar, to smear inside of the beehive which had been prepared to receive a new swarm, to attract and attach the colony to its new home. He also quoted other writers, however, as saying this had the opposite effect. Ibn Baithar said if the whole plant, root, leaves, and seed, were dried, put into a piece of linen, sewed with a silk thread, and worn under one's dress it would make one beloved and agreeable to those one met. Besides, such a wearer would have all his wishes fulfilled, be gay, and happy as long as he wore this, and why not under such conditions?

It was mentioned in Stearns' "The American Herbal" in 1801.

USES

Medicine. Balm tea was thought to be good for fevers, headaches, and asthmas. It is said to be carminative and antispasmodic. The oil from the plant was in salves for healing wounds. According to Parkinson, the juice of it was made into a tansy with eggs, sugar, and rose water and given to women to bring on the afterbirth, others said it increased the flow of the milk. It was steeped in baths in summer. The "National Standard Dispensary" says it is official in most pharmacopoeias, although it is not in the one of the United States.

Perfume. The oil distilled from the leaves and young shoots enters into the manufacture of *eau des carmes*, which had a great reputation as a restorative, and is the ancestor of *eau de cologne.*

Food. Evelyn in his "Acetaria" says of balm, ". . . and the sprigs fresh gathered and put into wine or other drinks during the heat of summer give it a marvellous quickness. This noble plant yields an incomparable wine made as is that of cowslip flower." It was steeped in sack.

CULTURE

It is grown a little in the United States. Balm comes readily from seed. I sowed mine out-of-doors in early May and it germinated but did not flower the first summer. It seems to like a warm, sheltered position and should not have rich soil.

Harvest. The leaves and tops are used for preparing the oil, drug, or tea. They are picked early in the morning and when used for tea are dried in the shade to preserve their color.

MENTHA PIPERITA, L.

PEPPERMINT

Labiatae Perennial

The peppermint is a perennial, native to Europe, and

has been introduced into the United States, where it grows wild in wet places. The plant is heavier than spearmint and has a reddish undertone throughout, even the small leaves near the flower spikes having red on their margins.

Root. The plant produces many creeping stolons which spread in favorable environments.

Stem. The branches are spreading, two to three feet long, and curve out instead of standing up straight. The stem is square, reddish, and with the tips often entirely red.

Leaf. The leaves are darker than those of the spearmint, larger, and not as crinkly. The margins are toothed and there are tiny glands on the upper surface of the leaves which are without hairs as are the stems. The scent is exhilarating as well as aromatic, and is given off without bruising the leaves, and it is delicious, stimulating, and cool, a little heavier than that of spearmint; more pepperminty. The leaves taste of camphor, a little bitter, and leave a cool pepperminty feeling behind in one's mouth.

Flower. The flowers come in late July and August and are borne in cylindrical, or club-like spikes, and are a pretty shade of rosy lavender.

Seed. There are no seeds, says Vilmorin.

HISTORY AND LEGEND

It is mentioned by Theophrastus, Dioscorides, and Ovid in his story of Philemon and Baucis told how Baucis rubbed mint on the table before setting it when she was entertaining Jupiter and Mercury, unaware of their divinity:

"She rubb'd it o'er with newly gathered mint
A wholesome herb, that breath'd a grateful scent."

It was first distilled in America in 1816, in Wayne County, N. Y., by a Mr. Barnett, who collected the wild plants, and the oil was called "pipmentol." In 1835 the industry was established in Saint Joseph's County, Michigan, at first with crude machinery which was later improved. The principal peppermint plantations are on the muck lands of southern Michigan and northern Indiana, but the New York oil is better. The annual production of peppermint oil in the United States is around 300,000 pounds. Besides the *Mentha piperita*, a var. *vulgaris* and a kind called *Mentha officinalis* are also cultivated.

USES

Medicine. The oil for medicine is expressed from the dried leaves of flowering plants. It is in most pharmacopoeias, and the tea is antispasmodic, and also a powerful analgesic, and is used to check the secretions of all glands, except those of the skin and kidneys.

Perfume. The oil is a flavoring in tooth powders, pastes, and washes.

Food. The stems are bitter, and only the leaves and tops should be infused in drinks. In Pennsylvania a tea is served to the farm hands in the fields instead of cold water, or the once popular schnapps, perhaps because peppermint is good for heat prostration.

CULTURE

The wild plants prefer a moist soil, but in the garden a deep soil which is a little moist is satisfactory. The largest supply of peppermint oil comes from America and Japan, but it is also cultivated in Europe.

Mint is propagated by pieces of the runners. All the mints can be increased from slips planted in sand in cold frames.

MENTHA SPICATA, L.

SPEARMINT

Roman Mint, Green Mint

Labiatae Perennial

The spearmint is native to Europe, but now grows throughout the temperate regions of the world. It produces the most fragrant leaves when growing in damp soil. The whole plant is dark green, crisp, and smooth, and there is a grace about the way it carries its slender flower spikes. There are, besides, two horticultural varieties, *gentilis* and *viridis*.

Root. It sends out stolons which root as they run and, in favorable soil, spread considerably.

Stem. The stems are square, smooth, without hairs, rampant, and grow two to three feet high, and spread out instead of standing up straight. They are sometimes light green near the tops without any red, but again they may have the reddish coloring all the way up.

Leaf. The leaves are in opposite pairs with little stems and leaves growing in pairs from their axils. The leaves are almost sessile, have gland-like humps, and there are tiny, irregular, pointed indentations along the margins. They are smaller and more crinkly than the leaves of *Mentha piperita;* they smell slightly of lemon and mint; when fresh they taste bitter, sharp, and camphory.

Flower. In late July and August come the spires of tiny white flowers marked with purple, and looking gray.

Seed. The seed is very scant, exceedingly fine, roundish and brown, says Vilmorin.

HISTORY AND LEGEND

It was in nearly all the early lists of plants and was probably in American gardens by 1739, for Clayton mentioned it.

USES

In Pennsylvania, bundles of mint are packed in with the grain to keep rodents away.

Perfume. The oil extracted from the plants flavors chewing gum, dental preparations, and soaps.

Food. The leaves are minced in vinegar with sugar for mint sauce; and used to flavor cold drinks: minced, they are scattered over green peas and glazed carrots. As a tea it is less harsh than peppermint leaves. The oil flavors confectionery, too.

CULTURE

I planted seed but it did not germinate. A plantation of mint will last a long while if the stems are cut off close to the ground every autumn and a layer of good soil or compost placed over them.

This is generally from pieces of the runners which root readily in any fertile, slightly moist soil. When it grows in dry soil the leaves are not as fragrant.

Harvest. As the plant flowers the leaves and flowering tops are collected and dried in the shade. If the plants are dried before distilling, the oil is more fragrant.

It is grown commercially in Michigan and Indiana, where it is known as "Green Mint." The annual market requirement for the oil is 50,000 pounds in the United States. The yield of oil varies from ten to twenty pounds per acre.

Varieties. The list of mints is a long one and I have grown over twenty kinds. There are many gray-leaved mints. All of them are fragrant and a few are handsome, but on the whole they are too weedy for the garden. The following are the ones useful for flavoring:

Mentha citrata Ehrh, called bergamot mint, lemon mint, orange mint, is native to Europe and naturalized in America. It is deliciously fragrant and tastes of lemon. Although it is naturalized in America, no plants were to be obtained, so mine came to me from Edinburgh. These have a purplish corolla and are more reddish than most mints, have smooth flower stalks and decumbent smooth stems to two feet long. The leaves are ovate, two inches long, and toothed. The flowers are in the uppermost axils of the leaves in a dense terminal spike up to one inch long.

Mentha crispa. The seed of this came from Kew, and the plant is a red-stemmed, crisp-leaved mint, smelling resinous, almost turpentiny, but pleasantly, and not too strongly. It is a handsome plant with vigorous curled leaves. A variety of it which also came from abroad has light green, crisped leaves and smells of mint.

Mentha arvensis, field mint, is the one from which the Japanese distill their oil, and it is said to have only a slight odor of peppermint. The flowers are in the axils of

Menthe spicata, spearmint
Menthe piperita, peppermint

the leaves instead of in terminal spikes. The variety grown in Japan is said to be var. *piperascens*, and in China it is said to be var. *glabrata*.

Mentha arvensis var. *canadensis* is generally known as *Mentha canadensis* and grows wild from Maine to California. It gives off an essence of mint, and was used by the first colonists and by the Indians.

Mentha rotundifolia Huds., apple mint, or the round-leaved mint, is a woolly plant. The cool, green leaves are glandular, rough, and hairy; so are the stems, which are not sharply squared and smell unpleasantly of ether and peppermint. It makes a handsome garnish to drinks flavored with mint or mixed in with old-fashioned flowers in a bouquet. It has creamy flower spikes. The plant grows about fifteen to eighteen inches high, and dies down to the ground in the winter but rises again in the spring. It is easily increased by slips planted in sand. A variety called *variegata* has irregular white patches on the green leaves—quite dashing and modernistic in effect.

HISTORY AND LEGEND

In olden days the different mints were not always specified.

Mint was one of the herbs with which the Pharisees paid their tithe; it was employed by the Greeks in their mysteries, perhaps because it reanimates the spirits; it was also one of the strewing herbs. All the old-time writers thought it prevented milk from curdling, and that its flavor gave a zest to the appetite, and hence it was much used in sauces and was mixed in puddings. It was thought good with salt against the bite of mad dogs. The mints, balm, and other herbs were infused in baths, and one notes that although the ancients did not indulge in frequent bathing, when they did they must have had a most luxurious experience.

Prince mentioned *M. rotundifolia variegata, M. californica,* and *M. piperita,* and Bartram listed *M. canadensis, M. viridis, M. piperita,* and *M. citrata.* Josselyn spoke of spearmint.

MONARDA DIDYMA, L.

BEE BALM

Oswego Tea, Fragrant Balm, American Melissa

Labiatae Perennial

The bee balm is a handsome plant native from Quebec to Michigan, and south to Georgia. It has conspicuous, raggedy, red flower heads, and exceedingly fragrant leaves and flowers. The whole plant except the stems feels soft and woolly.

Root. Each stem has a woody root with many fibers and can easily be pulled apart from the clump.

Stem. The stems are four-angled, and two to three feet or more high.

Leaf. The leaves are of a thin texture, dentate and with red at the margins. They are ovate, come to a gradually diminishing point, and measure about two to four inches long. When fresh the leaves taste bitter; their scent is lemony with a slight peppery tang. Sawyer quite correctly says the leaves smell of bergamot mint, and some species, of salvia.

Flower. The flowers come in July and August. The

heads are composed of clusters of flowers and are at the terminations of the stems, and of a few side shoots. The calyx is hairy in the throat and the teeth are narrowly awl-shaped; the corolla is nearly smooth, scarlet red, and one and one-half to two inches long. There are varieties with differently colored flowers:

M. didyma var. *rosea* has magenta-colored flowers.

M. didyma var. *violacea* has deep scarlet ones.

Monarda fistulosa, L., wild bergamot, has grayish lavender flowers.

Monarda fistulosa alba has white flowers.

M. didyma var. Cambridge, is the most popular for gardens, and is scarlet.

Monarda citriodora. The whole plant is tinted reddish in its youth. I received a salmon-pink one from a friend, probably *salmonea.*

HISTORY AND LEGEND

The plant was named for the Spanish botanist, Monardes, who lived at Seville in the sixteenth century. It was a popular plant in early American gardens. Prince listed *Monarda didyma, M. mollis,* and *M. gracilis;* while Bartram listed *M. didyma, M. fistulosa, M. oblongata, M. chenopodium,* and *M. punctata.*

USES

Medicine. Poucher, in the "Medical Botany of the United States," 1867, said it possesses valuable medicinal properties; the oil of it rubbed on the head was a counter-irritant, and sometimes employed as a liniment; the dried leaves were good for nausea, and vomiting in bilious fevers.

Perfume. The oil from it is said to resemble the odor of ambergris and for a while it was used as a fixative in perfumes.

Food. The dried leaves of *Monarda fistulosa* make an aromatic tea, while tea of *Monarda citriodora* has a pleasant, peppery taste.

CULTURE

The monardas grow on dry, well-drained soil and thrive in sun or a little shade. They can be raised from divisions of the roots, or from seed. Plants and seeds can be purchased.

MYRRHIS ODORATA, SCOP.

SWEET CICELY

Myrrh

Umbelliferae Perennial

The sweet cicely is native to the mountains of Savoy, and has become naturalized in England, Scotland, and Ireland.

Stem. The stems are hairy, marked with longitudinal lines, and are two to three feet high and one-quarter of an inch across.

Leaf. The leaves are fern-like, or tansy-like, much divided, each little division having its margins cut and being hairy.

Flower. The flowers are small, whitish, and polygamous in a strict compound umbel, two and one-half inches across, and with unequal rays of the typical umbelliferous flowers.

Seed. The seed is very long, about three-quarters of an inch, and narrow, strongly ribbed, and cleft.

HISTORY AND LEGEND

Pliny referred to it, and Gerard mentioned it as did Parkinson, who said it gives a better taste to any other herb put with it. The root in wine was a remedy for spider bites, and also against the plague and pestilence. It is not grown much in the United States, nor is it mentioned by the early American writers.

USES

The seeds, full of oil, have a pleasant taste and in olden times were crushed and used to scent and polish oaken floors and furniture. It had a certain vogue in the sixteenth and seventeenth centuries and was mentioned by Claude Mollet, but now is rarely cultivated in gardens.

Food. The seeds are eaten fresh and green, and are sliced and put with other herbs to give them a better taste. In Savoy the seeds are infused into certain brandies, especially in the *elixir des* Chartreuse (the liqueur of the *Grande Chartreuse*), and its use seems to have come down from the gardens of the ancient solitary monks. Boulestin and Hill say its leaves are faintly flavored of anise, and that it is too weak to be of much use in the kitchen, while Miss Bardswell says they taste of paregoric and were formerly put into the salads, and Sturtevant says it has fallen into disuse in Europe.

CULTURE

According to Burr's "Field and Garden Vegetables of America," the seeds should be sown in the autumn, as they germinate better if they have been frozen. Once established the seedlings will yield abundantly, and thrive in almost any soil or situation. Our seed came from England, but our plants died the first summer. They are said, however, to be quite hardy.

NIGELLA SATIVA, L.

FENNEL FLOWER

Black Caraway, Black Cumin, Nutmeg Flower, *Mille* or *Toute-épice*

Ranunculaceae Annual

This little annual grows wild from Gibraltar to India, but probably came originally from the Mediterranean regions. It is a small, dainty plant with much cut leaves and subtly colored flowers.

Root. It has a long slender, single root, branching a little at the base.

Stem. The stem is about fifteen inches high and ridged, roughly hairy, erect and branching.

Leaf. The leaves are alternate, yellow-green, very like some of the buttercups, much cut into fine, slender divisions, and are woolly and hairy above, and a little below.

Flower. The flowers are well over an inch across of a soft whitish-green with dull blue markings and are not conspicuous from afar, but if we look down in the flower's face we first see the five petal-like bracts, then eight odd-shaped small blue, white, green, and gold bracts. Between each of these the stamens spread out in twos or threes like the spokes of a wheel. They have bluish anthers and light gold filaments. More stamens curve up and out around the ovary which sends out five pistils to form a pattern something like a swirling swastika.

Seed. The seed pod is quite large, a green, bulging, somewhat spherical affair except that it is flat on top. It is roughly five-sided, the green arms forming the stigma, and project like antlers from each of the angles on top. The fruit turns brown when ripe.

The seeds ripen in August, and are black, triangular, having two flat and one convex surface and a rough skin. Their germinating power lasts three years. They taste aromatic, spicy, and sharp.

HISTORY AND LEGEND

It is said to be the *Gith* of Charlemagne, and the word comes from the Hebrew *Gesah,* which is mentioned in the Bible. It is mentioned by Calumella and by Pliny.

USES

The seed is an ingredient in snuff tobacco.

Medicine. The seeds were formerly held in the mouth for toothache.

Perfume. The oil expressed from the seeds is fragrant, is said to taste of camphor, and is used for perfume.

Food. The seeds were strewn on bread, like poppy seeds, and are used as a spice in Europe, Africa, and the Orient. In Germany they are put into bread instead of cumin, as they are in Turkey and Egypt. They are used in cakes like anise and sesame and also to flavor wine. In Upper Egypt, mixed with ambergris, cinnamon bark, ginger, sugar, and other ingredients, they are made into a conserve which is said to be popular with the Arab and Turkish women because it is fattening, but even in Asia

Minor it does not seem likely that any woman still wishes to be fat. Miss Shapleigh pounded the seeds, steeped them in vinegar, and found they gave a relish to sauces for fish.

CULTURE

The plants come readily from seed and seem to like a well-drained, sunny situation.

OCIMUM BASILICUM, L.

SWEET BASIL

Labiatae Annual

The basils are almost the most delightful of all seasoning herbs. Most of them are native to India. Bailey says there are from fifty to sixty species in the warmer parts of the world. They are neat little shrubs, fragrant and pleasant to the palate, each differing a little from the other in looks and flavor. The sweet basil is a small, green, bushy plant, eighteen inches to two feet high.

Root. It has a main central root from which numerous side branches shoot off.

Stem. The stem is hairy, stiff, rounded, a little ridged and slightly branched.

Leaf. The leaves are pointed, yellow-green, slightly serrated, and, as in all basils, look as if some one had taken them between his fingers and pinched them together along the central vein, and as if they had remained with the two sides partially folded, turning their backs to the

Ocimum minimum, bush basil

world. The leaves are opposite, each pair at right angles to the pair above, and covered with a bloom, yet glisten on both sides with the dots of the oil glands. They are slightly downy on the under surface. They taste of liquorice, and spice when fresh, and when dried there is a lemony quality to the fragrance, also something of anise, resin, and spice.

Flower. The flowers come at the end of July and August, and are greenish-white, labiate, less than half an inch long, inconspicuous, in pairs of opposite clusters which give the impression of a whorl. The whorls one above the other form a leafy raceme. A few open at a time.

Seed. The seed is small, roundish, and black and covered with a mucilaginous substance which expands in water. The germinating power, according to Vilmorin, lasts eight years.

OCIMUM MINIMUM, L.

BUSH BASIL

Dwarf Basil

Labiatae Annual

According to Bailey, this is probably a variety of *Ocimum basilicum*, and it, too, is a neat, bushy little plant from eighteen inches to two feet high but more branched, more compact, dwarfier, and having smaller leaves than the sweet basil.

It is a charming little plant, fragrant of lemon and spice, and having a bitter, resinous, and stimulating taste.

It is delightful in bouquets or for bordering beds of vegetables or of other herbs.

Stem. The stems are ridged and slightly hairy.

Leaf. The leaves are not over one-quarter of an inch long and pointed at the tips, also folded up and having toothed margins, while the surface glistens with the glandular dots.

Flower. It flowers the same time as the sweet basil, and the white blossoms, less than one-quarter of an inch long, have the lower lip much extended and crinkled. The buds are creamy and a little greenish.

Other basils are:

Small-leaved green basil, *le basilic fin vert* of the French seed catalogues.

The whole plant is crisp and fresh looking and is about fifteen inches high.

Stem. The stem is slightly ridged and angled.

Leaf. The leaves are larger, measuring one-half to three-quarters of an inch in length and are pointed at the tips, of a shiny yellow green and with the margins entire except for the faintest nick here and there. As in the others, the leaves are turned up on either side of the central vein, and are hairy on their under surface. It smells, like the others, of lemon and spice, and when fresh tastes peppery, bitter and of fragrant oil.

Flower. The flowers are whitish in whorls forming a raceme, and are about the same size as those of *O. minimum.*

Seed. The seed is round, purplish-brown, tiny, plump, with a little tannish dot at one end, and has no smell or taste.

Compact green bush basil, *basilic fin nain compact,* is

a low, very leafy plant, about fifteen inches across and eight inches high. The leaves are one-quarter of an inch to half an inch long with entire margins and pointed at the tips. It is a buxom plant and smells and tastes much like the others.

Lettuce-leaved basil, *basilic a feuille de laitue.*

This is a coarser plant and is from eight to twenty inches high, sweetly and strongly fragrant of resin and spice.

Stem. The stem is downy, with short little hairs.

Leaf. The leaves are large, up to three inches long, and one and one-half inches across. They are a shiny, light green, slightly notched at the margins, pointed at the tips, and turn up, but not as much as the other varieties. They are covered with almost microscopic hairs.

Flower. The flowers are greenish and inconspicuous as in the others.

Curled leaf basil, *basilic frisé.*

This is a round plant with stiff and squarish stems. It is temperamental looking with its yellow-green leaves, twisted, and having the margins denticulated a little. It is not pretty but is most pleasantly fragrant of spice and anise.

Purple bush basil, or large purple sweet basil, *basilic grand violet*, is about eighteen inches high in my garden and handsome, with large dark red leaves and pinkish flowers. Some plants are less red than others and have green leaves and stalks, others are all purplish-red except for a slight green tinge which gives a bronzy tone to the upper surface of the leaves.

Stem. The stems are purplish and red, slightly ridged and tomentose.

Leaf. The leaves point out and turn their backs.

Flower. The flowers are pinkish, less than one-quarter of an inch long, chunkier than most others, otherwise similarly shaped.

Compact purple basil, *basilic fin violet,* is a small, dark red plant, which grew eight inches tall in my garden with tiny leaves one-half to one-quarter of an inch long. The stems were reddish, quite purple at the tips, and round. The leaves stand up and point out and the margins are bright green with a nick in them here and there. The plant smells spicy.

O. gratissimum, L., the East Indian, or tree basil. It is just coming up in the garden now, too late to be described in this book. It is grown in India for medicine. According to Vilmorin it is worth while in the vegetable garden, is an annual, forming a pyramidal bush from twenty inches to two feet high and one foot to sixteen inches in diameter. It has an agreeable perfume, but is late growing and therefore more suitable for a warm climate.

Ocimum sanctum, L., the Tulsi of India, is said to be grown out of a hollow pillar before every Hindu dwelling and in gardens near temples. It is the most celebrated of the basils in history and legend. The root is made into beads and worn around the neck and arms of the Vishnu-Brahmans. It is sacred to Vishnu and Lakshmi, his wife, and a leaf of it is placed on the breast of every dead Hindu. Unfortunately, although we obtained several packets of seed of this basil, we were unable to keep it alive after it had germinated.

HISTORY AND LEGEND

The Greeks and Romans thought one should curse

when sowing the basil to insure its germination, and hence the French expression, *"semer le basilic,"* which means using abuse. Pliny says it is an aphrodisiac and was given to horses and asses at the mating season, and furthermore that to stimulate rapid germination it should be watered with boiling water after sowing it.

In Italy the women wear it because of its supposed efficacy in engendering sympathy. A young peasant going to call on his beloved often wears a sprig of it behind his ear. A pot of basil is placed in the window by the lady as a signal to her lover that she is expecting him. Isabella, immortalized in Keats' poem, kept the head of her lover in a pot of basil.

Ibn Al Awam mentions many kinds with instructions for growing them. Ibn Baithar mentions *O. minimum* as being good for medicine, and *O. pilosum* to counteract the effects of inebriation if taken in a decoction, but says if too much is taken it will darken the face.

Bacon says, "It is strange which is reported that basil too much exposed to the sun doth turn into wild thyme"; and Culpeper adds that it will not grow near rue, and continues, "This is the herb which all the authors are together by the ears about and rail at one another like lawyers: Galen and Dioscorides hold it fitting to be taken inwardly; and Chrysippus rails at it with downright Billingsgate rhetorick, Pliny and the Arabian Physicians defend it."

It was offered for sale in the *Virginia Gazette* in 1775, and Bartram had it in his catalogue.

USES

Basil is a popular flavoring herb. In France it is used

in turtle soup and stews, and in Italy it is an important ingredient in bean soup, and many other dishes. The dried leaves are put into snuff.

Medicine. An oil distilled from *O. basilicum* is said to be antiseptic and stimulant.

Perfume. The above oil is used in concocting the perfume of mignonette, which it recalls, and also in bouquets of violet and jonquil.

Food. I find it a pleasant flavoring in all dishes having tomatoes, in cheeses, fruit drinks, and in soups with other herbs. The flavor is flower-like.

CULTURE

All the basils except *O. sanctum* and *O. gratissimum,* are easily raised from seed sown out-of-doors when danger from frost is past. They germinate readily and produce sizable plants from which a few leaves can be cut in about six weeks after planting. They seem to like a well-drained, sunny exposure.

Harvest. The leaves can be cut off as soon as the plants are big enough to stand the operation, but they are cut in quantities for drying when the flowers begin to open. French growers advise stirring a little fertilizer around the roots to stimulate them after cutting back the leafy stems, and, like most annuals, the more they are cut the thicker they grow. A few plants could be potted up and brought indoors for the winter.

ORIGANUM MAJORANA, L.

SWEET MARJORAM

Knotted Marjoram, Annual Marjoram

Labiatae

Perennial in the south
Annual in the north

The sweet marjoram is native to the Mediterranean region and the Orient, but not in the tropics. It is now cultivated in southern Europe, Arabia, and Spain and by the Jews in North Morocco as a condiment. It is one of the most pleasantly scented herbs to have in the garden. The whole plant is of a dainty texture, glaucous, velvety to the touch, and bearing little green balls from which the flowers come.

Root. It is fibrous and spready.

Stem. The main stem is square and purplish-brown, but the side branches are round, wiry, and tinted reddish. In my garden it grew to from eight to twelve inches high.

Leaf. The leaves are rounded at the tips, elliptically shaped, from one-eighth to three-eighths inches long. They are covered with down, as is the whole plant, are in opposite pairs, at right angles to the pair above, and of a soft textured gray-green.

Flower. The flowers come at the end of July and have a peculiarly formed inflorescence. It consists of a tiny green, nobby, velvety growth, "the knots," about one-eighth of an inch across. These knots are single or in groups of several and stand on their own stems, which rise from the leaf axils along the stems, and at the tips of the stems, too. Each knot is four-sided, made up of tiny, sepal-like leaves, each folded over the next like a shutter, and out from each leaf of the shutter comes the tiniest of creamy, untidy flowers, a few at a time.

Seed. The seed is tiny, brown, and has no scent.

To me the plant smells of pine, spice, and heliotrope. Poucher, the perfumer, says the scent is reminiscent of nutmeg and mint, but quite characteristic. When fresh, the leaves have a sharp, aromatic, pleasant, bitter, and camphory taste; when dried it is delicious, like a perfume.

HISTORY AND LEGEND

The sweet marjoram was grown as a potherb by the Egyptians, and Hippocrates praised *origanum.* The Greeks and Romans crowned young married couples with it; in Crete it was the symbol of honor, and in Sicily is said to possess the gift of banishing sadness, in India it is sacred to Siva and Vishnu. Ibn Baithar mentions it, and Ibn Al Awam says when it is used for seasoning meat it removes the bad odor of corruption. Culpeper says it is much used "in all odoriferous water, powders, etc., that are for ornament or delight."

USES

The juice was formerly used to clean furniture.

Medicine. The fresh leaves and flowers in a tea were thought to open obstructions, and to be tonic and stimulating. The oil distilled from the leaves and flowers is tonic and carminative, and taken internally is said to hasten the eruption of measles and scarlet fever.

Perfume. The oil from the plant is very fragrant and exceedingly powerful, resembling the attars from certain of the thymes, and has been present in perfumes and unguents from the earliest times and to-day is used for perfuming French soaps more than the English, also for scenting hair pomades.

Food. In many parts of the world the leaves are used as a seasoning and when mixed in the food are said to assist the digestion. In Germany sweet marjoram seasons sausages, hence its name *Wurstkraut,* or sausage herb; in Italy sweet fritters made with spinach are flavored with it, and it figures as a dressing for roast chicken, as a garnish, and also in the salad bowl.

CULTURE

It is best to start the seeds indoors in a cold frame or hothouse and transplant the seedlings to the garden after danger from frost is over. In my garden the plants grew on a sunny, dry, well-drained exposure, and did well. One might stir the ground, and feed a little, if one keeps cutting the leaves too severely, to help it to continue to produce. Sweet marjoram is a charming pot plant. Although when growing in the ground the stems stand up quite straight, in a pot they droop over the sides most gracefully. The leaves of the potted plants, however, are not nearly as fragrant as those grown out-of-doors. The seed germinates in two weeks.

Harvest. Just as the flowers appear, the leaves and flowering tops are cut. The leaves are stripped off the stems and dried in the shade.

ORIGANUM VULGARE, L.

POT MARJORAM

Wild Marjoram

Labiatae Perennial

Pot marjoram is native to Europe and is so hardy it positively ramps over the ground. It smells thymier than sweet marjoram, and is a much bigger, coarser, and hairier plant. It is somewhat straggly with sprawling, leafy stems and pinkish or white flowers, and in certain situations would make a fine ground cover.

Root. The roots are many and shallow.

Stem. The stems are somewhat recumbent, but rise to two feet or more, are leafy, and much branched.

Leaf. The leaves are entire, sometimes slightly hairy on the margins and on the under ribs, rounded at the base, somewhat pointed at the tips; are one inch long, have short stalks, and smell thymey when crushed.

Flower. The flowers come in July and are in many flowered, flat-topped clusters. Each flower is subtended by a little brownish bract and has a three-parted pinkish lower lip and a two-parted upper one, the corolla is longer than the calyx. Two of the stamens are exserted. The flowers are very fragrant with something of the sweetness of *Clethra alnifolia,* which blooms at the same time, a bit of heliotrope, and an undertone of spice. Some plants bear white flower heads, and some pink.

Seed. The seeds are very small, oval, reddish, or dark brown, and, according to Vilmorin, the germinating power lasts five years.

HISTORY AND LEGEND

This plant is mentioned by Pliny for its medicinal uses, also by Ibn Al Awam and Ibn Baithar. Because of its supposed antiseptic quality it was strewn over church floors at funerals and placed in sick chambers. Origanum is mentioned as being in Adrian van der Donck's garden in Yonkers in 1653. In the *Virginia Gazette* of 1774 sweet marjoram is recommended as a tea with a little mint. *O. heracleoticum* and *O. virens* were in American gardens in 1806.

USES

The flowers add a pleasant note to a potpourri.

The leaves were formerly used to dye linen reddish brown and the Russian Cossacks color the wood of their lances with it. The flowers are loved by the bees and improve the taste of honey. Miss Rohde says the marjoram was put into sweet bags to scent the linen. The dried leaves were used in tobacco.

Medicine. The fresh leaves are more valuable than the dried and are made into tea, which is said to strengthen the stomach, cure headaches, and nervous complaints. The oil distilled from the plant is tonic, excitant, emenagogue, and is used for skin diseases, toothache, neuralgia, and in liniments, for rheumatism and bruises.

Perfume. In Provence and Spain the dried flowers only are sent to the perfumer, and produce the "oil origanum," which is made from several species of origanum. The oil of thyme is often called "oil of origanum."

Food. The leaves are condiments, but I found they were not nearly as pleasant or attractive as the sweet marjoram, and do not recommend them.

CULTURE

The plant was sown from seed late in May out-of-doors and did not flower the first summer. It can be grown from seeds or propagated by cuttings and will last for many years. The pink and white flowers are attractive in a somewhat weedy fashion, and are so delightfully fragrant that they deserve a place in some corner of the garden, perhaps as a ground cover in a fairly wild space.

Variety. There seem to be about thirty marjorams, and one of these is called dwarf pot marjoram. It is mentioned by Vilmorin who says it makes a good edging plant, that it does not grow taller than twelve to fourteen inches, and always comes true from seed. Perhaps this is the one I grew under the name of *Origanum onites,* which Dr. Merrill says is a form of *O. vulgare*. It looks exactly like it and smells the same too, except that the whole plant is smaller, being from twelve to fifteen inches high in my garden. Sown indoors in March, it was transplanted into the garden in May and flowered the first summer. Either it is an annual or not hardy, for it died during the winter.

Other plants came to me under the specific names of *O. heracleoticum* and *O. virens*, which, when examined by Dr. Merrill, were reported as being forms of *O. vulgare,* from which they only differed in size, leafiness, or perhaps in scent.

A golden-leaved one is reported, var. *aureum*.

PAPAVER SOMNIFERUM, L.

OPIUM POPPY

Papaveraceae Annual

The poppy is native to the Mediterranean and sparingly naturalized in North America. I had always thought the big Oriental poppy was the one from which the opium came, and was surprised when I found that this plant with its grayish foliage and finely textured, crinkly white petals was the source of the powerful drug. Seed sold for opium poppy may produce single or double flowers and the colors range from white through to pink or soft brownish lavender, and some have fringed petals. In some localities, however, notably India, the white-flowered variety is grown as a source of opium, while elsewhere colored varieties are favored. The whole plant is gray-green with a bloom on it, and is smooth except for sharp hairs on the upper half of the flower stem.

Stem. It is twenty inches or more high in my garden, but according to Bailey, rises to four feet.

Leaf. The leaves are irregularly and roundly toothed; the radical ones are narrowed into a short stem, but the stem leaves have none, and partially encircle the flower stem. The leaves grow shorter as they ascend the stem.

Flower. The flowers come in July at Peekskill, and last for about ten days. They are white, single, solitary, of light or purple pink, varying in color and form, measure three to four inches across, and are delicate and charming.

Seed capsule. This is longish, narrow, two inches long and one inch across, and as one looks at it one cannot help but think that the first man to make a Chinese lantern must have been inspired by the shape of the opium poppy's seed pod.

Seed. The seeds are roundish, black in some forms, and

white in others, and have a pleasant, nutty flavor, and are quite free from any opium.

HISTORY AND LEGEND

The Greeks represented the God Hypnos (sleep) with his head wreathed in poppies, or with poppies in his hand, also the Gods of Death and Night. From the earliest times it was used as a narcotic.

The competitors in the Olympic Games in Greece ate poppy seeds mixed with wine and honey, and Pliny says this decoction was served at the second course on the tables of "the ancients."

Ibn Baithar says when opium is dissolved in vinegar and put up a donkey's nose, it makes him weep and he will bray. I do not doubt him, but merely wonder why one should do this at all.

USES

The opium comes from the shell of the seed capsule, or wall of the fructified ovary called the pericarp. When this turns yellowish and is slightly soft to the touch (according to Lloyd, "Origins and History") the workers take a knife with a fine saw edge and incise it. They must be careful not to cut into the interior of the capsule or the juice will flow inside. Several hours are allowed to elapse between the cutting and gathering, then the drops, called tears, after being scraped off, are kneaded into opium balls of a uniform consistency, packed into cylindrical baskets lined with linen, each being kept apart from the others either by seeds or wild rumex leaves. Smyrna was the principal port of export. In Europe and North America the crop of opium failed because of the climate and the expense of the labor.

Medicine. The opium is highly important in medicine to produce sleep and relieve pain by numbing the perceptive centers of the brain.

Food. The seeds, as mentioned earlier, are scattered on top of cakes and breads, especially a kind called seed twists, and made into a filling of a bread called Swiss roll. For these purposes they are grown in almost every German vegetable garden.

CULTURE

The opium poppy likes a fairly rich soil and sunlight; comes readily from seed; and if necessary should be thinned. Poppies are notoriously difficult to transplant. In their native lands they are sown in the fall and flower in April and May. In the North we sow them after frost and they flower in July.

PELARGONIUM GRAVEOLENS, L'HER.

ROSE GERANIUM

Geraniaceae Shrub (in warm climates)

The rose geranium comes from the Cape of Good Hope and is an attractive shrubby plant. It grows four feet high in warm climates, but where the winters go below freezing it has to be grown in a pot and does not reach its full height.

Root. The root is spreading and fibrous.

Stem. The stems are much branched, round, and covered with soft, short hairs.

Leaf. The leaves are opposite, darker above and lighter below, yellow green, much cut and divided generally into three divisions, which are again subdivided. They are subtended by bracts, and have long stems. The surface of the leaf curls up and down onto several planes, is covered with soft hairs, and is rough to the touch. It measures one and three-quarter inches in length and two inches across. When touched or bruised the leaves smell of roses and a dash of spice, and when cooked give the flavor of the roses to the food.

Flower. The flowers are about three-quarters of an inch across, pinkish-lavender, in umbels at the termination of the branches. Each umbel is subtended by six pointed sepal-like bracts. They are large enough to add to the beauty of the plant, the two upper petals being erect and marked with dark reddish-purple, while the three lower ones have no dark markings. The pistil has a five-parted, branching, insect-like stigma of reddish purple. The stamens are whitish, inconspicuous, placed around the base of the style, fairly numerous,—maybe ten.

Variety. E. M. Holmes, Genus *Pelargonium* in *Perfumery and Essential Oil Record,* July, 1913, lists forty-six different kinds of scented geraniums, most of which, he says, are native to the rocky slopes of South Africa.

The *P. odoratissimum, Ait.,* called apple or nutmeg geranium, is a charming plant with gray-green, rounded, frilled, velvety leaves and small, white, fluttery flowers marked with magenta. It smells, when crushed, of camphor, rose, and geranium, but not as strongly as the rose

Pelargonium graveolens, rose geranium

geranium. There are others scented of lemon, mint, strawberry, peppermint, pennyroyal, fruity, of tansy, rose, and so on, some of them having handsome foliage and flowers. If one has a good place in which to store them over the winter, it is amusing to collect as many varieties as one can.

HISTORY AND LEGEND

The geranium was introduced into Europe in 1690. The plants were brought to Grasse, in southern France, in 1800, and to Algiers from France in 1850. A haphazard and unsuccessful experiment of growing it for the fragrant oil was made in Florida, in 1914–17.

USES

Perfume. The rose geranium and its relatives are grown commercially for the fragrant oil distilled from the leaves, and Holmes says the growers keep as secret as possible the particular varieties grown. Sawyer says they grow varieties of *P. odoratissimum, P. capitatum,* and *P. roseum* (which is a variety of *P. radula, l'Her.*). The oil of geranium is used in perfumery to replace the attar of roses and perfumes tooth powders and ointments, and blends in with floral bouquets. Porcher says no well-perfumed soap of good quality is complete without a liberal quota of this raw material. In Provence a superfine oil is made by adding rose petals to the still.

Food. The leaves when cooked give the taste of the rose to puddings, custards, and jellies. They make pretty garnishes and add to the fragrance of bouquets.

CULTURE

When grown commercially, the cuttings are set out in

well-sheltered beds in October and are planted out in terraces in April where they soon grow into bushes, three to four feet high. They are grown commercially in North Africa, Spain, Italy, Corsica, Réunion, and Provence. Different localities produce oils of varying odor values. The Spanish oil is considered the finest because the plants are not irrigated.

In the north the pelargoniums are grown in pots or as bedding plants for the pleasure of their fragrance, and to have the leaves for flavoring. I make my cuttings from November to January in a greenhouse from plants brought indoors. A friend brings her plants through the winter, but so far I have not been able to do this. Cuttings started in January make plants a foot tall by the end of June. I fill my pots with humus and leaf mold and give them a handful of sheep manure. In the ground they require a well-drained soil, and I often place them in the borders where they do well in ordinary garden soil. If cut back the plant forms a thickish bush.

PETROSELINUM SATIVUM, HOFFM.

PARSLEY

Umbelliferae Biennial

This plant is called *Petroselinum hortense,* Hoffm. by Bailey, and elsewhere *Petroselinum apium,* L. The species is seldom grown, the moss-curled and fern-leaved varieties being more popular for garnishes.

Root. It has a white taproot which grows slenderer as it descends into the ground.

Stem. The stem is pithy, inside, smooth, with tiny raised

lines along it, growing slenderer as it rises, which is as high as three feet when in flower.

Leaf. The leaves are large, measuring seven inches in length and about six inches across. They are smooth, bright green, whitish, or light green at the tips of the teeth, and are divided into three divisions which in turn are each divided into three more. The ultimate segments are wedge-shaped, ovate, and deeply cut. The stalks are hollow, and concave on the outside. The flowering stem does not appear until the second year, and the leaves on the flowering stem are very small, more like bracts, but are also divided, and with deeply cut margins. Parsley leaves when fresh smell of camphor, sharp, and a bit of turpentine. They taste, as every one knows, characteristically of green herbs with an undertone of something dark and not the least flowery.

Flower. The flowers are tiny, of a greenish-yellow with exserted stamens, come during the second summer in late June and early July, and are borne in umbels which are flat across the top. The large umbel is composed of many smaller ones on rays of unequal length. They smell very pleasantly, a little like Queen Anne's Lace.

Seed. The seeds are one-sixteenth of an inch long, rounded at the base, flat on two sides, with three prominent ribs, and their germinating power is said to last three years. They are strongly fragrant like the rest of the plant.

Variety. It seems to be the general opinion that the moss-curled kinds are the most attractive to grow for garnishes, although I prefer the fern-leaved to all others. In the breeding of parsleys a dark green color and a cut or curled texture seem to be desirable qualities. One moss-curled variety in which the divisions of the leaves overlap and curl up at the end came from Vilmorin's and was named *persil nain très frisé,* and its counterpart from Sutton's was called moss-curled. The leaves have a sharp, bitter, penetrating, and distinctive taste.

A double-curled dwarf from England sounds like the champion moss-curled, or Stumpp and Walter's exhibition curled parsley from the United States. The leaves are much cut and divided, the segments touching one another and giving the leaf the appearance of a humpy, frilly moss. The stalks are so short that the leaves almost lie upon the ground and form a low, thick tuft. It is fragrant as the others are.

The fern-leaved parsley has the leaves divided into a great number of small thread-like segments and these are not curled but spread out, and seems to me the most dainty and decorative of them all. This one is attractive when scattered through the salad or mixed into cheese balls. It tastes less sharp than the others.

The Hamburg parsley, or turnip-rooted parsley, called var. *radicosum,* is grown for its thick parsnip-like tapering roots, which are cooked to flavor soups.

HISTORY AND LEGEND

Parsley is one of the herbs long known to mankind. Theophrastus mentions it as a coronary plant. In Greek and Roman days it was worn in chaplets to absorb the fumes of wine and so delay inebriation. The Greeks also decorated their tombs with it. Calumella mentioned it and Pliny, who says it was made into wreaths for the victors of the Nemean Games, and "cooks correct the flavor of vinegar in their dishes with parsley, and our butlers employ the same plant enclosed in sachets for removing the bad odor of wine." Ibn Baithar mentions its medicinal use and says it is good eaten with salad.

In the South the Negroes consider it unlucky to transplant parsley from an old home to a new one, as did the gardeners in olden times in England. In Pennsylvania the gardeners believe parsley should not be planted in the house for fear some one would die. A pregnant woman is supposed to have better success planting the seeds than any one else. Josselyn mentioned it as *Apium petroselinum*, and Bartram as parsley in 1814.

USES

Medicine. The dried ripe seed and also the root are in the United States Pharmacopoeia. The action of the root is diuretic. The seed is diuretic, febrifugal, emenagogue, and insecticidal. The herb is used externally as a vulnerary.

Cosmetics. The "Toilet of Flora" has a recipe to prevent baldness, which is as follows: "to powder your head with powdered parsley seed three nights every year and the hair will never fall off."

Food. The parsley leaves decorate almost every meat platter. It is minced and strewn over potatoes, carrots, or peas; and a sprig gives the taste to most soups, for it is almost always in with the "soup greens." Parsley soup is delicious.

CULTURE

The parsley makes a pretty edging for beds of vegetables and likes a rather moist soil. In cool climates the plants are generally started indoors to have them early because of their slow germination. The seed takes from a month to six weeks to germinate, and soaking it beforehand in tepid water for twenty-four hours hurries it a little. The plants are quite hardy but not of use the second year, for they seem to shoot into flowers unless the stems are cut back. It might be a good plan to feed the plants a little, if they are cut back too hard, but I have never found this necessary. Some bring parsley indoors to have it in the winter, but since it is obtainable at every grocery store throughout the land, this seems a bit foolish, especially when there are so many other plants one might prefer to have at the kitchen window.

Harvest. The leaves are cut as they are needed in the kitchen and seeds should be collected as soon as they are ripe. The roots may be dug at the end of the second season, washed, dried, and then stored.

PIMPINELLA ANISUM, L.

ANISE

Sweet Alice, Heal-Dog, Heal-Bite

Umbelliferae Annual

The anise is native to Greece, Asia Minor, and Egypt. It is a graceful, attractive plant, adding to the beauty of the herb garden.

Root. It has a taproot.

Stem. The stem is shiny green, ridged, and slightly tomentose. In my garden it grew to two feet high, but in Europe it is reported as reaching four feet.

Leaf. The leaves are of two kinds; the radical ones are roundish with deep margins having fairly deep pointed teeth. The stem leaves are divided into three toothed divisions; these vary somewhat in the shape of their divisions, some being narrower than others. The raw leaf tastes at first of liquorice, then of camphor, of fresh greens, and, quite characteristically, of anise. When crushed it smells of anise.

Flower. The flowers are small, whitish, and borne in lacy, white, fairly dense umbels which measure about two and a half to three inches across and are at the terminations of the stalks.

Seed. The seeds are one-eighth of an inch long and have the stem adhering to them. They are straw-colored, roundish, ridged, and carry the remains of the style in a button-like finish at the tip, and taste strongly of anise.

HISTORY AND LEGEND

Anise is mentioned in the Bible, by Theophrastus, and Dioscorides. Pliny says that if suspended to the pillow, to be smelt by the sleeper, it will give him a youthful look and prevent disagreeable dreams. In classical days the source of anise was Egypt and Crete. It is on Charlemagne's list, and was mentioned as of medicinal value by Ibn Baithar. In the reign of Edward I, 1305, it was one of the drugs to be taxed when carried across the Bridge of London, and "little bags of fustian stuffed with iris and anise" perfumed the royal linen of Edward IV's household. Mrs. Le Boiteaux mentions that in 1619 the first Assembly of Virginia decreed that "each man, as he is settled upon his division, plant (amongst other plants specified) six aniseeds and that each are to make trial thereof the nexte season." Josselyn mentions "annis."

USES

The oil distilled from the seeds is said to destroy lice, and be excellent as a bait for mice. The seeds are used in drag hunts when there is no fox.

Medicine. The anise seed is mentioned in the United States Pharmacopoeia. The action is aromatic, stimulant, carminative, and it increases the flow of the milk.

Perfume. The oil of the seed is a popular flavor for dental preparations, and is often blended with peppermint. Soaps are perfumed with it, and pomatums, but, as Piesse says, it does not do nicely in compounds "for handkerchief use."

Food. The seeds flavor bread, cake, and confectionery, and the green leaves are good in salads, or as a garnish. The Portuguese are fond of it as are the Neapolitans, who put it into everything. In a portion of southwestern France a pancake flavored with it is a specialty of the region. Recipes for anise cookies and anise bread were brought from Germany by my grandmother.

The oil flavors many liqueurs, such as absinth, *anisette, ratafia d'Anis, eau de vie d'Hendaye, pferfermünze* liqueur, *kalmus* liqueur, *roscan aromatique,* and in Italy the *rosolio de Torino,* and in England, *usquebaugh.*

CULTURE

Fresh home-grown anise seed is far more potent than the bought ones, and is therefore well worth the slight trouble of growing it, for anise comes readily from seed. It prefers a moderately rich, well-drained loam, which has been carefully prepared, and a warm, sunny exposure. The seed is sown in May, and when the plants are a few inches high they should be thinned if too thick. My plants flowered in about six weeks after sowing.

Harvest. As soon as the seeds turn grayish I cut off the umbels and dry them in the shade; then bottle them in glass containers.

It is grown commercially in France, Germany, Russia, and Spain, whence comes the best anise known as *alicante*. It is also grown in the United States, chiefly in Rhode Island.

PRIMULA VERIS, L.

COWSLIP

Lady's Keys, Saint Peter's Wort

Primulaceae Perennial

The cowslip is a hardy little plant which colors the dry meadows and pastures of Europe and Russian Asia to the Caucasus and Altai Mountains with the sunny flowers resembling a bunch of keys. The name primula is a contraction from the Italian *fiore de primavera,* flower of spring. The plant is low, soft, pubescent, four to eight inches tall.

Root. The roots consist of thready fibers.

Leaf. The leaves are crinkled, ovate, or ovate-oblong, two to three inches long, hairy beneath, with a winged leaf stem. Each leaf rises from the ground and all of them together form a rosette.

Flower. The soft yellow flowers are sweetly fragrant, of a fresh woodsy scent, and come in early spring. They are three-eighths to one-half an inch across. The calyx is three-quarters of an inch long, hairy, with short ovate-acute tips, and the tube of the corolla is concave. The petals form overlapping folds at the mouth of the flower, which is slightly open. The flower stem bears an umbel of several flowers. The root and flowers are said to have the odor of anise. This plant differs from the *Primula vulgaris,* primrose, which has a radical and single-flowered stem; and from the *P. elatior,* oxlip, which has the limb of the corolla broad and flat.

HISTORY AND LEGEND

In Greek mythology the primula was Paralisos, son of Flora and Priapus, who died of a broken heart over the loss of his sweetheart and was changed by the Gods into this yellow flower of spring. There is a superstition that if planted upside down the primroses will come up variegated. *Primula veris* and *Primula auricula* are both mentioned in Prince's catalogue in 1790, and in Bartram's of 1814.

USES

Medicine. The whole plant is known to be gently narcotic, the flowers more so than the leaves. The "National Standard Dispensary," 1916, says, however, the primula is unimportant medicinally.

Cosmetic. Parkinson says: "Of the juice, or water from the flowers of cowslips divers gentlewomen know how to cleanse the skin from spots or discolourings therein as also to take away the wrinkles thereof and cause the skin to become smooth and faire . . ."

Food. Mrs. Leyel says a tea of the flowers at night has a decided narcotic tendency.

John Evelyn gives a recipe for cowslip wine, which requires three pecks of the flowers, "being used to two gallons of water." The leaves are made into salads, and the English, according to Eleanour Rohde, used both leaves and flowers constantly for a potherb, in cowslip cream, puddings, and tarts, as well as in wine. In olden days, and perhaps even now, they candied and pickled the flowers, and made cowslip tea, syrup, and conserves. Cowslip wine is said to resemble the muscatel wines of southern France.

CULTURE

Primula veris can be raised from seed or increased by dividing the plants. It likes a good garden soil and some protection from cold winds. In my garden it has always done best when shaded for part of the day.

ROSA DAMASCENA, MILL.

DAMASK ROSE

Rosaceae Shrub

The damask rose is of course not a herb, but because of its beauty, Old World associations, and constant use in cooking, it rightly belongs in our garden. When I bought the damask rose twelve years ago, none were obtainable in the United States, and mine came to me from a famous rose grower in France, but now they can be bought in American nurseries. This is the rose of Damascus, the petals of which furnish the most fragrant of all rose oils. It is the parent of the gallicas, or French roses. It is grown in Bulgaria, whence the finest attar of roses comes. It is not a vigorous grower in our climate, rising to three feet, but elsewhere to five to six feet, and is a gracefully curving shrub.

Root. The roots are strong and woody.

Branch. The branches rise from low down, are covered with unevenly-sized thorns, and are woody and spreading.

Leaf. The leaves are dull green above and lighter below, and are tinted brownish toward the edges above. The margins are indented and are compounded into seven leaflets each about two and one-half inches long.

Flower. The blossoms are pale pink, crinkly, thin-textured, semi-double, not showing the stamens and pistils at first. They come in a two- to three-flowered cyme and there are seven flowers to a branch and sometimes as many as thirteen. According to the season, they flower from the middle of June to the middle of July and are in bloom about ten days. The bud stems, buds, and calyx are covered with tiny bristles. The flowers and stems are only faintly fragrant of the true rose odor when fresh, but when dried are strongly fragrant. They fade quickly after cutting.

CULTURE

The roses are pruned in the fall, hilled up, covered with straw for the winter, and severely pruned again in the spring. They can be increased from cuttings by planting these in sand out-of-doors over the winter, and the following spring they will have rooted.

Harvest. The petals are picked early in the morning, dried in the shade, and then cleaned for potpourris; not, however, if rose-petal jam is to be made, when fresh rose petals are used.

ROSA GALLICA, L.

ROSE DE PROVENCE

French Rose

Rosaceae Shrub

The bushes came to me from France by special permit, too, although they are now obtainable in the United States. This rose is an ancestor of the hybrid perpetual roses, and with the damask rose is the principal rose used for perfume. The bush is low, two to three feet high when in flower and growing taller later in the season. It is short in comparison with other rose species.

Branch. The branches are light green and thorny, with small thorns of a light green color shaded reddish.

Leaf. The leaves are compounded into five leaflets, each sharply serrated, dark above and lighter below, and there are sharp little pricks along the midrib on the under side.

Flower. The flowers blossom from the middle of June for about ten days, and then not again all season. The sepals have much divided margins like a compound leaf. The petals are all crushed together in the bud and are a deep reddish-rose color, and show their stamens and pistils, which makes them look almost single, but they are semidouble, having about fifteen petals. They smell a little of pine when fresh and strongly of roses when dry. They are very hardy in my garden and have grown into the hedge behind.

CULTURE

I grow them exactly as I do the damask roses.

HISTORY AND LEGEND

This applies to all of the old roses. Much has been written about how the Romans imported roses from Egypt for their grand parties, and how the petals carpeted the floors of the banqueting rooms, and rose water played in the fountains. The aesthetes of those days slept on mattresses stuffed with rose petals, and the sturdy Romans, no longer quite so sturdy, bathed in rose wine. Pliny says the rose petals were charred and used as cosmetics for eyebrows, and that the dried petals made into a powder were sprinkled on the body after the bath to check perspiration.

Avicenna is said to have been the first to extract the oil from roses by distillation. In Arabic Spain the clothes of the Emirs were rinsed in rose water. The rose was on Charlemagne's list, and is in every herbal. To the Greeks it was a symbol of love, beauty, and happiness, and said to derive its red color from Aphrodite's blood. It is also the emblem of silence, whence the expression, "sub rosa"; and the Mohammedans thought it holy.

The rose de Provins was introduced into Provence in 1254 by Thibault, Comte de Champagne, and at that time the commerce of dried rose petals, conserves, syrup, and honey of roses began and they were considered products of great value.

The roses were in American gardens quite early. Mrs. Logan's "Gardener's Calendar" mentions white, monthly, and sweet briar roses. Prince lists the Damascena red, Damascena white, and large Provence rose in 1790. In an article on tea in the *Virginia Gazette* of January, 1774, a recipe is given for a tea of "Red Rose bush leaves, and cinquefoil which recruits the strength, mitigates pains, and inflammations, and is beneficial to consumptives and feverish people, healing wounds and serviceable in spitting blood."

Before the war the center of culture for the damascena roses, where the finest attar of roses was produced, was Kezanlik in Bulgaria. For miles the land was given over to the culture of this plant and the fragrance when they were in blossom was said to be almost overwhelming. There the soil is sandy and porous, and slopes toward the south, and the bushes were planted close together to form hedges, in long rows with six feet between the rows, and were renewed every five years. A rose plantation was established near Leipzig in 1886 to furnish rose oil, but the cold climate was not favorable. At Grasse a fine oil is obtained from the roses.

USES

Medicine. The *Rosa gallica* is mentioned in all editions of the pharmacopoeia from 1820 to 1920. Rose petals are mildly astringent and carminative.

Perfume. In France the attar of roses is extracted by *enfleurage,* but in Bulgaria through distillation. One drop of rose oil will perfume one quart of water. The essence of rose is present in practically every perfume, and the dried petals are in every potpourri.

Food. Rose water and rose petals enter into many recipes, for the flavor of roses gives a smooth, sweet taste, and blends in well with other condiments. Crystallized rose petals are of Oriental origin and pleasant to behold as well as to eat.

At Nanking, according to Bois, "Les Plantes Alimentaires," a rose is grown for eating, which seems to be a variety of the *Rugosa* rose. The dried petals perfume not only teas and drinks, as is commonly done in other parts of China, but bakers use a large amount for their cakes, and brewers prepare a kind of liqueur of roses.

ROSMARINUS OFFICINALIS, L.

ROSEMARY

Labiatae Shrub

The rosemary is perennial in warm climates, but winter kills it in severe climates. In my garden it grows to eighteen inches or more and is treated as an annual, whereas in its home it is a woody evergreen shrub three to six feet high, and is often planted as a hedge. The whole plant, especially the leaves and flowering tops, is fragrant, the leaves more so than the flowers.

Root. The roots are fibrous and spreading.

Stem. The stems are a lighter green than the leaves, woody below and the upper ones are tomentose and very much branched.

Leaf. The leaves are evergreen, without stalks, very thick along the stems, in pairs, and from their axils other pairs grow out. They are long, narrow, obtuse, and covered with short hairs above, and about three-sixteenths of an inch across and one and one-half inches long. The whole surface is roughish and uneven, the under surface is lighter and covered with tiny glands, the margins roll tightly under like a "French roll" in sewing. They are fragrant without touching, but more so when rubbed, of nutmeg, pine needles, and heliotrope, all combining into a

Rosmarinus officinalis, rosemary

distinctive smell of their own. They taste bitter, resinous, of camphor, warm and distinctive.

Flower. My plants have never flowered, but along the Mediterranean they blossom from January to May and they are in axillary clusters, a pale blue, about one-half an inch long, and have the stamens exserted.

Seed. The seeds are light brown, oval, with a large white hilum at one end, and Vilmorin says the germinating power lasts four years.

Variety. The following varieties are mentioned: the common narrow-leaved rosemary; the broad-leaved rosemary; the silver-striped rosemary; and the gold-striped rosemary, which last can only be propagated by cuttings, and is said to be hardier than the silver. There is a variety known as Miss Jessup's upright.

HISTORY AND LEGEND

Rosemary was called *Rosmaris* by Ovid, and *Rose Marinus* by Pliny, which means sea dew. In olden days it was used at funerals instead of the more expensive incense. Later, however, the Mary in the name associated it with the Mother of Jesus, and the legend arose that when the Virgin Mary washed her sky-blue cloak she spread it over a rosemary bush to dry and the flowers were thenceforth blue.

Dioscorides, Galen, and Charlemagne mention it. Ibn Baithar says hunters stuffed their prey with the herb after they had taken out the entrails to keep it from smelling badly and that is was a well-known plant in Andalusia where the ovens were heated with it, as they still are to-day, and this nutmeg-like fragrance mingled with olive oil which greets us as we step off the ferry from Gibraltar to Algeciras, tells us we are in Spain. Narbonne honey is flavored with rosemary.

Rosemary is the emblem of remembrance and fidelity, as Ophelia says to Laertes, Act IV, Scene V:

> There's rosemary, that's for remembrance;
> Pray, love, remember . . .

It is supposed to bring good luck, prevent witchcraft, and to have disinfecting powers. Perhaps that is why it was used at funerals. In France it is even now placed in the hands of the dead, and in French hospitals it is the custom to burn rosemary with juniper berries to correct impure air and prevent infection.

Josselyn mentions rosemary in 1672, and it appears in Bartram's catalogue in 1807, and in Stearns' "The American Herbal" in 1801.

USES

Medicine. Rosemary oil is in all pharmacopoeias. The flowers are a stimulant, antispasmodic, emenagogue, and rubefacient, while the leaves are rubefacient and carminative.

Perfume. The oil of rosemary is secured by distilling the leafy tips and leaves, either fresh or dried. It gives the characteristic note to Hungary water, which was first made in 1370, *eau de cologne* cannot be made without it, and it is now used in cheap perfumery and in soaps. In Greece, Turkey, and southern France the rosemary in flower is so fragrant that the baths are perfumed with it and it is used in hair washes and tooth washes.

CULTURE

The plants come readily from seed which should be

started as early as possible, indoors, if the plants are to grow large enough to cut the leaves early in the season. Cuttings can be made in January or later from plants carried over the winter indoors. Plants bought did not survive the journey and died. As the leaves are constantly cut one should occasionally stir the soil a little and feed with sheep manure, or other plant food. My plants are in a dry, sunny situation, in well-drained soil. The leaves of plants brought indoors in the winter are not as strongly fragrant.

Harvest. For drying, the leaves are picked as the plants flower, and dried in the shade, but when used fresh they can be picked at any time.

The commercial oils come from southern France, Spain, and the Dalmatian Islands. It is said, during the harvest season one can smell the rosemary off the Spanish coast long before sighting land.

RUTA GRAVEOLENS, L.

RUE

Common Rue

Rutaceae Perennial

Rue is one of the bitter herbs, and comes from southern Europe. It is a pretty plant with its grayish-green, much cut leaves and yellow-green flowers, and is in the garden because of sentiment, not for any present-day use. The whole plant has a dry, acrid, strong scent, as of a stinging thing. When I get only a faint whiff of it, it reminds me of old ladies in the nineties of my childhood or of old druggists' shops, but if I get too much of it, it nauseates me, but that is probably entirely and peculiarly personal, for many like it exceedingly.

Root. There is a thick main root from which fibers grow out.

Stem. Several stems grow out from where the root rises from the ground. They grow up to two feet and are round and covered with a bloom which comes off as one touches them.

Leaf. The leaves are covered with a bloom, not hairy, and give off the characteristic scent when touched. They are compounded into about nine leaflets, each of which is again divided into deeply cut segments rounded at the tips. The longest are five inches long and they grow shorter as they ascend the stem. Some of them are shaped like a druggist's spatula. Their taste is very bitter.

Flower. The flowers are in short, few-flowered, flat-topped, terminal clusters and open early in June for me and continue for a long time. Four light yellow green pointed sepals subtend the greenish-yellow corolla about half an inch across, having four petals which curl up all around the edges, so much so as to form a hood at the tips. The stamens stand out stiffly and are dark green. The conical ovary is made up of four united sections from the center of which rises the tiny green pistil.

Seed. The seeds are black, crescent-shaped, and keep their germinating power for two years.

Variety. There is a variegated form in which the leaves are splashed with white.

HISTORY AND LEGEND

The Greeks and Romans thought if rue were stolen

from a neighbor's garden it would thrive better than if raised at home. Rue is said to have been the antidote Mercury gave to Ulysses to preserve him from the effects of Circe's enchanted beverage, and Parkinson says that King Mithridates of Pontus, to offset the effects of possible poisoning, began every day by eating a concoction made up of twenty leaves of rue, a little salt, a couple of walnuts, and a couple of figs beaten together in a mass. My comment to this is that the king must have loved life very much.

Rue is mentioned in the Bible. Because of its penetrating odor it was considered a prophylactic, and it was the custom to place a bunch of rue upon the bar of the central Criminal Court in England to preserve the judges from being infected with gaol fever from the prisoners brought before them from Newgate Prison. Shakespeare says:

> Reverend Sirs:
> For you there's rosemary and rue; these keep
> Seeming and savour, all winter long.
> Grace and remembrance be to you both.

Ibn Baithar, amongst other virtues attributed to rue, says if it is rubbed on bald spots it will restore the hair. Josselyn mentioned rue, and it is in Bartram's catalogue of 1807, and in Stearns' "The American Herbal" of 1801. It was grown in peasant gardens to be used as a preservative against the plague, and was an ingredient in the vinegar of the four thieves.

USES

Perfume. Rue oil is obtained by distilling the leafy portions, and enters into sweet-pea attars to which it gives a characteristic aroma, and in the manufacture of aromatic, toilet, hygienic, and cosmetic vinegars.

Food. Boulestin and Hill say the chopped leaves with brown bread make good sandwiches, and that rue is a powerful stimulant for a failing appetite, but that the leaves should be used sparingly, for they are biting, which only goes to show how differently people respond to tastes and smells. Bois says if too many leaves are eaten they are poisonous. The Italians and Greeks, however, season their food with it and eat it in salads.

CULTURE

Plants of rue can be bought in nurseries in the United States. It comes readily from seed, which, when sown out-of-doors, germinated fairly quickly for me, but the plants did not flower the first summer. I read it can be propagated from cuttings. Rue is a husky, hardy plant and although it dies down considerably in the winter, it comes up quite perkily again in the spring. It seems to like a well-drained, rather moist situation, but will grow in any good garden soil.

SALVIA OFFICINALIS, L.

SAGE

Labiatae Perennial

Sage is a hardy plant native to the northern shores of the Mediterranean and is one of the herbs universally employed as a flavoring. It is said to be grown in the gardens of every village in Europe.

Root. The root is woody with wiry fibers, and spreading.

Stem. The stems are of a soft, woody texture, growing from eighteen inches to two feet high, are squarish, and covered with woolly down. They are somewhat spready and recumbent, and grow quite untidy unless cut back from time to time.

Leaf. Ibn Baither says the Greek name for the plant means camel's tongue, and the oval leaves terminating in a point, with their glandular uneven surface covered with a fine network, do resemble the tongue of some animal. They are soft to the touch, dark above and lighter below, and of a "sage green" changing from grayer to greener at different seasons. They are covered with short, soft white hairs, are opposite at right angles to the pair above, and bracts rise from their axils. They are very fragrant of sage, which is a mixture of thyme, turpentine, with a dark quality, a pungent one, and altogether pleasant.

Flower. The flowers come in late June and grow in a long raceme, are quite gaping, of a lavender blue and look a little like a parrot's beak. They grow in whorls, and form nearly leafless spikes. Two strongly marked white spots on the lower lip are surrounded by a dark lavender patch. The style is whitish; the stigma two-parted at the tip, blue-purple, and curves out from the hooded upper lip; and the four stamens are whitish with golden anthers; the four sepals are brownish, pointed, ribbed, and hairy.

Seed. The seeds are nearly spherical, blackish-brown, and, according to Vilmorin, the germinating power lasts three years.

Variety. There are many varieties. The one described above is the narrow-leaved sage, the Sage of Virtue. There is the broad-leaved sage or balsamic sage, rarely used in cookery, but rather in medicine. The red-leaved sage, or red top, is much esteemed in cookery. The ribs and nerves of the leaves are purple, and so are the young stalks and the young leaves, but with age these change to green. Green-leaved sage, green top, is a variety of the red-leaved; the young shoots, leafstalks, and the nerves of the leaves being green. Then there is a variegated red-leaved sage and a sage with white flowers, which has smaller leaves than most of them, and is quite hardy.

HISTORY AND LEGEND

Theophrastus, Dioscorides, and Pliny mention sage. Sage in the garden is said to prolong life, and there is another saying that sage grows according to the wealth of the family who own the land, and another that it only prospers where the wife rules. In French, sage means wise. This meaning and our English one are said to come from the belief that the plants have the property of strengthening the memory. Salvia planted with rue was thought to keep toads away.

At one time the Dutch carried on a profitable trade in it. They procured the leaves of the narrow-leaved sage from the south of France, dried them in imitation of tea, and shipped these to China, where for each pound of sage they received four pounds of tea in exchange.

USES

Sage, tansy, or black walnut leaves are said to keep ants away. Sage leaves can be smoked, as is tobacco.

Medicine. To a mild degree it possesses astringent and tonic properties. Sage tea has been a favorite household remedy to cure colds and sore throats, and as a gargle.

Perfume. The oil distilled from the whole plant has a camphoraceous odor and is used in soap perfumes.

Food. Dried sage leaves flavor pork, and stuffings of duck, goose, veal, sausages, and cheeses. They should be used discreetly, as sage is strong and apt to override other flavorings. Too much sage gives some people indigestion.

CULTURE

Sage plants can be bought from nurseries in the United States. The plants grown from seed are said to be generally the narrow-leaved variety. They can be increased from cuttings planted in sand which should be made in spring. The plant should be allowed to go into the winter with a full head of leaves and not be cut back too late to prevent these from growing out again. My plants grow in a very dry situation in clay soil, but most likely *Salvia officinalis* will grow in any good, well-drained garden loam.

Harvest. The first year the plants should not be cut too much. The leaves are harvested by stripping from the stems and drying in the shade to prevent their turning black. The drying should proceed continuously. Dr. Stockberger says the American leaf sage usually brings higher prices than the European.

SALVIA SCLAREA, L.

CLARY

Clary Sage

Labiatae Biennial

Clary is a native of southern France, Italy, and North Africa, and has become naturalized a little in Pennsylvania. It is a coarse but handsome plant, and clumps of it planted at pivotal points are effective, especially if the pinkish *sclarea* var. *turkestanica* is mixed with whitish sturdy stalks of *Salvia sclarea.* The unusual scent of the flowers is so strong it is the first to greet us from way across the garden.

Root. The root is spready and several stems rise from it.

Stem. The stems are about one inch across, square, ridged, covered with glistening hairs, almost like shiny wires, and measure three feet or more to the tip of the inflorescence.

Leaf. The leaves are opposite, the largest about eight inches long and six inches wide, growing smaller as they ascend the stem, puckered, with little humps all over their surfaces, and fairly wide with the margins crisped, unevenly and roughly indented. The upper surface is gray with hairs which are longer than those on the under surface. The leaf stems are square, ridged and hairy. The leaves smell, but not at all strongly, of paregoric, camphor, and benzoin, but when cooked seemed to have no noticeable taste, which may be owing to the climate.

Flower. The flowers come the second season, in late June, last a long time, and are greenish-white, labiate, and are borne in long, numerous, stiff, conspicuous spikes twelve inches or more long at the upper half of the plant. Two or three flowers form opposite whorls and are each subtended by a whitish, green-margined, wide, almost circular bract. The spur, or upper lip, curves high above the under lip, and out of the tip of it projects a bluish-tipped, forked stigma like the feeler of an insect. The flowers are half an inch long with the furry, four-pointed, cup-like calyx. They are overpoweringly fragrant and to me smell warm, piny, spicy, and camphoraceous. Porcher says the perfume has a musky, amber character.

Seed. The seeds are round, brownish, and four are produced together. They retain their vitality for two years.

Variety. The var. *turkestanica* is stunning with the flowers and bracts of an iridescent, pinkish-lavender, blue, and white.

HISTORY AND LEGEND

The name comes from *sclarus*, clear, because the seeds were used to clear the eyes. Clary was thought to be good for "weak backs and to straighten the reins being made into tansies and eaten otherwise." Parkinson gives a recipe for cooking clary leaves: "The leaves taken dry and dipped into a batter of the yolk of eggs and a little milk and then fried with butter until they be crisp serve of a dish of meat accepted by manie and unpleasant to none." The tops were put into soups, and John Evelyn says of it: "in short it is a plant indu'ed with so many wonderful properties as the assiduous use of it is said to render men immortal," and suggests using the summits of the young leaves and the flowers "in our cold sallet; yet so as not to domineer." Josselyn mentioned it as did Bartram, and it is in Stearns' "The American Herbal."

USES

Perfume. The plant is now grown for the oil, called clary sage oil, distilled from the inflorescence, and from the whole plant. It is used in violet compounds, in face-powder perfumes, in compounding chypre, and as a fixative in perfume. The dried leaves are put into sachets.

Food. The leaves formerly flavored all homemade wine, metheglin, ale, and beer. The German name of clary is *mustcateller sallier*, which means muscatel sage, and comes from the custom of using the leaves, along with elder flowers, to impart the flavor of muscatel raisins to Rhenish wines. Omelettes are made with clary leaves, and the flowers are used in aromatic teas.

CULTURE

The natural habitat of the plants is rocky, dry soil where nourishment and moisture are down deep. The French growers say manure improves the flavor of the oil and increases the flowers. My plants were grown from seed and throve in an average garden soil. The plant flowers the second summer, after which it should be pulled out by the roots and replaced with young plants from the seed-bed. As soon as the leaves are large enough they can be harvested, beginning the first season and continuing on into the following July, when the plant flowers.

SANGUISORBA MINOR, SCOP.

BURNET

Rosaceae Perennial

The burnet, also called *Poterium sanguisorba, L.*, is a hardy plant native to Europe and Asia, and naturalized a little in this country, and is sparingly cultivated here for the young leaves. It is included because it is one of the old-time herbs and not for its beauty, or present-day value. The plant forms rosettes of leaves, which spread out low on the ground, eighteen to twenty-four inches across. Because of the sharp-pointed leaf margins, it is reminiscent of the old-fashioned silks finished off that way.

Root. The root is woody and spreading.

Stem. The flower stems rise from the heart of the plant twelve to fifteen inches high, are ridged, hairy, and branched, and bear little leaflets along them.

Leaf. The leaf stems are thin, begin at the root, and have one furrow and three ridges and the leaves are compounded into opposite, oval, rounded leaflets, set in pairs along each side of the stem. The margins of the leaflets are notched regularly as if they had been pinked on a machine, and each leaf turns inward from either side of the midrib. They are glaucous, lighter below and darker green above. They smell of fresh greens, and taste pleasantly, as hay smells.

Flower. The flowers come in June in my garden and are rose-red, less than one-eighth of an inch across and are borne in an inflorescence somewhat like a green pine cone, about three-quarters of an inch high and half an inch across. The lower flowers are staminate and the upper ones bisexual, and as the lower ones ripen their stamens hang down like tiny, untidy-looking threads.

Seed. The fertile flowers produce a four-sided brown and wrinkled seed.

Variety. Burr mentions three varieties, the hairy-leaved burnet, the large-seeded burnet, and the smooth-leaved burnet.

HISTORY AND LEGEND

Burnet does not seem to go back to ancient history. Josselyn speaks of it, and Eleanour Rohde tells this story about it: It is called Chabairje (Chaba's slave) in Hungarian and thereby hangs the tale. Its virtues were first discovered by King Chaba who, after he had engaged in a terrible battle with his brother, is said to have cured the wounds of fifteen thousand of his soldiers with the juice of this plant.

USES

Bailey says it is mentioned as a sheep forage.

Medicine. It is not in any pharmacopoeia as far as I know, but the pulverized, dried roots are said to be astringent, and good for cases of internal hemorrhage.

Food. The leaves are supposed to convey the flavor of fresh cucumbers, but either our climate or my palate may be to blame for not detecting this. Formerly the leaves were steeped in cool tankards and the Pennsylvania Germans used it in a drink called cool cup. A few of the leaves added to a cup of wine, we are told, "helpe to make the heart merrie." We picked the young leaves and put them in with the lettuce for the salad, where they added a pleasant flavor. The old leaves are hard and a little tough.

CULTURE

The plants come readily from seed, or they can be propagated by root divisions. They are quite hardy and not the least finical. Vilmorin says it does not require much attention and others say it likes a chalky soil. It did not flower much the first season from plants started indoors in March and transplanted later. At first I thought the rosettes of leaves would make a pretty ground cover, but the flowers are so uninteresting and untidy looking that I have removed it from the decorative part of the garden. In Europe it is sometimes used as an edging to other vegetables.

SATUREIA HORTENSIS, L.

SUMMER SAVORY

Labiatae Annual

The summer savory, also called *Calamintha hortensis*, is native to southern Europe and has escaped on poor soils in Ohio, Illinois, and Nevada. It is a dainty, spreading plant, the branches being more conspicuous than the sparse leaves. This is one of the sweet herbs and has a pleasant, spicy fragrance pleasanter than the winter savory, and better for cooking, although the other, too, is good.

Root. It has a long main root, somewhat tough and whitish.

Stem. The stems are brown, turning yellowish, and are rounded, hairy, and twelve to eighteen inches or more high.

Leaf. The leaves are very slender, almost linear, obtuse, less than half an inch long, and soft to the touch. They taste of camphor, pepper, sweet and resinous. On drying they smell sharp, peppery, not as sweet as the basils, but very pleasant indeed.

Flower. The flowers are tiny, one-eighth of an inch long, pale pinkish-lavender, borne in loose spikes made up of whorls in the axils of the leaves, and have pale-colored stamens with deeper lavender anthers. They open one after another over a considerable period and give a fluffy, light appearance to the whole plant.

Seed. The seeds are small, deep brown, and their germinating power lasts from two to three years.

USES

The bees like it. I put the branches in with bouquets.

Medicine. Both savories were made into teas in olden days to cure intestinal disorders, colds, and fevers.

Food. The leaves and flowering tops are put into stuffings, on salads, and boiled with peas, for stuffing sausages or a pork pie, or used as a garnish. Boulestin and Hill say it is everywhere put into broad beans (hence its German name, *bohnenkraut*), both in the first boiling and in the final preparation either *à la poulette,* or *au lard,* when it is chopped with parsley. We use it with string beans, and it gives an indescribable aromatic taste to them.

CULTURE

The plants stand transplanting when they have been started indoors, but this is merely a waste of time since they come up so satisfactorily when sown out-of-doors early in May in a well-prepared soil and a sunny situation. If they are coming up too thickly they should be thinned to about six inches or a little less, apart, each way. Summer savory does not stand cutting back very well, and some people advise cutting down the whole plant at once when it is beginning to flower, and then drying the tips and leaves in the shade. Dried and pulverized, it is a delicious condiment. The seed is sold by many American seed houses.

SATUREIA MONTANA, L.

WINTER SAVORY

Labiatae Perennial

The winter savory, also called *Calamintha montana, Lam.*, is native to Europe and North Africa, is hardy, and one of the most decorative plants in the herb garden with its little white florets scattered amongst the bright green leaves as if it had just begun to snow. It smells pleasantly of resin and spice. The plant grows to two feet across and about twelve inches high.

Root. The root is white, twisted, and firmly attached to the soil, and sends up stems as it pushes its way along.

Stem. The stems are woody, brown on the lower portions, but light green above and hairy.

Leaf. The leaves are evergreen, smooth, dark green, shiny, and covered with tiny glands. They are half an inch long, very narrow and pointed at the tip, about one-sixteenth of an inch across; the margins are hairy, entire, and the central rib is prominent. The leaf turns up on either side of this midrib. They stand out, straight up from the stems, and are arranged in opposite pairs, each pair at right angles to the one above it with a pair of tiny leaflets in the axils of each leaf. The leaves taste sharp and spicy when fresh.

Flower. The flowers begin to open in July, are white with a bit of pink, and are one-eighth of an inch across, and three or more of them rise on the tiny stem from the leaf axils, only one in each cluster opening at a time. From a distance it looks as if the blossoms had been strewn over the plant.

Seed. The seeds are brown, triangular, ovoid, finely shagreened, and their germinating power lasts three years.

Variety. The species of savory are many; Bailey says one hundred and thirty.

HISTORY AND LEGEND

Palladius mentions *Satureia hortensis* in the third century, and Turner in 1561. Ibn Baithar mentions *Satureia capitata* and says *Satureia hortensis* was grown in Andalusia and Egypt. Josselyn mentions winter and summer savory. Claytonius, "Flora Virginica," 1762, mentions *Satureia foliis ovatis serratis.*

It is said to be an aphrodisiac.

USES

The leaves and young shoots are delicious as a condiment in foods, and in several liqueurs. They stay green all winter, although the leaves are not nearly as pungent as they are in summer.

CULTURE

The plant is very hardy and comes readily from seed, which can be sown out-of-doors in May in a well-prepared seed bed, or indoors in a frame and later transplanted. This transplanting seemed to act, for me, as a stimulus to the plant's growth. It is said to like a fairly high altitude. Vilmorin says, to encourage a vigorous supply of young shoots cut the stems down in spring to four inches above the ground. I have to do this to keep the plant from taking up too much space, for it spreads considerably.

Winter savory is a decorative plant, charming as a

border or edging. It can be increased by divisions, or by slips planted in sandy soil. The seed of winter savory is sold at American seed houses.

SESAMUM ORIENTALE, L.

SESAME

Bene

Pedaliaceae Annual

Sesame, or bene, also called *Sesamum indicum, L.*, is native to the tropics and is a pretty plant with its almost furry, whitish, foxglove-like flowers.

Root. The root is fleshy, white, and has one main stem.

Stem. The stem is round, ridged, hairy and glistening, and grows to three feet high.

Leaf. The lower leaves are opposite, toothed, three inches long, fleshy, hairy, and with glands on them. The upper leaves are not toothed, slender, and alternately placed along the stem.

Flower. The flowers come from July to September and are lavender shaded white, thimble, or foxglove-shaped, very hairy, soft to the touch, one inch long, the upper lip with two lobes and shorter than the three-lobed lower lip.

Seed. The capsule is tetragonal, oblong, four-celled with numerous seeds which are tiny, one-sixteenth of an inch, cream-colored, flat, two-sided, leaf-shaped, terminating in a point at one end. Drury, "Useful Plants of India," says there are plants with black seeds and that the white-seeded varieties are not so common. The seeds taste like nuts, and give a pleasant flavor to cookies and biscuits.

HISTORY AND LEGEND

According to Brahma Purana, sesame was created by Yama, God of Death, after a long penitence, and is used in funerary and expiatory ceremonies as a purifier and symbol of immortality. Sesame was mentioned by Theophrastus, in The "Anabasis," and by Dioscorides.

We all remember Ali Baba and the Forty Thieves and how Ali Baba hiding in a tree heard the robber chief standing before the treasure cave, say: "Open sesame" and when he came out: "Close sesame." Then when Ali Baba's brother followed after him to the cave to steal some of the treasure, how in his greed he forgot the password and called "Open barley" and other grains in vain, and so was caught and strung up by the robbers when they returned. Ibn Baithar, who must have been bald himself, he writes so much about curing it, says that sesame oil in a concoction with olive and myrtle oil is a good cure for dandruff. Parkinson says: "The seed in ancient times was much used in bread for a relish and makes it sweet, as also in cakes with honey as poppy seeds." The sesame seed, called "bene" in the South, was introduced by the African Negroes into Florida.

USES

To extract the oil the seed is bruised and immersed in hot water, and the oil which rises to the surface is then skimmed off. At Marseilles it figures in the manufacture of soap.

Medicine. It is in all pharmacopoeias. The oil is mild, laxative, and is a soothing external application.

Food. In China, Egypt, and India the oil extracted from

the seeds is used like olive oil in cooking. Moore and Rock, "Chinese Recipes," say that fat in Chinese recipes is always sesame oil. The Negroes parch the seeds over a fire, mix them with water, stew other ingredients with them, and so make a hearty meal. In South Carolina the seeds are used by the Negroes to make broths, and are also eaten parched, and often candied with sugar and molasses. The Hindus roast them and grind them into a meal which they eat. We have made the sesame cookies we give amongst our recipes and find they taste delicious. The seeds are good in cakes, too.

CULTURE

Sesame comes readily from seed, which can be purchased in American seed establishments. Planted the first week in May in a sunny, well-drained situation, by July 23d it was up to two feet. It probably grows more vigorously in southern countries than in northern ones.

Harvest. When ripe the seed is picked and cleaned.

TANACETUM VULGARE, L.

TANSY

Cow Bitters, Button Bitters, Tansy

Compositae Perennial

Tansy, also called *Chrysanthemum vulgare*, Bernh., is native to Europe and naturalized in the eastern United States and Canada, along roadsides, and around farmyards. It is a robust, weedy plant which soon grows into thick clumps. The whole plant is pleasantly fragrant, of a sharp quality, a little resinous, and slightly reminiscent of the daisy. I have eaten it with no ill effect, but, since it is said to be poisonous, do not advise any one else to indulge in it.

Root. It forms a thick main root creeping along, from which grow thin, wiry rootlets.

Stem. The stems die down yearly, but new ones come up again in the spring. They grow three feet or more high, are ribbed, slightly furry, and leafy all the way up.

Leaf. The leaves are a deep green, finely cut and divided and twice toothed, looking something like ferns, slightly furry on the under sides and smooth above.

Flower. The flowers come in late summer, have only the disk florets, and are like waxy yellow buttons when they first open. These buttons are quite numerous and in flat-topped clusters.

Seed. The seeds are small and brownish and retain their vitality two years.

Variety. Tanacetum vulgare var. *crispum* came from seed sent from the Chelsea Botanic Garden. They are ornamental and handsome plants worthy a place in the flower garden. The dark green leaves bend down and have their margins crisped and feathered, are considered more aromatic than those of other varieties, and are grown for distillation.

Tanacetum var. *hurohensis*, the seed of which came from Correvon, has smaller leaves, narrower and more delicate than those of the *Tanacetum pseudoachillea*, which has fleshy leaves. Both of them are darker green than *T. vulgare.* The *T. pseudoachillea* seed came from Kew. *T. herderi* is a dwarf, gray-green plant with much cut leaves imported from Europe. *T. boreale* has a ferny leaf which droops, is distinctively cut, and has a broader leaf surface than most of the tansies. There is said to be a variety with variegated leaves.

HISTORY AND LEGEND

Culpeper says every one must drink tansy in the spring so as not to be sick in summer. Parkinson tells how the young leaves should be shredded small with other herbs, or else the juice of it and other herbs fit for the purpose should be eaten in the spring, some say at Easter. Mrs. Earle says tansy was highly esteemed in old-time gardens, was rubbed over raw meat to keep flies away and prevent decay, and was put inside the coffins at funerals, and that the yellow flowers keep their color when used in "winter posies." Josselyn mentioned it and Prince had it in 1790, also *T. californicum,* and Bartram in 1814.

USES

Tansy leaves spread about are supposed to be efficacious in destroying fleas.

Medicine. The "National Standard Dispensary" says it has no medicinal use and that it is quite poisonous, a violent, virulent irritant to the stomach and intestines, and that many deaths are caused by it annually. The Pennsylvania Germans, however, used the sap in a poultice and the leaves as a stomachic in tea, also for urinary troubles, and it has been used as an abortive. It is made into a drink for cattle when they are said to have "lost their cud."

Perfume. Small quantities of tansy oil from the distilled tops and leaves are used in toilet waters from time to time.

Food. I give a recipe for tansy pudding which is very good.

CULTURE

Tansy can be grown from divisions, but it also comes readily from seed. It likes the sun and rather heavy soils, but will grow in any good garden soil. A few of the crisp-leaved tansies are handsome in any garden, but the common tansy should be planted in the pasture, or on the edge of a meadow where we can enjoy its fragrance on a hot day as we pass by.

In the United States the center of the production of tansy is in Michigan, where 2,500 pounds are distilled annually. For home consumption the leaves should be cut off as they appear, and one writer says cutting off the flower heads seems to prolong the production of the leaves.

THYMUS VULGARIS, L.

THYME

Labiatae Subshrub

The *Thymus vulgaris* is native to southern Europe and is a dainty subshrub with grayish, evergreen leaves and woody stems growing about six inches high. The broad-leaved English and the narrow-leaved French are botanically *Thymus vulgaris*, as is the German thyme. They all look so much alike it is difficult to see their differences even when grown side by side in my garden. They die back somewhat in the winter but come out again early in spring, and from the whole plant, without being crushed, comes a delicious scent of thyme with also something of camphor and spice in it.

Root. The roots are woody and grow under the ground for a considerable distance, and from their woody stems grow little hair-like brown threads.

Stem. The stems are woody below and above are shiny as of translucent amber. The English thyme is somewhat taller and stronger than the French.

Leaf. The leaves are one-quarter of an inch long and shine with glistening glands; they are wider at the base, narrowing at the tip, and slightly furry. Owing to their hairiness they have a grayish tinge. The French narrow-leaved thyme has leaves an infinitesimal bit slenderer and a little more glaucous than the English broad-leaved variety. The leaves of both have a sharp, bitter, strong, aromatic, flower-like taste and burn a little, but the English thyme has a sharper, less flower-like taste than the French.

Flower. The flowers come late in May but last a long while, and when cut back, flower again in July. They are carried in loose, conically shaped spikes at the terminations of the branches. The buds are a rosy pink; the flowers have a tinge of lavender on the pink base. The stamens and pistils are not exserted. The flowers of the French thyme are a bit larger than those of the English.

Variety. Other varieties of thyme grown for flavoring are *Thymus serpyllum* var. *Citriodorus* Hort., which I grew on the rocks. The stems hang down in strings and the plants are not very fragrant. The flowers are purple, come early in June and last a long time afterwards, the leaves are dark, tiny, glossy, bristly haired, with bristles on the margins of the lower half of the leaves only. The flowers are one-quarter of an inch across, a true lavender with a purple marking on the lower lip.

Thymus serpyllum var. *citriodorus aureus*, golden lemon thyme, a variety of the above, is a pretty, recumbent plant with leaves the color of subdued gold. Some of them are spotted a true, light gold. The flowers, coming late in June, are pale lavender. The stems of my plants had tiny fluffs on them. They smelt of lemon and spice.

Thymus serpyllum, L., wild thyme, mother-of-thyme, serpolet, is a recumbent plant as are its varieties, one of which is called *coccineum* and has bright magenta-purple flowers; another called *splendens,* with pinkish-lavender flowers, tastes of camphor, spice, and thyme, while a var. *album* has white florets and tastes a bit of anise.

Thymus azoricus, whose scent, according to Boulestin and Hill, suggests the tangerine orange, while I think it smells of Ivory Soap, is also used for flavoring and as a substitute for lemon thyme, or in combination with it. It comes from seed and has slender leaves, one-eighth of an inch long, woolly stems, lavender-pinkish flowers in July, and makes round little humps like a vigorous moss in the rocks.

HISTORY AND LEGEND

Thyme was mentioned by Theophrastus, Horace, Virgil, and Pliny. Ibn Baithar tells how thyme kills lice, expels the dead foetus, and, drunk with violet oil, clears the head. There was a superstition that if a branch of serpolet, *Thymus serpyllum*, were carried into a sick man's house it would cause his death. Parkinson speaks of its being used in baths, for strewing, in most broths, with forcing herbs, to make sauces for fish and flesh, invariably to stuff goose, and with roasted or fried fish. It is used in these fashions to-day. Josselyn mentions "time." Sturtevant says it was in North America in 1721. Bartram in 1807 listed *Thymus vulgaris* and *T. serpyllum.*

USES

Medicine. It is in all pharmacopoeias and its action is said to be antiseptic, antispasmodic, carminative, and antipyretic. To cure a cough the Swiss used it with boiled milk.

Perfume. The oil of thyme is distilled from the flowering tops of *T. vulgaris, T. zygis* var. *gracilis,* and *T. capitatus* from plants grown in southern France and Spain, and is used in *eau de cologne,* soaps and liquid dentifrices, while the dried herb with others, perfumes sachets.

Food. The broad-leaved English thyme is used principally for seasonings, but I like the more flowery, narrow-leaved French thyme, too.

In Seville, a decoction of thyme washes out the wine vessels. In winter the Irish put the branches in whey, which they say makes an excellent drink; while in Iceland, *T. serpyllum* flavors sour milk; and in Switzerland it is rubbed over cream cheese, called "banon," made of goat's milk, to which it gives a peculiar flavor. To preserve them longer, the German Swiss put it with the fruits when they are dried, and a little thyme in the wine is delicious. Correvon says *T. serpyllum* imparts a good taste to rabbit meat.

CULTURE

Most of the thymes come readily from seed except the ones with variegated foliage, or other horticultural peculiarities, and these should be raised from cuttings, or pieces of stems with roots clinging to them. *Thymus vulgaris* seems to grow in any good garden soil. The recumbent ones root as they creep along, so are easily increased from bits of the stems with roots clinging to them. They like to nestle against warm, dry stones. *T. vulgaris* makes a neat and pretty border plant.

In southern Europe thyme grows on rocky and sunny hillsides, and they all like well-drained and sunny situations. I sowed some of mine out-of-doors in May and they did very well. Others were started indoors, and later transplanted, and this seems a safer plan for the rarer kinds. Some writers say the plants should be renewed every three or four years, but I find that the creeping kinds grow so vigorously they have to be severely sheared back if they are not to crowd out other plants.

It is said that the warmer the climate the stronger the fragrance.

Harvest. The plants should be cut when they are in full flower and then dried in the shade to preserve their color as much as possible. The flowers and leaves are both used for flavoring and in potpourris.

TROPAEOLUM MINUS, L.

NASTURTIUM

Cress of Peru, Cress of India, Yellow Lark's Heels, Dwarf Nasturtium, Tom Thumb Nasturtium.

Tropaeolaceae Annual

The tall varieties of the nasturtium are climbing and of a sturdier growth, and are called *Tropaeolum major, L.*

T. minus flowers more abundantly and does not require any support, and therefore is the better for the herb garden. It is native to Peru, and some writers are of the opinion that it is a perennial at home. It is a leafy, spreading, low plant, with almost circular leaves and conspicuous flowers from yellow and orange through to dark red. The plant is about twelve inches high, succulent, and covered with tiny down. It smells pleasantly of spice.

Root. The root is tenuous and small.

Stem. The stems are crisp, round, of light green and fastened to the under side of the leaves, which they support like a large floppy hat balanced on one's head.

Leaf. The stem joins the leaf one-third the way up on the lower surface and directly over this on the upper surface is a light green circle from which seven to eight veins radiate like spokes in a wheel. The leaves are two and one-half inches across with the margins nicked where the veins cut them, and otherwise more or less wavy. On the under sides they are a lighter green than the upper. They are smooth and hold the drops of water on them like glistening jewels after a rainfall.

Flower. The flowers are two and one-half inches across, either of solid colors, or of a light color striped and marked in a darker tone. They have a heel, and the five sepals and five petals are of a bright color, as are the six stamens, which are irregularly shaped and arranged. Fernie says that in the warm summer months the flowers at about sunset have been noticed to give out electric sparks.

Seed. The seeds are light green, later turning light brown, three-parted, ridged and wrinkled, from one-quarter to three-quarters of an inch across to much larger.

They taste peppery, pleasantly and stronger than other portions of the plant. The germinating power lasts five years, says Vilmorin.

Variety. There seems to have been much selecting and crossing among the nasturtiums. Particularly handsome are Sutton's Sunset, of an orange pink, and Sutton's Salmon Pink, both dwarfs.

HISTORY AND LEGEND

The first mention of them in Europe is by Lobelius in 1564, as *Tropaeolum* species, and a creeping variety is pictured. They were described by Monardes in 1574; Gerard says they first came to Spain from the Indies. Quintinye grew them in the royal kitchen garden in 1690; Evelyn tells how to pickle them.

USES

Medicine. They are mentioned in the "National Standard Dispensary" of 1916.

Food. The flowers decorate salads and the stems and young leaves are eaten either in salads or sandwiches. The seeds chopped up can be used in sauces, as capers are, where a peppery, spicy taste is desired, and the seeds and flower buds are used in pickles.

CULTURE

The seeds are planted out-of-doors early in May in a sunny situation; not too closely together, for the seedlings do not stand transplanting. In very dry weather the plants are sometimes subject to aphids and can be cured by pouring cooled, soapy, dish water over them a few times a day for several days. The flowers come five to six weeks after sowing and produce seeds two to three months after planting. If the soil is too rich the plants will run to leaves and stems. The trailing varieties are often planted in pots.

VIOLA ODORATA, L.

VIOLET

Garden Violet, Florist's Violet

Violaceae Perennial

The sweet violet is no longer used as extensively as formerly in flavoring, but its fragrance and the aura of poetry about it entitle it to a place in every herb garden. Many varieties of the fragrant violets are hardy in northern gardens. The plant is native to Europe, Africa, and Asia.

Root. The roots are rhizomatous, and the plant sends out runners which root.

Stem. The flower stems are radical, simple, uniflowered, smooth, with several little bracts, about four or six inches high. The leaf stems are concave or hollow in front and rounded at the back, and one leaf is borne on each stem.

Leaf. The leaves are radical, long-petioled, heart or palmately shaped, with almost even, round indentations along the margins, sometimes slightly pointed at the tips, green and covered with tiny hairs. They measure two inches across at the widest point and one and one-third inches in length.

Flower. The flowers are borne on stems coming directly from the roots, and are partly hidden under the leaves. They are nodding, a deep violet, have five overlapping petals, two lower and three upper ones, and a heel. Their fragrance is the typical violet scent, pervasive, poetic, and never to be forgotten, but when the cut flowers are old they smell vilely.

Variety. There are white, pale lavender, pink, single, and double varieties.

Seed. The seed is in a capsule with three concave valves containing a number of yellowish-brown, rounded seeds.

In Italy and the French Riviera a very fragrant variety with pale blue flowers, the *Violette de Parme,* is cultivated. This variety is not hardy.

HISTORY AND LEGEND

Homer, Theophrastus, Dioscorides, and Pliny mention the violet as the favorite fragrant flower, and it has always been regarded as the emblem of modesty and humility. Ibn Al Awam says that loud thunder weakens the plants and causes them to be spotted with stars. Ibn Baithar says the fresh flowers put in a compress stop headache and that the dried plant weakens the heart, troubles the soul, and causes fright. In the Middle Ages in South Germany, the finding of the first violet was a cause for rejoicing and festivities. It was tied to a stake as a symbol of the coming of spring, and young and old danced around it and sang. There were recipes for conserves, vinegars, honey, and cakes of violets in the old cook books. Prince lists *Viola odorata* and many blue and white ones, and Bartram lists *Viola odorata* and *Viola* var. *flore pleno* in 1807.

USES

It is used technically as a dye.

Medicine. It is not important, although a syrup of violets is sometimes given as a mild laxative.

Perfume. The double purple and double blue varieties are the ones cultivated for their perfume, says Sawyer. The violet scents pomades, soaps, toilet waters, and perfumes. A pure violet extract is rare, being generally composed of a tincture of orris root, which resembles the violet as closely as the rose geranium does the rose.

CULTURE

In my garden the violets grow both in the rocks and in beds in partial shade. They increase very rapidly from runners and make charming ground covers. They are said to like a chalky soil. In the south of France, where they are grown for their perfume, they are planted under orange, lemon, and olive trees; in the north, if violets are planted in a cold frame protected with glass, they will flower all winter.

Harvest. To dry them the petals are separated from the calyces and dried indoors. They should be kept in an air-tight place, as dampness has a bad effect on their color. The plants are said to yield the most the second and third years.

OVER THE STOVE AND IN THE ICE BOX

COOKING WITH HERBS

Judging by the conversation in most American homes during meals, the food might be as nonexistent as the Emperor's new clothes in the fairy story. Even though I would not recommend sitting down to the table and rubbing one's hands in joyous anticipation, followed by the loud smacking of lips and bringing the meal to a grand finale by swabbing up every last bit of sauce with a piece of bread, as I have often seen South Europeans do, yet discerning comments upon the fine shadings in flavor encourage the hostess to be creative about her menus. The habitual silence on the subject may be one of many reasons why so few housewives are imaginative in the preparation of foods and the decoration of the platters.

To be adventurous about food one need not go beyond the garden gate, but can cook bamboo shoots, Chinese bean sprouts, sorrel, or basil at home provided they are growing in the garden. Dishes can be prepared which come to us from far-away lands, from distant times, and from recipes which, like Sleeping Beauty, have been slumbering for years in some old cook book on the shelf in the library.

People with delicate or nervous digestions are apt to be diffident about eating new foods, and I will not try to override their fears but will concentrate on those who enjoy new sensations of the palate and the nose.

In flavoring with herbs the same discretions must be exercised as with any condiment. There should be merely a *soupçon,* that is, a suspicion, of a hot, aromatic, or a pungent flavor in a dish, and this should merge in with the taste of the eggs, meat, or soup and enhance their natural flavor and not disguise or dominate it. The herb flavoring should have a subtle, intriguing quality, and never be so strong that one is instantly aware of it, except where the dish is named for the herb as in rosemary soup, or eggs *à l'estragon,* when it quite properly prevails over any other savors. Until one has used the aromatic herbs as condiments one cannot conceive how such commonplace dishes as veal stew, chopped meat, or pea soup can be changed into a delicacy of flower-like fragrances to delight the palate of the most fastidious gourmet. But the herbs should not enter into every dish served at a meal. If they flavor two courses, that is sufficient.

To cook with herbs no special equipment outside of the usual kitchen utensils is necessary except a mortar and pestle for pounding certain of the seeds and leaves. Although rose water, the Eastern spices, and pepper are included in some of the recipes, in general, when the herbs are used, no other condiments are required except salt, sugar, and at times a little of the juice or peel of lemon or orange, which seem to heighten the herb flavorings. A bit of onion should be present in meats, soups, and salads, for, like the pedal point in a chord of music, it is the base upon which all other flavorings vibrate. One takes a pinch of finely minced leaves, as much as can be held between the thumb and forefinger, for a dish for four people, and about the same amount of seeds. After the herbs have been in the dish for a time the flavor becomes stronger, so one cannot judge whether enough has been used merely by the taste when the herbs are first dropped into the pot. It takes a little practice to learn exactly how much is required and, as our French cook used to say, one has to have *l'habitude* of cooking with herbs.

In flavoring meat balls, or dressings for chicken or veal, the dry or fresh herbs are generally mixed with the ingredients before they are cooked. If they are allowed to soak for an hour or two in the milk, stock, butter, or water, however, the flavor is drawn out more fully. For example, when a dash of coriander seeds in biscuits is desired, the crushed seeds are soaked in the milk before making up the dough; when cooking mackerel *aux fines herbes*, the herbs are mixed in with the creamed butter. Butter, cheese, and eggs take on the taste of herbs well. In soups, when using fresh parsley or rosemary, the finely chopped herb is dropped in at the last minute and the aroma is quickly transfused through the hot dishes and floats up to us as we drink it. To flavor cold drinks with mint, marjoram, thyme, or borage, the herbs are wrapped in a cloth and bruised, and then steeped in the liquid for some time. In making iced tea or drinks from hot fruit juices, the herbs are steeped in the hot liquid, which is then cooled. When a sprig of mint is perched on top of a glass of iced tea, it is fresh and green to look upon, but this last-minute association does not suffice to impart any of its spicy quality to the liquid.

The tops of sweet woodruff and the leaves of burnet, or costmary, and any of the other plants formerly steeped in cool tankards add to the relish of cold fruit drinks. The flowering tops of borage impart a cucumbery flavor, but this herb is very strong and should only be allowed to steep for a few minutes. For decorating fruit drinks flavored with herbs I lift the sky-blue corollas of the borage right out of its calyx and float them in the pitchers where they look more delicate than the usual maraschino cherries.

Dried herbs, in most cases, are as effective as the fresh ones, but not as pretty. The herbs, after being steeped, are strained out before finishing the dish, unless one prefers to see them scattered through the food.

The French use four herbs for the *fines herbes,* and when an *omelette aux fines herbes* is ordered in France, as the fork breaks into the golden surface dotted with the tiniest of green specks, the fragrance exhaled from the combined herbs is entirely different from the scent of the spurious copies flavored only with parsley found in American restaurants.

After experimenting with various combinations of herbs, Miss Shapleigh concluded that thyme, basil, summer savory, and chives form a delicious partnership for flavoring omelettes, soups, or meats.

Chives with thyme, winter savory, and fennel give a mild taste to fish when mixed into a hot fish stock and a little butter.

Basil, thyme, sweet marjoram, and parsley are delicately aromatic—the thyme and sweet marjoram predominating.

Chives, with parsley, summer savory, and basil are not as sweet as the above, but grateful, too.

If enough of any of these mixtures is stirred into a cream cheese to speckle the luscious surface thickly and is then allowed to stand overnight, if possible, by the next morning the whole cheese is permeated with the fragrant essences and can be spread over thin slices of bread and covered with another slice. Cottage cheese, too, becomes a delicacy if herbs are stirred into it in the same fashion. This mixture, laid on lettuce leaves and served with a cup of tea, some pieces of crisp toast, and a slice of cake, provide an entirely feminine supper to have on a tray in front of the fire when the family have left the mistress of the house to dine in blissful solitude.

Herbs are pleasant for filling sandwiches and particularly appropriate for a garden party or any other out-of-door meal. Jasmine or linden tea served with them and a bowl of sweet-smelling herbs placed on the table would compose an aromatic repast. Watercress chopped and mixed with a little lemon juice, sugar, and mayonnaise makes another pleasant sandwich filling, as do the finely chopped leaves of fresh mint, mixed with butter and a little sugar. Where thyme, mint, watercress, or parsley have been mixed into the sandwiches a few sprigs of them are pretty and appropriate for decorating the platters.

The common parsley or the moss-curled variety are not as attractive for a garnish as the fern-leaved one with its finely cut dark green leaves. Strangely enough, parsley seems to have displaced all other herbs as a decoration of platters, except for an occasional appearance of watercress, the "spring greens" which accompany roast meat in England. With a herb garden to draw from, we can have attractive garnishes of sprigs of thyme, the savories, sweet marjoram, and the basils or balm lying beside roasts or spread all through a dish of mixed vegetables *jardinière* served on yellow or green Italian pottery platters. Mint would make a fitting garnish for roast lamb, especially if it has been chopped into the sauce. Where rosemary or thyme have flavored the soup, a tiny sprig consisting of two or three leaflets can be floated in the hot soup after it has been poured into each plate, as a reminder of what has happened in the kitchen.

A few leaves of rose geranium are attractive placed around a custard, rice pudding, or fruit jelly, which has been flavored with rose water or geranium leaves; the mint, nutmeg, or oak-leaved geraniums are pretty, too, as garnishes. The leaves of these scented geraniums and of the lemon verbena are floated in finger bowls and when taken between the fingers the same effect is obtained as when the Turks pour rose water over the guests' hands after a meal.

In preparing a fresh, crisp salad of herbs one need never repeat oneself. Before dinner I walk along the paths between the rows of herbs and with a sharp knife cut a leaf here and another there and drop them into a bowl filled with cold water which I carry. Upon returning to the house I set this in a cool place until it is time to arrange the salad platter. The foundation is of pale green lettuce leaves and on these I place whatever I have picked that day. It may be a few leaves of anise, caraway, the very young leaves of sorrel, mustard, or the stems of nasturtiums cut into small pieces. Sometimes I take the tips of the burnet leaves, or bits of fern-leaved parsley, or watercress; or, if I feel like being flowery, the buds of nasturtiums are disposed among the greens, and the salad garnished with the open blossoms. Whenever I think it will go well, a dash of chopped chives, which taste delicately of onion, are added. Over a mixture only of lettuce and endive, dark green tarragon leaves are sometimes minced and scattered as a last-minute gesture. This herb has a characteristic taste that does not blend well with the others so it must be used alone.

For these salads, all in different shades of green, I prefer a colorless French dressing to a yellow mayonnaise or a red Russian one. Nestling amongst the greens are snowy cream-cheese balls speckled with fragrant herbs. This is a dish to savor slowly, turn about on one's tongue, and wonder out loud of what it is composed.

When the fresh herbs are not available, their flavor can be introduced into the salad by using a vinegar in the dressing which has been aromatized variously with tarragon, thyme, dill, or fennel. Dill or fennel soaked in vinegar, is very sour.

The leaves of dill and fennel when stirred into a mayonnaise do not impart any noticeable taste, but the pale green strands are pretty scattered through the golden sauce. Half a cup of mayonnaise will take half a teaspoonful of chopped herb leaves.

Chopped chives, all alone without other herbs, are good mixed into cream or cottage cheese as well as in omelettes and scrambled eggs and scattered over boiled potatoes.

Dill leaves, besides flavoring pickles, lend piquancy to hot or cold fish sauces as do the leaves of fennel, which also give a good flavor to soups and omelettes, provided one likes their strong taste of anise.

The thickened stem bases of *Foeniculum dulce*, called *finocchio*, are eaten as a vegetable, either boiled and served with a hot butter sauce, or baked and scattered over with Parmesan cheese.

Basil gives a delightful relish to dishes where tomatoes predominate as in spaghetti with tomatoes and cheese.

Thyme has always imparted its fragrance to chicken stuffings and some cooks think it is the best herb for turkey dressings. It is a necessary ingredient for New York clam chowder and either fresh or dried adds to the pleasure of eating broths, cream cheese, chopped meat, and stews. It is an ingredient in *fines herbes* or mixed seasonings.

Sage is present in stuffings for veal, pork, and of course where a goose is to be cooked. The fresh, crumply leaves are delicious in cheese.

Winter savory is called *bohnenkraut*, bean herb, in Germany, and until one has tried a few sprigs of it with string beans one has no idea how it ennobles this ubiquitous vegetable.

Sweet marjoram combines well with other herbs, but has not been featured alone. The French like chervil, which tastes like a mild parsley. They also like tarragon, which gives the special note to lobster *thermidor, sauce Bearnaise.* It is good in brown stock and *hollandaise sauce,* and *eggs à l'estragon,* where two whole leaves are laid cross-wise over each little poached egg before it is immortalized in the aspic jelly.

In the South most people think of mint in relation to juleps and everywhere it is used with lamb. Some like it

Artemisia dracunculus, tarragon

minced over green peas, but few know how pleasant it is scattered over glazed carrots, and that minced and scattered over sliced oranges or other chilled fruit salads, it is pretty and has a refreshing scent. A little of the herb with a dash of nutmeg stirred into creamed spinach will change that much maligned dish into a delicacy. Spinach is also luscious when one-third of the quantity is made up of slightly sour, but pleasantly tasting, sorrel leaves, to which is added a little rosemary or nutmeg. Borage leaves make a palatable spinach.

The yellow petals of marigold flowers as a flavoring seem odd to moderns. Before cooking them the petals should be crushed in a mortar to bring out their flavor, which is a little bitter, but when mixed with other ingredients such as macaroons, nutmeg, allspice, and rose water is delicate and unusual. Miss Shapleigh used these ingredients in her marigold custard.

I make a jam of rose petals from a Turkish recipe. Turkish rose petal jam is not solid, but mine generally is and both jams are of an old rose color, taste as the roses smell, and truly seems like the ambrosia the Gods ate on Mount Olympus.

I give a recipe of "Pastils of Roses" from the "Toilet of Flora" as follows:

> Pulverize one pound of the marc or residuum left in the still after making angelica water, add a large handful of roses and with a sufficient quantity of gum tragacanth dissolved in rose water, beat them into a stiff paste which is to be rolled out upon a marble with a rolling pin and cut into lozenges or formed into pastils; if you have in mind to ornament them cover them with leaf gold or silver.

Since angelica water is mentioned in the above we give a recipe for candying the stems:

> Boil the stalks of angelica in water till they are tender; then peel them and put them in other warm water and cover them. Let them stand over a gentle fire till they become very green; then lay them on a cloth to dry; take their weight in fine sugar with a little rose water and boil it to a candy height. Then put in your angelica and boil them up quick; then take them out and dry them for use.*

From the candied stems of angelica grow the sugared roses and violets atop the snowy icing on elaborately decorated cakes.

The stems are faintly flavored, but the seeds are stronger and give a pleasant savor to custard, blanc mange, or floating island.

Besides the leaves and stems of the herbs, the seeds of caraway, coriander, dill, fennel, or poppy, and fennel flower, *Nigella sativa,* are all delightful condiments when whole, or crushed. They are crushed and the oils extracted to scent liqueurs and perfumes; this process, however, is a little beyond the skill of most amateur cooks. In addition to the well-known and long-practiced ways of employing them I flavor biscuits, cup cakes, and baked apples with coriander seeds. Caraway comfits can be bought and probably coriander comfits too, to decorate short bread and sprinkle on top of cookies. The seeds of fennel flower, almost unknown in America, have a sharp, spicy taste. Powdered and steeped in vinegar they add a dash of spice

* From Eleanour Rohde, who quoted it from "The Recipe Books of John Nott," 1723.

to fish sauces. Dill and fennel seeds are savory in pickled beets and a change from caraway seeds. Opium poppies yield seeds for sprinkling on breads and cakes, and are easy to grow, but they should be the black-seeded varieties.

The roots of herbs, notably the horseradish, are used, too, as flavoring. To make a horseradish sauce, the young root is grated as finely as possible and sugar, vinegar, and salt are added. Into this is stirred cream or oil; if the latter, orange rind should be added.

These are merely a few of the possibilities of flavoring with herbs and they have been presented as preliminary suggestions to the beginner. Moreover, once the imagination has begun to function in regard to the preparation of foods, undoubtedly many other combinations and ways of using these pleasantly aromatic or tart flavors will be found, for with so many varieties available why cling to the old-time chocolate and vanilla, delightful and agreeable as these undoubtedly are?

The herbs, besides flavoring food, can be combined into sachets and potpourris. I have not as yet ventured into working with alembics and stills, weights and measures, but since I have been asked so frequently to give recipes for sachets, I have looked up the subject and found some which seem simple and inexpensive to prepare for one who is growing many of the ingredients in his back yard.

Every perfume must have an element known as a fixative in it to keep the essential oils from evaporating and thereby losing its fragrance. Since Theophrastus' day, and probably earlier, these have been ambergris, castorium, civet, musk, and gum benzoin, all of them except the last being very expensive. They can be bought from wholesale druggists, as can the ingredients mentioned in the recipes.

Piesse, in his "The Art of Perfumery," says the materials employed in the manufacture of sachet powders are only those which retain their odor in a dried state and these include what are termed "herbs"—lemon, thyme, mint, and so on, also a few leaves of plants such as the orange and lemon trees. Few blossoms except lavender, rose, and cassia have any fragrance when dried. Surprisingly enough, the jasmine, tuberose, violet, and mignonette lose theirs.

Piesse's recipe for lavender sachet:

lavender flowers ground	1 pound
gum benzoin in powder	1/4 pound
attar of lavender	1/4 ounce

and another:

dried thyme	1/4 pound
dried lemon thyme	1/4 pound
dried mint	1/4 pound
dried marjoram	1/4 pound
dried lavender	1/2 pound
dried rose heels	1 pound
(this means the petals from which the white base has been removed)	
ground cloves	2 ounces
calamus powder	1 pound
musk in grain	1 drachm

another from Piesse is called "a mixture of dried flowers and spices not ground":

dried lavender	1 pound
whole rose leaves	1 pound

crushed orris (coarse)	½ pound
broken cloves	2 ounces
broken cinnamon	2 ounces
broken allspice	2 ounces
table salt	1 pound

The salt is only used to increase the bulk and weight of the product, says Mr. Piesse, in order to sell it cheaply.

After reading some charming recipes for potpourris in "The Toilet of Flora," 1775, it seems one could concoct one's own kind of potpourris from the herb garden provided the correct amount of fixatives are included and that the ingredients are kept dry.

Bags to scent linen, from "The Toilet of Flora":

Take a thin Persian muslin and make into little bags about four inches wide in the form of an oblong. Take rose leaves dried in the shade, cloves beat to a gross powder and mace scraped; mix them together and fill the little bags with this composition.

Potpourri from "The Toilet of Flora":

Take one pound of fresh gathered orange flowers, ½ pound of common roses, ½ pound of lavender seeds, ½ pound musk roses, ¼ pound sweet marjoram leaves, ¼ pound clove-July-flowers picked, 3 ounces of thyme, 2 ounces of myrtle leaves, 2 ounces of melilot stalks stripped of their leaves, 1 ounce rosemary leaves, 1 ounce cloves bruised, and ½ ounce of bay leaves. These ingredients mixed all together in a large pan covered with parchment, if exposed to the heat of the sun during the whole summer season for the first month stirred about every other day with a stick and taken indoors in rainy weather, will towards the end of the summer produce an excellent composition to perfume little bags by adding thereunto in order to heighten the fragrance, a little scented cypress powder mixed with coarse violet powder.

Piesse gives a lavender water made from the flowers to wash the face for beauty and fragrance, as follows:

English oil of lavender	4 ounces
Spirit	3 quarts
Rose water	1 pint

and "An excellent recipe to clear a tanned complexion":

At night when going to rest bathe the face with the juice of strawberries and let it lie on the part all night and in the morning wash yourself with chervil water. The skin will soon become fair and smooth.

As a last toilet preparation we give the recipe of Galen's cold cream called *Ceratum Galeni* from Piesse which although it is seventeen hundred years old is as good a cold cream as I have ever used.

Almond oil	1 pound
Rose water	1 pound
White wax	1 ounce
Spermaceti or Boric acid	1 ounce
Attar of roses	½ drachm

Manipulation: Into a well-glazed, thick porcelain vessel capable of holding twice the quantity of cream to be made place the wax and soda. Now put the jar to boiling in a bath of water; when the materials are melted add the oil and again heat until the flecks of wax and soda are liquefied. Let rose water run in slowly and stir all the time. Keep stirring the whole mixture. In winter the rose water should be heated so as not to cool the wax. When the whole of the water has been incorporated and the cream is cool, add the attar of roses. This is done so that the cream will not evaporate.

RECIPES

MINT JULEP

Fresh mint leaves (should not be bruised or cut)
Whiskey or brandy
Finely crushed ice

In a tall glass have mint leaves and as much whiskey or brandy as needed for the people to be served. In another glass have the ice. Pour the ice into whiskey, or brandy, and the mint leaves, and continue to pour the mixture from one glass to the other until the spirit is thoroughly flavored with the mint.

Pour the liquid into small glasses which should rest in larger ones containing crushed ice. Serve when the glasses are frosted.

Miss Shapleigh.

FRESH TOMATO JUICE COCKTAIL

(Four or five cocktails)
(Fresh tomatoes)

1 pint tomato juice
2 tablespoons lemon juice
1 tablespoon orange juice
½ teaspoon salt
few grains cayenne
1 teaspoon sugar
1 teaspoon finely cut tarragon leaves
1 teaspoon finely cut basil leaves
1 teaspoon finely cut chives

Mix the tomato juice with the herbs and seasonings, and allow it to stand for one or two hours in a cold place. Add lemon and orange juice and strain into glasses.

Miss Shapleigh.

CANNED TOMATO JUICE COCKTAIL

1 pint juice
2 tablespoons lemon juice
½ teaspoon salt
few grains cayenne
1 teaspoon sugar
few drops of onion juice (may be omitted)
2 teaspoons each of tarragon and basil

Heat the tomato juice and herbs; add salt, cayenne, and sugar, and allow the mixture to stand for an hour or more; add lemon juice and onion juice, if it is used; strain and serve.

Miss Shapleigh.

MINT COCKTAIL

4 tablespoons finely cut fresh mint leaves
2 tablespoons sugar syrup
2 tablespoons lemon juice
1 tablespoon orange juice
1 bottle "extra dry" ginger ale

Put mint leaves, sugar syrup, and fruit juices in a bowl; add a pinch of salt, and allow the mixture to stand, closely covered, for one hour.

Strain into cocktail shaker over ice, add ginger ale, shake, and pour into glasses. It will be the color of pale sherry. Green coloring may be added if preferred.

Adapted by Miss Shapleigh.

FRUIT AND HERB DRINK

Juice of 3 oranges and 2 lemons
½ cup of sugar syrup
1 cup of strong tea infusion
1 sprig of balm (pounded in a mortar)

5 sprigs of borage
bunch of mint
1 sprig burnet
3 anise leaves
pinch of salt

Pour hot tea and syrup over the fruit juice and herbs. Cover the dish and allow the mixture to stand an hour or two. Strain into a tall glass pitcher over ice, add wine, or loganberry juice and ginger ale, or White Rock. In the mouth of pitcher put a bunch of mint.

Miss Shapleigh.

BALM WINE

1 peck of balm leaves (*Melissa officinalis*)
2 pounds granulated sugar
whites of four eggs
1 cake of yeast

Take a peck of balm leaves, put them in a tub or large pot, heat four gallons of water scalding hot, ready to boil, then pour it through the leaves, let it stand so all night, then strain them through a hair sieve, put to every gallon of water two pounds of fine sugar, and stir it very well; take the whites of four or five eggs, beat them very well, put them into a pan and whisk it very well before it be overhot, when the skin begins to rise take it off and keep it skimming all the while it is boiling, let it boil three quarters of an hour then put into the tub, when it is cold put in a little new yeast upon it, that it may head the better, so work it for two days, then put it into a barrel and stop it up close and when it is fine, bottle it.

From Moxon, "English Housewifery," 1775.

This is delicious and good as a flavoring to fruit drinks.

MAYDRINK OR MAITRANK

Take a handful of the fresh young branches of sweet woodruff, cut off the lower leaves and stems. Then wash the leaves and tops and strew sugar over them. Use as many bottles of wine as are needed. White wine is always used and half the quantity is of a light wine and half of a heavy wine. Add a few slices of oranges, and just before serving a bottle of sparkling champagne is poured into this delightful drink.

From German Anna.

RESEDA BOWLE

Although not made with herbs, the following is given:

A *Bowle* of Reseda.

To one bottle of wine one takes fifteen fresh flower spikes of the mignonette and three-quarters of a cup of sugar. The little blossoms are removed from the spike. It takes a little longer to draw out the flavor of the mignonette than of the sweet woodruff.

A *Bowle* can be made with Maréchal Niel roses, substituting the rose petals for the mignonette.

From German Anna.

A COOLING DRINK MADE WITH BARLEY AND ALMONDS

One ounce of French barley, boil in one quart of water; strain and add to barley one quart of fresh water, and boil for one hour; strain, and combine the two waters.

Blanch one cup of almonds to a paste with one tablespoon of rose water; add to barley water with the juice of one lemon, two tablespoons of rose water, a little salt, and sugar to taste.

Strain and cool.

From "The Queen's Closet Opened."

THE KING'S MEAD

For a small amount, take one quart of water, one cup of honey, one lemon cut in slices, one half a tablespoon of nutmeg. Boil until no scum comes to the top, removing the scum as it rises. Add a pinch of salt, the juice of half a lemon. Strain and cool.

This is a good drink as it is, but should stand until it is fermented.

From "The Queen's Closet Opened."

GREEN PEA SOUP WITH MINT

1 quart of fresh peas
1 onion
1 large or 2 small sprigs of mint
1 teaspoon of spinach juice
1 teaspoon of salt
1 teaspoon of sugar
4 tablespoons of butter
2 egg yolks
½ cup of cream

Shell the peas, and break up the pods; wash the pods and boil for two or three hours in the water in which other vegetables have been cooked if possible. Strain and add the peas, the onion, mint, salt and sugar, and three pints of water in which the pods were cooked. Cook until the peas are tender, then rub through a sieve, add butter, spinach juice (for color) and bring to boiling point. Season more if needed, and just before serving add the egg yolk diluted with the cream. Cook, stirring constantly for five minutes, but do not allow the liquid to boil. Strain and serve with croutons.

Adapted by Miss Shapleigh
from Leyel and Hartley,
"The Gentle Art of Cookery."

TOMATO SOUP

1 can or 4 cups of tomatoes
1 onion, 1 laurel leaf, 2 sprigs of thyme
2 or 3 basil leaves
1 teaspoon salt, a little pepper

Stew the above ingredients for one hour, then strain through a very fine strainer.

Make a sauce using:

2 tablespoons butter
2 cups milk

2 tablespoons flour
½ teaspoon salt

To the sauce add the strained tomatoes and cook in a double boiler for one hour.

When serving put a bit of basil in each plate.

Marie.

FRENCH HERB SOUP

3 tablespoons butter
1 small head lettuce (shredded)
1 small bunch watercress (cut fine)
1 cup sorrel (cut fine)
2 sprigs chervil (finely chopped)
6 cups chicken stock
½ cup cream
1 egg yolk
1 teaspoon salt and a little pepper

Cook the herbs in the butter, for five minutes, being careful not to brown the herbs; add chicken stock, salt and pepper, and cook for one-half hour; add cream mixed with egg yolk, and stir until heated, but not boiled. Season to taste, serve without straining, with croutons.

From Mrs. Le Boiteaux in the Garden Club of America Bulletin.

ROSEMARY SOUP

Follow the recipe for French Herb Soup, but use a little rosemary and leave out the chervil and watercress.

ITALIAN SOUP

1 pint of old green beans cut into small pieces
1 cup spaghetti
1 small onion, thinly sliced

2 beans garlic, finely chopped
6 leeks with stalks, cut in small pieces
12 marigold blossoms (use petals only)
50 leaves of large leaf basil, chopped
3 bay leaves (small)
3 large potatoes, pared and cut into small cubes
1 cup olive oil
2 quarts veal or chicken stock, or water
1½ teaspoons salt

Fry onion, leeks, garlic, and beans in olive oil for twenty minutes. Add potatoes, spaghetti, marigold blossoms, and seasonings, and stock. Cook slowly for two hours. Season to taste with salt and pepper, remove bay leaves and serve.

Crosby Gaige.

PARSLEY SOUP

2 cups milk
1 cup water
1 teaspoon salt
2 tablespoons butter
2 tablespoons flour
1 medium-sized onion

Melt butter, add flour and salt, and the liquids and onion. Boil for one hour. Remove the onion, add one-half a cup of cream mixed with the yolks of two eggs. Cook until thickened. Just before serving add one-half a cup of finely chopped parsley. Stir well, and serve at once.

Marie.
Called Soupe à la Bonne Femme.

HERB AND VEGETABLE SOUP

2 quarts white stock, chicken or veal
6 small heads of lettuce, cut fine
1 small handful of chervil, same of purslane

1 small handful of sorrel, same of parsley
1 bunch of green onions
1 pint of peas, when in season
¼ pound or ½ cup of butter

Cook the above in butter, gently, for one-hour, add stock and two carrots, cut into small pieces; add three cucumbers, cut into quarters; two pieces of toast, broken into small pieces; one and one-half teaspoons salt and a little pepper. Cook one hour, rub through a sieve, and add one cup of cream and two egg yolks. Bring to boiling point, but do not boil; strain; season to taste; and add, just before serving, one tablespoon of finely cut parsley.

From Dalgairns, 1830.
Called Nun's Broth.

EGGS WITH SWEET HERBS IN RAMEKINS

4 eggs, cooked in shells until hard
2 tablespoons of mixed fresh herbs (thyme, basil, summer savory, sweet marjoram, and parsley)
2 tablespoons of butter
salt and pepper
2 raw eggs well beaten
½ cup of cream
remove eggs from shells and mince finely.

Cook the herbs in butter for five minutes, being careful not to brown the butter. Add to this the minced cooked eggs, salt and pepper, well-beaten raw eggs, and cream. Fill well-buttered ramekins with the mixture, and bake for twenty minutes. Serve at once.

Adapted from John Evelyn's "Acetaria."

OMELETTE *AUX FINES HERBES*

4 eggs slightly beaten
4 tablespoons of cream
1 tablespoon of olive oil
2 tablespoons of mixed herbs

½ teaspoon salt
⅛ teaspoon pepper

Various combinations of herbs may be used, but for the omelette the following is good: thyme, basil, summer savory, and chives. If fresh herbs are used, chop them finely and mix, adding to the omelette just before folding or mixing them with the eggs before cooking the omelette. If dried herbs are used, soak in cream or water, drain and chop.

The omelette is made by slightly beating the eggs, and adding for each egg one tablespoon of cream, salt, and pepper. Cook in olive oil or melted butter.

Mix all the ingredients, put oil into a hot omelette pan, pour in the egg mixture and shake the pan slightly during the time of cooking. Fold and serve immediately.

The French or Spanish omelette is never brown.

Miss Shapleigh's recipe adapted from the French.

EGG TIMBALES WITH TOMATO SAUCE

4 eggs slightly beaten
1 cup of milk or thin cream
1 teaspoon salt, a little pepper
1 tablespoon finely chopped and mixed fresh thyme, savory, chives, and parsley

Mix the above and bake in well-buttered timbale moulds until firm to the touch, about twenty minutes. Have the moulds set in a pan of hot water, and do not allow the water to boil during the baking, unmould, and serve with a tomato sauce.

TOMATO SAUCE

2 cups of tomatoes
1 tablespoon of oil or butter
1 slice of onion
1 teaspoon sugar
2 sprigs of basil
½ teaspoon salt

Simmer until reduced nearly one-half. Strain, rubbing all the pulp through a sieve, season more to taste, if necessary. Pour over the timbales just before serving. This same is good over fish or meat dishes.

Miss Shapleigh.

EGGS À L'ESTRAGON IN ASPIC

Cook as many eggs as you wish to serve either by boiling or poaching them. Allow them to become very cold. Make aspic jelly by cooking for twenty minutes: 1 quart of white stock (chicken or veal), 2 tablespoons of chopped herbs, using thyme, sweet marjoram, parsley, chives, and basil.

Strain, add one teaspoon of salt, a few grains of cayenne, one tablespoon of tarragon vinegar, and two tablespoons of granulated gelatine which has soaked in half a cup of cold water. Cool and add the slightly beaten white of two eggs, and eggshells. Stir constantly over the fire until boiling point is reached, then allow the broth to cook without stirring for ten minutes. Strain through double strainers and cheesecloth.

Wet individual moulds, and pour in the liquid to a depth of one-third inch. When set, which will be in a few moments if the mould is placed in ice, place several leaves of fresh tarragon on the jelly. Cover with just enough liquid to set the tarragon in place. In the center place the egg, and add jelly to set it. After it is set, fill the mould with jelly, and allow the eggs to become cold and firm. Unmould, garnish with lettuce, and serve with mayonnaise to which has been added some chopped tarragon and parsley.

Miss Shapleigh's recipe adapted from the French.

FRIED EGGS WITH YELLOW RICE

½ cup of washed rice
2 tablespoons olive oil
½ bean of garlic, chopped
1 teaspoon of cumin seed
1 teaspoon Spanish saffron soaked in water

1½ cups hot stock or water
½ teaspoon salt
4 eggs fried lightly in olive oil

In the olive oil cook the garlic and rice until the rice is slightly brown. In a mortar pound the cumin seed, add the water in which saffron has soaked, and strain over the rice. Add water or stock, and cook until the rice is soft, adding more liquid if necessary. Serve on a dish with fried eggs on top. A sauce may be added if desired.

Adapted from a Spanish recipe.

TANSY PUDDING

4 eggs slightly beaten
1 cup of cream
¾ cup of spinach juice mixed with a tablespoon of tansy juice
1 cup of cracker crumbs
½ cup of sugar
½ teaspoon nutmeg

Mix all together and bake in a buttered dish until firm. It may also be cooked like an omelette. It looks green.

Adapted from Mrs. Randolph, 1831.

EGGPLANT À L'ITALIENNE

1 eggplant, peeled and cut into thin slices
thin slices of Italian bread
½ cup of olive oil
1 cup of tomato sauce, thick, flavored with basil
1 cup of freshly grated Parmesan cheese
8 eggs

When the olive oil is hot, fry the eggplant and bread in it. In a baking dish, put a layer of the fried bread, a layer of eggplant, two or three spoonfuls of tomato sauce; repeat until the material is used, or the dish is nearly full. Over it pour the slightly beaten eggs mixed with the grated Parmesan cheese. Bake thirty minutes in a quick oven. Cut into pie-shaped pieces for serving.

Miss Shapleigh.

SAVORY RICE

1 cup of rice, well washed
3 tablespoons of olive oil
1 tablespoon of finely chopped onion
1 bean of garlic finely chopped (may be omitted)
1 teaspoon each of chopped chervil, parsley, chives, summer savory, and sweet marjoram
1 teaspoon salt
3 cups water or stock

Cook the onion and garlic in olive oil for five minutes, add rice and cook until the rice is slightly brown. Then add salt and water, or stock, and cook until the rice is tender, and the liquid has been absorbed.

Note: This is a very good stuffing for chicken or capon; the herbs give a delicate flavor to the meat.

With a tablespoon of grated horseradish root added when the rice is cooked, the rice makes an excellent stuffing for tomatoes when baked.

Adapted from two modern English cook books.

RICE MAÎTRE D'HÔTEL

½ cup of rice, well washed
2 onions, finely chopped
¼ cup of butter
1 stalk celery, chopped
1 tablespoon of mixed herbs (thyme, parsley, sweet marjoram)
½ teaspoon salt
½ teaspoon paprika
white of one egg
1 potato, washed and peeled
1 pint or more of water

Cook the onion and rice in the butter for ten minutes, being careful not to brown the butter. Add celery, potato, and water and cook until the rice has absorbed the water. If the water is absorbed before the rice is soft, more water must be added. Stir into the rice the herbs and stiffly beaten white of egg. Turn into a buttered pudding dish and steam it for two hours. Serve hot with Maître d'Hôtel sauce.

MAÎTRE D'HÔTEL SAUCE

2 tablespoons of butter
2 tablespoons of flour
1 cup of chicken stock or milk
¼ cup of cream
¼ teaspoon salt, a little pepper

Mix butter, add flour, and cook until smooth. Add stock or milk, boil until thickened; add cream, a slight grating of nutmeg, two tablespoons of lemon juice, two tablespoons finely chopped parsley, salt and pepper to taste.

Adapted by Miss Shapleigh
from Leyel and Hartley,
"The Gentle Art of Cookery."

ITALIAN LUNCH DISH

4 cucumbers parboiled ten minutes and cut into one- to two-inch pieces
1½ cups tomato sauce (put basil in here)
1 cup Parmesan cheese

Put layers of tomato, cucumber, and cheese, having cheese on top and bake twenty to thirty minutes in a baking dish. Cook the tomato sauce down until quite thick. I usually use one can of tomatoes, and cook it down so that I have about two cups of sauce.

Miss Shapleigh.

NASTURTIUM SAUCE

6 tablespoons of butter
3 tablespoons of flour
1½ cups of water or broth

½ teaspoon salt
⅛ teaspoon pepper
3 tablespoons or more of pickled nasturtium seeds

Melt three tablespoons of butter; add flour, salt, and pepper, and when smoothly blended, add water or broth, and cook until thickened. Then add the remainder of the butter, bit by bit, and the nasturtium seeds. Season more if necessary. Serve with boiled mutton.

Adapted by Miss Shapleigh
from Leslie, "Directions for Cookery,"
Philadelphia, 1830.

MUSTARD PASTE

Dry mustard, 4 tablespoons (level)
Fresh tarragon, 1 teaspoon (chopped)
Fresh basil, 1 teaspoon (chopped)
White wine vinegar to mix to a paste about 1 teaspoon
A pinch of salt and 1 teaspoon sugar.

Miss Shapleigh.

SAUCE TARTARE

4 tablespoons of vinegar
1 teaspoon mustard
1 tablespoon of mixed parsley, chives, and tarragon

Cook the vinegar and herbs until reduced to one tablespoonful. Use this for making the mayonnaise, adding mustard to the egg yolks. When the mayonnaise is finished, add chopped fresh parsley, watercress, chives, tarragon, and chervil—the amount depending on the quantity of mayonnaise. Add one tablespoon of herbs to one pint of mayonnaise. Before chopping the herbs, pour boiling water over them, and then dry thoroughly.

Adapted by Miss Shapleigh
from Leyel and Hartley,
"The Gentle Art of Cookery."

MACKEREL *AUX FINES HERBES*

1 large mackerel, split down the back
¼ cup butter, salt, and pepper

minced parsley, fennel, mint, sweet basil, and thyme, using 2 or 3 sprigs of each
½ teaspoon salt, a little pepper, cinnamon, and nutmeg

Mix herbs and spices, and cream with the butter. Wipe the mackerel, sprinkle with salt and pepper, and cover all over with the seasoned butter. Grill, or fry in a hot pan, until the fish will flake apart. Remove to a platter; add to the butter in the pan two tablespoons of orange juice and strain over the fish.

If the fish was broiled, melt some butter, add chopped shallot and the juice of one orange, boil for one minute and pour over the fish.

From Leyel and Hartley,
"The Gentle Art of Cookery."

CUTLETS MAINTENON

Have cutlets from a leg of lamb cut about ¾ of an inch thick
1 egg slightly beaten and diluted with ¼ cup of water
bread crumbs mixed with chopped thyme, parsley, marjoram, grated nutmeg, salt, and pepper.

Season the cutlets with salt and pepper, dip in egg, roll in the seasoned bread crumbs, and wrap each one in paper which has been buttered, and broil for fifteen minutes. Remove the cutlets from paper, garnish with broiled or *sauté* mushroom caps and parsley. Serve with mushroom sauce.

MUSHROOM SAUCE

Fry 10 mushroom caps, cut into thin slices, butter, season, and add to one cup of brown sauce. One tablespoon of sauterne is an addition which improves this sauce.

Adapted by Miss Shapleigh from
"New System of Cookery," Boston, 1807.

CHACKLICK

Thin slices of beef cut into two-inch pieces. Thin slices of bacon the same size, and sage leaves cut in half. Arrange these on skewers, having beef, bacon, and sage, until the skewer is full, leaving only a small end to hold on to when frying in a hot pan. Put a bit of butter in pan first, after that the bacon fat is sufficient. Season with salt and pepper.

Note: These skewers strung with the meat, bacon, and sage are good to take on a picnic, being ready to cook. This is a Greek dish.

From Mrs. Le Boiteaux, in the
Garden Club of America Bulletin.

CHOPPED MEAT BALLS

½ pound chopped meat (beef, veal, and pork)
1 teaspoon each of chopped chives, thyme, marjoram, and parsley mixed
1 tablespoon flour mixed with salt and pepper
butter

Into the meat work the chopped herbs; form into balls; roll in seasoned flour; and fry in butter until well browned.

Miss Shapleigh.

CUBAN FRICASSEE OF CHICKEN

1 chicken, cleaned, washed, and cut into pieces for serving
3 tablespoons of olive oil
2 tablespoons of flour
½ teaspoon salt and a little pepper
1 bean of garlic
1 small onion
½ cup washed rice
1 teaspoon Spanish saffron soaked in a little hot water
1 quart water

Mix the flour, salt, and pepper, and roll the pieces of chicken in it. Heat the olive oil with garlic and onion, and fry in it the chicken until well browned. Remove the chicken to a casserole. Fry rice in the oil until the rice is slightly brown; remove the onion and garlic and pour oil and rice over the chicken; add liquid from saffron and water. Cook slowly until the chicken is tender. Season more to taste.

VEAL STEW WITH HERBS

2 pounds of veal cut into small pieces
1 onion thinly sliced
1 small bean of garlic, finely chopped
3 tablespoons olive oil
2 tablespoons flour
1 teaspoon Spanish saffron soaked in ¼ cup of hot water
1 teaspoon sugar
1 teaspoon salt
⅛ teaspoon cinnamon
1 teaspoon cumin seed pounded in mortar

Fry the onion and garlic in olive oil for five minutes; add veal, and fry ten minutes; add flour, seasonings, salt, sugar, and cinnamon; mix cumin with saffron, and strain the liquid into the meat; add three cups of water and cook slowly for two or three hours. Just before serving sprinkle two tablespoons of chopped parsley over the meat. Season more if necessary. Serve in a border of rice.

Miss Shapleigh.

MINT JELLY WITH FRUIT

6 lemons
1 cup of sugar
2 tablespoons of granulated gelatine soaked in ⅛ cup of cold water
3 large leaves of peppermint geranium
½ teaspoon of spinach juice
mint leaves
2 cups of water
1 cup of fruit

Boil the sugar and water together for five minutes, and pour it hot over the gelatine which has been soaked in cold water, and the leaves of peppermint geranium; cook for five minutes, strain, and add the juice of the lemons with the rind of one lemon, and spinach juice. When nearly set, add fruit, turn into moulds and chill. Unmould and garnish with whipped cream and fresh mint leaves.

Adapted by Miss Hartley
from Leyel and Hartley,
"The Gentle Art of Cookery."

MARIGOLD CUSTARD

1 pint of milk
1 cup of marigold petals
¼ teaspoon salt
3 tablespoons of sugar
small piece of vanilla bean
3 egg yolks
⅛ teaspoon of nutmeg
⅛ teaspoon of allspice
½ teaspoon of rose water

Pound the marigold petals in a mortar, or crush them with a spoon, and scald with the milk and vanilla bean. Remove the vanilla bean, and add slightly beaten yolks of eggs, salt, and sugar mixed with the spice. Cook until the mixture coats the spoon. Add rose water and cool. This makes a good sauce for a blanc mange. It may be poured into a dish without cooking, and then baked like a custard. Serve with beaten cream, and garnish with marigold blossoms.

Miss Shapleigh.

SUET PUDDING

2 cups of flour
4 teaspoons of baking powder
¼ teaspoon of salt
1 cup of suet finely chopped
2 eggs, well beaten

1 cup of sugar
1 cup of currants
1 handful of chopped marigold petals
1 handful of chopped marjoram

Mix the flour with baking powder and salt, rub the chopped suet into the flour with the tips of fingers. Add well-beaten eggs, sugar, currants, marigold petals, and marjoram, and enough water (about one cupful) to form a soft dough. Put into a floured cloth and steam for two hours. Garnish with flowers and serve with lemon sauce.

More or less from Suet Pudding in John Evelyn's "Acetaria," 1699, changed by Marie, 1931.

LEMON SAUCE

1 egg well beaten
½ cup butter
1 cup sugar
1 handful chopped marigolds
a speck of marjoram
2 drops lemon juice

Stir all to a cream, add one tablespoon of hot water, and cook over hot water until thickened. Serve at once.

Marie.

ROSE GERANIUM JELLY

Prepare the pulp of apples as for a plain jelly. Boil the juice thus obtained for twenty minutes. To each pint of juice add one pound of sugar and place in a preserving kettle over the fire. Stir until all the sugar has melted, then add two or three rose geranium leaves, bring to the boiling point, and boil rapidly for two minutes, removing any scum which may rise to the surface. Turn into jelly glasses, removing the leaves—but place a fresh leaf in each glass.

MINT JELLY

For mint jelly, add pounded mint leaves while boiling; color with a little green coloring, and put one or two fresh mint leaves in each glass.

Adapted from Leyel and Hartley, "The Gentle Art of Cookery."

ROSE PETAL JAM

The rose petals are gathered early in the morning from flowers which have just opened that day. The petals of the damask rose are the sweetest, although the petals of *Rosa gallica* and of General Jaqueminot have been used.

The white and yellowish base or heel is cut off with scissors and the petals are washed and drained, then to each cup of rose petals take one cup of water and a cup of sugar and boil until the syrup hardens on the spoon. At just the right moment a little lemon juice should be added and a bit of tartaric acid. If they are not done exactly the right way they are bitter. The jam is poured into little jars and allowed to cool, and the next morning it is sealed with wax and covered.

A Turkish recipe from Constantinople.

Another recipe says to plunge the petals into boiling water and gently agitate them until they become transparent, pass them through cold water, and then do them up as above.

SESAME COOKIES

1 cup of butter
2 cups of sugar
2 eggs
½ cup water
2 tablespoons sesame seeds
3 cups of flour
2 teaspoons of baking powder
½ teaspoon of salt

Cream the butter and sugar, and add the eggs very well beaten, and water and sesame seeds which have been cooked together for a few minutes. Then add flour sifted with baking powder and salt; thoroughly mix and chill, allowing the mixture to stand overnight or for several hours. If not stiff enough to roll out, add more flour, roll into a thin sheet, and cut into any desired shapes. Bake in a moderate oven for ten minutes.

Adapted from Moore and Rock,
"Chinese Recipes," 1913.

SEED OR SAFFRON CAKE

(with yeast)

1 pound flour (4 cups)
½ pound butter (1 cup)
1 pint milk (scalded and cooled)
1 yeast cake soaked in ¼ cup lukewarm water
½ teaspoon salt
1½ tablespoons caraway seed
¼ teaspoon each of cloves and mace
½ teaspoon of cinnamon
1 cup sugar
1 tablespoon of rose water
1 teaspoon saffron soaked in warm milk
3 eggs

Pour the milk, when hot, over the sugar, butter, and salt. When lukewarm add yeast and saffron juice. Add eggs slightly beaten, and flour sifted with the spices, rose water, and caraway seed. Beat well and let rise for six hours. Cut down, put the dough into a buttered pan, and let rise until light. Bake one hour in a moderate oven.

Adapted from Glasse,
"The Art of Cookery," circa 1758.

ANISE SEED COOKIES (*Springela*)

Four eggs, not separated but thoroughly beaten, then add 1½ cups granulated sugar and beat for thirty minutes. Add 2 heaping cups of flour and 14 drops of anise seed oil; drop from a teaspoon on well-buttered pans and bake in a moderate oven. It will improve them to let them stand from two to three hours in the pans before baking.

International Jewish Cook Book.

CARDAMON COOKIES

Boil 6 eggs hard. When cold, shell and grate the yolks, add ½ pound sugar, the grated peel of a lemon, and ½ wine glassful of brandy. Stir in ½ pound of butter which has been worked to a cream. Sift in as much flour as you think will allow you to roll out the dough; take as little as possible, a little over ½ pound, and flour the board very thick. Put in wine, 3 tablespoonfuls of cardamon seed, and a little rose water and cut out with a fancy cake cutter, and brush with beaten egg. Sprinkle pounded almonds and sugar on top.

International Jewish Cook Book.

CARAWAY AND ROSE COOKIES

½ pound of butter
½ pound of fine sugar
½ of a grated nutmeg
1 pound of sifted flour (4 cupfuls)
3 tablespoons of caraway seed
2 tablespoons of rose water

Rub the butter into the sugar and flour, add nutmeg, caraway seeds, and rose water. Moisten to a stiff dough with water. Let it stand, covered, for several hours, then roll out into a sheet one-fourth of an inch thick. Cut with a cookie cutter, lay in a well-buttered pan, and bake in a moderate oven until it is light brown in color.

Adapted by Miss Shapleigh
from Leslie, "Directions for Cookery,"
Philadelphia, 1830.

FRESH CURD CHEESE WITH SAGE

½ pound pot of curd cheese
small handful of fresh sage leaves
the same of spinach leaves
½ teaspoon chopped chives
or
1 teaspoon chopped onion

Pound the sage and spinach in a mortar, add a little water or milk and press through a sieve. Add the juice to the cheese, salt to taste, and stir in the chives.

FRESH CURD CHEESE WITH CARAWAY SEED

1 cup of pot cheese, or one cream cheese
Mix the cheese to a smooth paste with olive oil or cream, then add
½ teaspoon salt and few grains of cayenne
1 teaspoon of caraway seed pounded in a mortar
½ teaspoon of chives finely cut
½ bean of garlic minced

Mix all the ingredients together well, and shape into a cake or balls.

Miss Shapleigh's version of an old recipe.

FRESH CURD CHEESE WITH ALMONDS

2 tablespoons powdered sugar and a speck of salt
½ pound fresh curd or pot cheese
¼ cup blanched almonds
2 tablespoons rose water
⅛ teaspoon mace
2 tablespoons cream

Chop the almonds and then pound with rose water in a mortar

until almost like a meal. Add to the cheese with mace and remainder of rose water and a little salt and sugar.

Adapted from Harrison,
"Housekeeper's Pocket Book," London, 1740.

Suggestion: Serve with a slice of pineapple or mixed diced fresh fruit or with stewed fruit.

RECIPE FOR HERB POWDER

Take fresh marjoram, basil, bay leaf, and parsley and dry in the sun until crisp. Pick carefully off the stalks and rub into fine powder. Add a small quantity of dried and powdered lemon peel, and allowing to each ounce of herbs in powder one small saltspoon of salt and half this quantity of ground pepper. Sift through a piece of coarse muslin and store for use in small bottles.

This makes an excellent herb powder for flavoring purposes.

From Grieve, "Culinary Herbs."

BIBLIOGRAPHY

BIBLIOGRAPHY

This is not a complete list of books consulted but merely a list of the ones which have been quoted, for those who might wish to study the same subject or to verify a statement.

REFERENCE BOOKS

Arber, Mrs. Agnes (Robertson). "Herbals, Their Origin and Evolution." Cambridge, England, University Press, 1912.

Bailey, L. H. "Cyclopedia of America Agriculture." 4 vols. N. Y., The Macmillan Co., 1907-09.

Bailey, L. H. "Manual of Cultivated Plants." N. Y., The Macmillan Co., 1924.

Bailey, L. H. "The Standard Cyclopedia of Horticulture." 6 vols. N. Y., The Macmillan Co., 1914-17.

Bailey, L. H., and Bailey, E. Z. "Hortus." N. Y., The Macmillan Co., 1930.

Baillon, Henri E. "Dictionnaire de Botanique." 4 vols. Paris, Hachette et Cie., 1876-92.

Barrows, Anna, and Shapleigh, Bertha E. "An Outline on the History of Cookery." N. Y., Teachers College, Columbia University, 1925. (Technical Education Bulletin No. 28.)

Boulger, George S. "The Uses of Plants: A Manual of Economic Botany." London, 1889.

Elliott, Stephen. "A Sketch of the Botany of South Carolina and Georgia." 2 vols. Charleston, S. C., J. R. Schenck, 1821-24.

Gray, Asa. "Elements of Botany of the Northern United States." N. Y., American Book Co., 1887.

Hazlitt, William C. "Old Cookery Books and Ancient Cuisine." London, E. Stock, 1902.

Johnson, George W. "A Dictionary of Modern Gardening." Philadelphia, Lea and Blanchard, 1847.

Linnaeus, Carolus. "Amoenitates Academicae." 10 vols. Erlangae, J. J. Palm, 1787.

Rehder, Alfred. "Manual of Cultivated Trees and Shrubs." N. Y., The Macmillan Co., 1927.

Robinson, William. "The English Flower Garden." London, J. Murray, 1896.

Rohde, Eleanour Sinclair. "The Old English Gardening Books." London, Martin Hopkinson and Co., 1924.

Rohde, Eleanour Sinclair. "The Old English Herbals." N. Y., Longmans, Green and Co., 1922.

Sturtevant, Edward Lewis. "History of Garden Vegetables." (The American Naturalist, vol. 21, no. 1, Jan., 1887.)

Sturtevant, Edward Lewis. "Sturtevant's Notes on Edible Plants," ed. by U. P. Hedrick. Albany, J. B. Lyon Co., 1919.

FOLKLORE

Beals, Mrs. Katherine (McMillan). "Flower Lore and Legend." N. Y., Henry Holt and Co., 1917.

Bergen, Mrs. Fanny (Dickerson). "Animal and Plant Lore." Boston, Houghton Mifflin and Co., 1899.

Budge, Sir Ernest A. T. Wallis. "The Divine Origin of the Craft of the Herbalist." London, The Society of Herbalists, 1928.

Davies, R. E. "A, B, C of the Herb Garden." London, George Newnes, 1921.

Fernie, William T. "Herbal Simples." N. Y., Boericke and Tafel, 1897.

Fletcher, Robert. (Bulletin of Johns Hopkins Hospital. Baltimore, 1896.)

Gubernatis, Angelo de. "La Mythologie des Plantes." 2 vols. Paris, C. Reinwald et Cie., 1878-82.

Leyel, Mrs. C. F. "The Magic of Herbs." London, J. Cape, 1926.

Pergen, Ritter von. "Deutschen Pflanzen-sagen." 1864.

Reiling, H., and Bohnhorst, J. "Unsere Pflanzen." Gotha, 1904.
Skinner, Charles M. "Myths and Legends of Flowers, Trees, Fruits and Plants." Philadelphia, J. B. Lippincott Co., 1925.
Thiselton-Dyer, T. F. "The Folk-lore of Plants." N. Y., D. Appleton and Co., 1889.
Thomas, D. L. "Kentucky Superstitions." Princeton, N. J., 1920.
Wirt, Mrs. E. W. "Flora's Dictionary, by a Lady." 1837.

PERFUMES AND COSMETICS

Charabot, Eugène T. (An article in *La Parfumerie Moderne,* 1921.)
Hampton, Frank A. "The Scent of Flowers and Leaves." London, Dulau and Co., 1925.
Lamotte. "Avenir de la Lavande." 1908.
Mourré, Charles. "La Lavande Française." Paris, Gauthier-Villars et Cie., 1923.
Piesse, G. W. Septimus. "The Art of Perfumery." Philadelphia, Presley Blakiston, 1880.
Poucher, William A. "Perfumes, Cosmetics and Soaps." 2 vols. A. Van Nostrand Co., 1930.
Power, Frederick B. "Descriptive Catalogue of Essential Oils and Organic Chemical Preparations." N. Y., Fritzche Bros., 1894.
Rudelka, W. "Peppermint." (Botanical study in *Les Parfums de France,* July, 1927.)
Sawer, J. C. "Odorographia." London, Gurney and Jackson, 1892.
Schimmel and Co. "Report." 1907.
Thompson, C. J. S. "The Mystery and Lure of Perfume." Philadelphia, J. B. Lippincott Co., 1927.
"Toilet of Flora, The." (Anonymous.) London, 1775.

ETHNOBOTANY

Chamberlin, Ralph V. "The Ethnobotany of the Yosemite Indians." (Proceedings of Academy of Natural Sciences, Philadelphia, vol. 63, part 1, 1911.)
Chestnut, V. K. "Plants Used by the Indians of Mendocino County, California." (U. S. Dept. of Agriculture, 1900-02.)

Havard, Valery. "Drink Plants of the North American Indians." (Torrey Botanical Club Bulletin.)

Havard, Valery. "Food Plants of the North American Indians." (Torrey Botanical Club Bulletin, 1895.)

Palmer, "Food Plants of the North American Indians." (U. S. Dept. of Agriculture, 1871.)

Robbins, W. W., Harrington, J. P., and Freire-Marreco, Barbara. "Ethnobotany of the Tewa Indians." Washington, Govt. Printing Office, 1916. (Smithsonian Institution. Bureau of American Ethnology. Bulletin 55.)

Smith, H. H. "The Meskwaki." 1928.

Smith, H. H. "Ethnobotany of the Menomini Indians." (Bulletin of Public Museum of City of Milwaukee, Wisconsin, vol. 4, no. 1, Dec. 10, 1923.)

FRAGRANT FLOWERS

McDonald, Donald. "Sweet-scented Flowers and Fragrant Leaves." London, Sampson Low, Marston and Co., 1895.

Mott, Frederick T. "Flora Odorata." London, Orr and Co., 1843.

TEAS

Fortune, Robert. "A Journey to the Tea Countries of China." London, J. Murray, 1852.

Okakura, Kakuzo. "The Book of Tea." N. Y., Fox, Duffield and Co., 1906. (Dover reprint)

MEDICINE

Barton, Benjamin S. "Collections for an Essay Towards a Materia Medica of the United States." Cincinnati, Lloyd Library, 1900. (Bulletin no. 1 of the Lloyd Library. Reproduction ser. no. 1.)

Barton, W. P. C. "Vegetable Materia Medica of the United States." 2 vols. Philadelphia, 1817-18.

Flűckiger, Frederick August, and Hanbury, Daniel. "Pharmacographia, A History of the Principal Drugs of Vegetable Origin in Great Britain and British India." London, Macmillan & Co., Ltd., 1879.

"Merck's Index." N. Y., Merck and Co., 1930.

Millspaugh, Charles F. "American Medicinal Plants." 2 vols. N. Y., Boericke and Tafel, 1884-87.

National Standard Dispensary, 1916.

Newman, John B. "The Book of Herbs." Stratford, 1864.

Porcher, Francis P. "Resources of the Southern Fields and Forests; being also a Medical Botany of the Southern States." Charleston, S. C., 1867.

Stuart, Rev. G. A. "Chinese Materia Medica." 1911.

COOK BOOKS

"American Housekeeper or Domestic Cookery." Hartford, 1838.

Belle, Frances P. "California Cook Book." Chicago, Regan Publishing Co., 1925.

Bonnefons, Nicolas de. "Les Délices de la Campagne." Paris, 1662.

Boulestin, X. Marcel, and Hill, Jason. "Herbs, Salads and Seasonings." London, William Heinemann, 1930.

Brillat-Savarin. "Anthelme." Physiologie du Gout, Paris, Librairie de la Bibliothèque Nationale, 2 vols. in 1.

Child, Mrs. Lydia M. "The American Frugal Housewife." Boston, Carter, Hindus and Co., 1st ed. 1829; 16th ed. 1835.

"Court and County Cook Book." 1702.

Dalgairns. "Practice of Cookery Adapted to the Business of Everyday Life." Boston, Monroe and Francis, 1830.

Digby, Sir Kenelm. "The Closet of Sir Kenelm Digby Opened; newly edited with Introduction, Notes and Glossary by Anne MacDonnell." London, Philip Lee Warner, 1910.

Dumas, Alexandre. "Petite Dictionnaire de Cuisine." Paris, 1882.

Ellwanger, George H. "The Pleasures of the Table." N. Y., Doubleday, Page and Co., 1902.

Escoffier, André. "Le Guide Culinaire." Paris, 1902.

Evelyn, John. "Acetaria: A Discourse of Sallets." London, 1699.

Glasse, Mrs. Hannah. "The Art of Cookery." Circ. 1758.

Greenbaum, Florence Kreisler. "The International Jewish Cook Book." N. Y., Bloch Publishing Co., 1918.

Grieve, Mrs. Maud. "Culinary Herbs." 1918. (A pamphlet written for the British Guild of Herb Growers.)

Hale, Mrs. Sarah J. "New Cook Book." Philadelphia, 1857.

Harrison. "Housekeeper's Pocket Book." London, 1740.

Hodgkinson, Richard. "A Closet for Gentlewomen." London, 1641.

Leslie, Eliza. "Directions for Cookery." Philadelphia, 1830.

Leyel, Mrs. C. F., and Hartley, Olga. "The Gentle Art of Cookery." London, Chatto and Windus, 1929.

Markham, Gervase. "The English Housewife." London, 1649.

Mason. "The Lady's Assistant." 1777.

Moore and Rock. "Chinese Recipes." 1913.

Moxon, Elizabeth. "English Housewifery." 11th ed., 1775.

"New System of Cookery, by a Lady." Boston, 1807.

Nutt, Frederic. "The Complete Confectioner." London, 1790.

Pennell, Elizabeth R. "A Guide for the Greedy." Philadelphia, J. B. Lippincott Co., 1923.

"Queen's Closet Opened, The."

"Ramona's Spanish Cook Book."

Randolph, Mrs. Mary. "The Virginia Housewife." Baltimore, 1832.

Rhett, Mrs. Blanche S. "200 Years of Charleston Cooking," edited by Lettie Gay; gathered by Blanche S. Rhett. N. Y., Jonathan Cape and Harrison Smith, 1930.

Scott, Natalie. "Mirations and Miracles of Mandy." New Orleans, La., R. H. True Co., 1929.

Southworth, Mary E. "One Hundred and One Mexican Dishes." San Francisco, Paul Elder and Co.

VEGETABLES AND HERBS

Andrews, Edward D. "The New York Shakers and Their Industries." (N. Y. State Museum, Circular 2, Oct., 1930.)

Bardswell, Frances A. "The Herb Garden." London, Adam and Charles Black, 1911.

Batchelor, John, and Miyabe, K. "Ainu Economic Plants." April 12, 1893.

Bentley, Robert. *The Pharmaceutical Journal,* 1860.
Bois, D. "Les Plantes Alimentaires Chez Tous Les Peuples." Paris, Paul Lechevalier, 1927.
Boulger, G. S. "The Uses of Plants." 1889.
Bowles, E. A. "A Handbook of Crocus and Colchicum for Gardeners." London, 1924.
Brotherton, R. P. *The Gardeners' Chronicle,* Dec. 5, 1908.
Burr, Fearing. "The Field and Garden Vegetables of America." Boston, 1863.
Chalot, C. "Le Géranium Rosat." (*La Parfumerie Moderne,* June, 1927.)
Charabot, S. *Bul. Sci. Pharm.,* vol. 34, pp. 469-71, 1927.
Chevalier, Auguste. "On the Crocus." *Revue de Botanique.*
Clute, Willard N. "Useful Plants." Joliet, Ill., Willard N. Clute and Co., 1928.
Correvon, Henry. "Plantes et Santé." Paris, Delachaux et Nustle, S.A.
Delamer, E. S. "The Kitchen Garden." London, 1857.
Dicks, S. B. "Capsicum or Pepper." *The Gardeners' Chronicle,* Jan. 10, 1925.
Dicks, S. B. "The Parsley." *The Gardeners' Chronicle,* July 26, 1924.
Drury, Heber. "The Useful Plants of India." Madras, 1858.
Durham, H. E. "Tarragon." *The Gardeners' Chronicle,* Dec. 30, 1930.
Flint, Martha B. "A Garden of Simples." N. Y., Charles Scribner's Sons, 1900.
Flückiger, F. A. *The Pharmaceutical Journal,* 1877.
Gattefossé, R. M. "Culture et Industrie des Plantes." 1917.
Grieve, Mrs. Maud. "A Modern Herbal." 2 vols. London, Jonathan Cape, 1931.
Guillard, M. F. "Les Piments des Solanées." 1901.
Hardy, G. H. "Angelica." *The Gardeners' Chronicle,* Sept., 1918.
Heuzé, Gustave. "Les Plantes Industrielles." 4 vols. Paris, Librairie Agricole de la Maison Rustique, 1894.
Homes, E. "Genus Pelargonium." *Perfumery and Essential Oil Record.*

Kains, M. G. "Culinary Herbs." N. Y., Orange Judd Publishing Co., 1920.

Kronfeld, E. M. "Geschichte des Safrans." 1892.

Le Boiteaux, Mrs. Isaac. *The Garden Club of America Bulletin.*

Leclerc, Henri. "Les Epices." 1929.

Losch, Dr. Fr. "Kräuterbuch." Műnchen, J. F. Schreiber, 1924.

Loudon, Mrs. Jane Wells. "Gardening for Ladies." 1843.

Northcote, Lady Rosalind. "The Book of Herbs." London, John Lane, 1903.

Paillieux, A., et Bois, D. "Le Potager d'un Curieux." Paris, 1892.

Rohde, Eleanour Sinclair. "A Garden of Herbs," Boston, Hale, Cushman & Flint, 1936. (Dover reprint)

Rohde, Eleanour Sinclair. "Old English Herbals." London, Longmans, Green and Co., 1922.

Russel, G. A. *American Pharmaceutical Assoc. Journal,* Jan., 1921.

Saunders, C. F. "Useful Wild Plants of the United States and Canada." 1920.

Sievers, A. F. "American Medicinal Plants of Commercial Importance." U. S. Dept. of Agriculture, Publication no. 77.

Step, Edward. "Herbs of Healing." London, Hutchinson and Co., 1926.

Stockberger, W. W. "Drug Plants under Cultivation." (U. S. Dept. of Agriculture, Farmers' Bulletin, no. 663. Issued 1915, revised April, 1927.)

Vilmorin-Andrieux et Cie. "The Vegetable Garden." English ed. published under the direction of W. Robinson. 3rd ed. London, 1920.

HISTORY

Al Makkari. "Mohammedan Dynasties in Spain," tr. into English by Pascual de Gayangos. London, 1840.

Amherst, Alicia. "A History of Gardening in England." London, 1876.

Apuleius Barbarus. "The Herbal of Apuleius Barbarus; described by Robert T. Gunther." Oxford, England. Printed for Presentation to the Members of The Roxburghe Club, 1925.

Bacon, Francis. "Essay on Gardens," in *Essays Moral, Economical and Political.*

Barnham, A. "Hortus Americanus." Jamaica, 1794.

Bartram, John. "Catalogue." Philadelphia, 1790.

Bartram, William. "Travels." Vanguard Press, 1928.

"Bible, The."

Bidwell, Percy Wells, and Falconer, John I. "History of Agriculture in the Northern United States, 1620-1860." Washington, Carnegie Institution, 1925. (Publication no. 358.)

Bryant, Charles. "Flora Diaetetica; or, History of Esculent Plants." London, 1783.

Candolle, Alphonse L. P. P. de. "Origin of Cultivated Plants." London, Kegan Paul, 1884.

Carr. "Catalogue of Bartram's Garden." 1807 and 1814.

Carrier, Lyman. "The Beginnings of Agriculture in America." N. Y., McGraw-Hill Book Co., 1923.

Claytonius, Johannes. "Flora Virginica." London, 1762.

Cockayne, Rev. T. O. "Saxon Leechdoms, Starcraft, and Wortcunning." 3 vols. 1864-66.

Culpeper, Nicholas. "The English Physician; or An Astrologo-Physical Discourse of the Vulgar Herbs of this Nation." London, 1652.

Darlington, William. "Memorials of John Bartram and Humphrey Marshall." Philadelphia, 1849.

Drewitt, F. G. D. "The Romance of the Apothecaries' Garden at Chelsea." Cambridge, England, University Press, 1928.

Earle, Alice Morse. "Customs and Fashions in Old New England." N. Y., The Macmillan Co., 1893.

Earle, Alice Morse. "Home Life in Colonial Days." N. Y., The Macmillan Co., 1927.

Earle, Alice Morse. "Old Time Gardens." N. Y., The Macmillan Co., 1901.

Earle, Alice Morse. "Sun-dials and Roses of Yesterday." N. Y., The Macmillan Co., 1902.

Gerard, John. "The Herball; or, General Historie of Plantes." London, 1597.

Gibault, Georges. "Histoire des Légumes." Paris, 1912.

Hehn, Victor. "The Wanderings of Plants and Animals," ed. by James S. Stallybrass. 8 vols. London, Sonnenschein and Co., 1885.

Henslow, T. G. W. "History of Garden Vegetables." (Royal Horticultural Society Journal, 1912.)

Hill, John. "The Useful Family Herbal." London, 1770.

Hill, Thomas (Didymus Mountain). "Gardener's Labyrinth." 1586.

Hoskyns, Chandos Wren. "A Short Inquiry into the History of Agriculture." London, Bradbury and Evans, 1849.

Howe, Marshall A. "New York's First Botanical Garden." N. Y., March, 1929.

Ibn Al Awam. "Le Livre de l'Agriculture, traduit de l'Arabe par J. J. Clement-Mullet." Paris, Librairie A. Franck. Two vols. in one. 1864-67.

Ibn Baithar. "Heil und Nahrungs-mittel aus dem Arabischen, Übersetzt von Dr. Joseph v. Sontheimer." Stűttgart, 1840.

Jameson, J. F. "Narratives of New Netherland, 1609-1664." N. Y., Charles Scribner's Sons, 1909.

Jefferson, Thomas. "Notes on the State of Virginia." 1787.

Joret, Charles. "Les Plantes dans l'Antiquité et au Moyen Age." 2 vols. Paris, Librairie Emile Bouillon, 1897-1904.

Josselyn, John. "New-England's Rarities with an Introduction and Notes by Edward Tuckerman." Boston, William Veazie, 1865.

Kalm, Peter. "Travels in North America, translated into English by John Reinhold Forster." 1770. (Dover reprint)

Kellerman, Seb. "Zur Ersten Einfűhring Amerikanischen Pflanzen in 16 Jahrhundert, *Naturwissenschaftliche Wochenschrift,* März, no. 13, 1909.

La Quintinye, Jean de. "The Compleat Gard'ner in Six Books; made English by John Evelyn, Esquire," London, 1693.

Lick, David E., and Brendle, T. R. "Plant Names and Plant Lore among the Pennsylvania Germans." Egypt, Pa., T. R. Brendle, 1927.

Lloyd, John U. "Origin and History of all the Pharmacopical Vegetable Drugs with Bibliography." Cincinnati, Caxton Press, 1929.

Lloyd, J. W. and C. G., "Drugs and Medicines of North America." Cincinnati, 1884-85.

Logan, Mrs. Martha. "The South Carolina Almanack. 1756." (Called "Tobler's South Carolina Almanack.")

McClintock, Walter. "Old Indian Trails." Boston, Houghton Mifflin Co., 1923.

McMahon, Bernard. "The American Gardener's Calendar." 1806 and 1819.

Massachusetts, State Board of. *Nature Leaflet,* no. 19.

Miller, Phillip. "The Gardener's Dictionary." London, 1731.

Parkinson, John. "Paradisi in Sole; Paradisus Terrestris." London, 1629.

Parkinson, John. "Theatrum Botanicum; The Theatre of Plants." London, 1640.

Philipps, Henry. "History of Cultivated Vegetables." 1827.

Pliny. "The Natural History; translated with copious notes and illustrations by the late John Bostock and H. T. Riley." 6 vols. London, 1887-1900.

Prince, William. "Catalogue." 1771 and 1790.

Pursh, Frederick. "Florae Americae Septentrionalis; or A Systematic Arrangement and Description of the Plants of North America." 2 vols. London, 1814.

Randolph, John. "A Treatise on Gardening." (Reprinted by Appeals Press, Richmond, 1924.)

Sadler, Elizabeth H. "The Bloom of Monticello." 1926.

"Six Colonial Recipes." N. Y., City History Club of Colonial Dames of State of New York, 1908.

South Carolina Gazette. 1735 and 1738.

Stearns, Samuel. "The American Herbal," 1801.

Theophrastus. "Enquiry into Plants and Minor Works on Odours and Weather Signs, with an English translation by Sir Arthur Hort." N. Y., G. P. Putnam's Sons, 1926.

Turner, William. "A New Herbal." London, Stephen Meireman, 1551.

Vail, A. M. "An Old Physic Garden in New Amsterdam." (N. Y. Botanical Garden Journal, 2:183, 1901.)

Varro, Marcus Terentius. "Farming." (Translated with Introduction and Commentary by Lloyd Storr-Best. London, 1912.)

Virginia Gazette. "Article on Tea." Jan. 13, 1774.

Virginia Gazette. Sept. 9, 1775.

PERIODICALS CONSULTED

Agricultural Science Journal.
American Folklore, The Journal of.
American Naturalist, The.
American Perfumer and Essential Oil Review.
Garden, The.
Garden Club of America Bulletin, The.
Gardeners' Chronicle, The (London).
Gardening Illustrated.
Jardinage.
La Parfumerie Moderne.
Les Parfums de France.
Perfumery and Essential Oil Record.
Pharmaceutical Journal, The.
Revue de Botanique.
Revue Horticole.
Royal Horticultural Society Journal.
South Carolina Gazette (before 1800).
Virginia Gazette (before 1800).

INDEX

INDEX

NOTE: Page references in italics are to recipes in which the herb in question is used. Page references in roman type are to horticultural and general information.

A CATALOGUE OF SELECTED DOVER BOOKS IN ALL FIELDS OF INTEREST

A CATALOGUE OF SELECTED DOVER BOOKS IN ALL FIELDS OF INTEREST

WHAT IS SCIENCE?, *N. Campbell*
The role of experiment and measurement, the function of mathematics, the nature of scientific laws, the difference between laws and theories, the limitations of science, and many similarly provocative topics are treated clearly and without technicalities by an eminent scientist. "Still an excellent introduction to scientific philosophy," H. Margenau in *Physics Today*. "A first-rate primer . . . deserves a wide audience," *Scientific American*. 192pp. 5⅜ x 8.
60043-2 Paperbound $1.25

THE NATURE OF LIGHT AND COLOUR IN THE OPEN AIR, *M. Minnaert*
Why are shadows sometimes blue, sometimes green, or other colors depending on the light and surroundings? What causes mirages? Why do multiple suns and moons appear in the sky? Professor Minnaert explains these unusual phenomena and hundreds of others in simple, easy-to-understand terms based on optical laws and the properties of light and color. No mathematics is required but artists, scientists, students, and everyone fascinated by these "tricks" of nature will find thousands of useful and amazing pieces of information. Hundreds of observational experiments are suggested which require no special equipment. 200 illustrations; 42 photos. xvi + 362pp. 5⅜ x 8.
20196-1 Paperbound $2.75

THE STRANGE STORY OF THE QUANTUM, AN ACCOUNT FOR THE GENERAL READER OF THE GROWTH OF IDEAS UNDERLYING OUR PRESENT ATOMIC KNOWLEDGE, *B. Hoffmann*
Presents lucidly and expertly, with barest amount of mathematics, the problems and theories which led to modern quantum physics. Dr. Hoffmann begins with the closing years of the 19th century, when certain trifling discrepancies were noticed, and with illuminating analogies and examples takes you through the brilliant concepts of Planck, Einstein, Pauli, Broglie, Bohr, Schroedinger, Heisenberg, Dirac, Sommerfeld, Feynman, etc. This edition includes a new, long postscript carrying the story through 1958. "Of the books attempting an account of the history and contents of our modern atomic physics which have come to my attention, this is the best," H. Margenau, Yale University, in *American Journal of Physics*. 32 tables and line illustrations. Index. 275pp. 5⅜ x 8.
20518-5 Paperbound $2.00

GREAT IDEAS OF MODERN MATHEMATICS: THEIR NATURE AND USE, *Jagjit Singh*
Reader with only high school math will understand main mathematical ideas of modern physics, astronomy, genetics, psychology, evolution, etc. better than many who use them as tools, but comprehend little of their basic structure. Author uses his wide knowledge of non-mathematical fields in brilliant exposition of differential equations, matrices, group theory, logic, statistics, problems of mathematical foundations, imaginary numbers, vectors, etc. Original publication. 2 appendixes. 2 indexes. 65 ills. 322pp. 5⅜ x 8.
20587-8 Paperbound $2.50

THE MUSIC OF THE SPHERES: THE MATERIAL UNIVERSE—FROM ATOM TO QUASAR, SIMPLY EXPLAINED, *Guy Murchie*
Vast compendium of fact, modern concept and theory, observed and calculated data, historical background guides intelligent layman through the material universe. Brilliant exposition of earth's construction, explanations for moon's craters, atmospheric components of Venus and Mars (with data from recent fly-by's), sun spots, sequences of star birth and death, neighboring galaxies, contributions of Galileo, Tycho Brahe, Kepler, etc.; and (Vol. 2) construction of the atom (describing newly discovered sigma and xi subatomic particles), theories of sound, color and light, space and time, including relativity theory, quantum theory, wave theory, probability theory, work of Newton, Maxwell, Faraday, Einstein, de Broglie, etc. "Best presentation yet offered to the intelligent general reader," *Saturday Review*. Revised (1967). Index. 319 illustrations by the author. Total of xx + 644pp. 5⅜ x 8½.
21809-0, 21810-4 Two volume set, paperbound $5.00

FOUR LECTURES ON RELATIVITY AND SPACE, *Charles Proteus Steinmetz*
Lecture series, given by great mathematician and electrical engineer, generally considered one of the best popular-level expositions of special and general relativity theories and related questions. Steinmetz translates complex mathematical reasoning into language accessible to laymen through analogy, example and comparison. Among topics covered are relativity of motion, location, time; of mass; acceleration; 4-dimensional time-space; geometry of the gravitational field; curvature and bending of space; non-Euclidean geometry. Index. 40 illustrations. x + 142pp. 5⅜ x 8½. 61771-8 Paperbound $1.50

HOW TO KNOW THE WILD FLOWERS, *Mrs. William Starr Dana*
Classic nature book that has introduced thousands to wonders of American wild flowers. Color-season principle of organization is easy to use, even by those with no botanical training, and the genial, refreshing discussions of history, folklore, uses of over 1,000 native and escape flowers, foliage plants are informative as well as fun to read. Over 170 full-page plates, collected from several editions, may be colored in to make permanent records of finds. Revised to conform with 1950 edition of Gray's Manual of Botany. xlii + 438pp. 5⅜ x 8½. 20332-8 Paperbound $2.50

MANUAL OF THE TREES OF NORTH AMERICA, *Charles Sprague Sargent*
Still unsurpassed as most comprehensive, reliable study of North American tree characteristics, precise locations and distribution. By dean of American dendrologists. Every tree native to U.S., Canada, Alaska; 185 genera, 717 species, described in detail—leaves, flowers, fruit, winterbuds, bark, wood, growth habits, etc. plus discussion of varieties and local variants, immaturity variations. Over 100 keys, including unusual 11-page analytical key to genera, aid in identification. 783 clear illustrations of flowers, fruit, leaves. An unmatched permanent reference work for all nature lovers. Second enlarged (1926) edition. Synopsis of families. Analytical key to genera. Glossary of technical terms. Index. 783 illustrations, 1 map. Total of 982pp. 5⅜ x 8.
20277-1, 20278-X Two volume set, paperbound $6.00

IT'S FUN TO MAKE THINGS FROM SCRAP MATERIALS,
Evelyn Glantz Hershoff
What use are empty spools, tin cans, bottle tops? What can be made from rubber bands, clothes pins, paper clips, and buttons? This book provides simply worded instructions and large diagrams showing you how to make cookie cutters, toy trucks, paper turkeys, Halloween masks, telephone sets, aprons, linoleum block- and spatter prints — in all 399 projects! Many are easy enough for young children to figure out for themselves; some challenging enough to entertain adults; all are remarkably ingenious ways to make things from materials that cost pennies or less! Formerly "Scrap Fun for Everyone." Index. 214 illustrations. 373pp. 5⅜ x 8½. 21251-3 Paperbound $2.00

SYMBOLIC LOGIC and THE GAME OF LOGIC, *Lewis Carroll*
"Symbolic Logic" is not concerned with modern symbolic logic, but is instead a collection of over 380 problems posed with charm and imagination, using the syllogism and a fascinating diagrammatic method of drawing conclusions. In "The Game of Logic" Carroll's whimsical imagination devises a logical game played with 2 diagrams and counters (included) to manipulate hundreds of tricky syllogisms. The final section, "Hit or Miss" is a lagniappe of 101 additional puzzles in the delightful Carroll manner. Until this reprint edition, both of these books were rarities costing up to $15 each. Symbolic Logic: Index. xxxi + 199pp. The Game of Logic: 96pp. 2 vols. bound as one. 5⅜ x 8.
20492-8 Paperbound $2.50

MATHEMATICAL PUZZLES OF SAM LOYD, PART I
selected and edited by M. Gardner
Choice puzzles by the greatest American puzzle creator and innovator. Selected from his famous collection, "Cyclopedia of Puzzles," they retain the unique style and historical flavor of the originals. There are posers based on arithmetic, algebra, probability, game theory, route tracing, topology, counter and sliding block, operations research, geometrical dissection. Includes the famous "14-15" puzzle which was a national craze, and his "Horse of a Different Color" which sold millions of copies. 117 of his most ingenious puzzles in all. 120 line drawings and diagrams. Solutions. Selected references. xx + 167pp. 5⅜ x 8.
20498-7 Paperbound $1.35

STRING FIGURES AND HOW TO MAKE THEM, *Caroline Furness Jayne*
107 string figures plus variations selected from the best primitive and modern examples developed by Navajo, Apache, pygmies of Africa, Eskimo, in Europe, Australia, China, etc. The most readily understandable, easy-to-follow book in English on perennially popular recreation. Crystal-clear exposition; step-by-step diagrams. Everyone from kindergarten children to adults looking for unusual diversion will be endlessly amused. Index. Bibliography. Introduction by A. C. Haddon. 17 full-page plates, 960 illustrations. xxiii + 401pp. 5⅜ x 8½.
20152-X Paperbound $2.50

PAPER FOLDING FOR BEGINNERS, *W. D. Murray and F. J. Rigney*
A delightful introduction to the varied and entertaining Japanese art of origami (paper folding), with a full, crystal-clear text that anticipates every difficulty; over 275 clearly labeled diagrams of all important stages in creation. You get results at each stage, since complex figures are logically developed from simpler ones. 43 different pieces are explained: sailboats, frogs, roosters, etc. 6 photographic plates. 279 diagrams. 95pp. 5⅝ x 8⅜.
20713-7 Paperbound $1.00

PRINCIPLES OF ART HISTORY,
H. Wölfflin
Analyzing such terms as "baroque," "classic," "neoclassic," "primitive," "picturesque," and 164 different works by artists like Botticelli, van Cleve, Dürer, Hobbema, Holbein, Hals, Rembrandt, Titian, Brueghel, Vermeer, and many others, the author establishes the classifications of art history and style on a firm, concrete basis. This classic of art criticism shows what really occurred between the 14th-century primitives and the sophistication of the 18th century in terms of basic attitudes and philosophies. "A remarkable lesson in the art of seeing," *Sat. Rev. of Literature.* Translated from the 7th German edition. 150 illustrations. 254pp. 6⅛ x 9¼. 20276-3 Paperbound $2.50

PRIMITIVE ART,
Franz Boas
This authoritative and exhaustive work by a great American anthropologist covers the entire gamut of primitive art. Pottery, leatherwork, metal work, stone work, wood, basketry, are treated in detail. Theories of primitive art, historical depth in art history, technical virtuosity, unconscious levels of patterning, symbolism, styles, literature, music, dance, etc. A must book for the interested layman, the anthropologist, artist, handicrafter (hundreds of unusual motifs), and the historian. Over 900 illustrations (50 ceramic vessels, 12 totem poles, etc.). 376pp. 5⅜ x 8. 20025-6 Paperbound $2.50

THE GENTLEMAN AND CABINET MAKER'S DIRECTOR,
Thomas Chippendale
A reprint of the 1762 catalogue of furniture designs that went on to influence generations of English and Colonial and Early Republic American furniture makers. The 200 plates, most of them full-page sized, show Chippendale's designs for French (Louis XV), Gothic, and Chinese-manner chairs, sofas, canopy and dome beds, cornices, chamber organs, cabinets, shaving tables, commodes, picture frames, frets, candle stands, chimney pieces, decorations, etc. The drawings are all elegant and highly detailed; many include construction diagrams and elevations. A supplement of 24 photographs shows surviving pieces of original and Chippendale-style pieces of furniture. Brief biography of Chippendale by N. I. Bienenstock, editor of *Furniture World.* Reproduced from the 1762 edition. 200 plates, plus 19 photographic plates. vi + 249pp. 9⅛ x 12¼. 21601-2 Paperbound $4.00

AMERICAN ANTIQUE FURNITURE: A BOOK FOR AMATEURS,
Edgar G. Miller, Jr.
Standard introduction and practical guide to identification of valuable American antique furniture. 2115 illustrations, mostly photographs taken by the author in 148 private homes, are arranged in chronological order in extensive chapters on chairs, sofas, chests, desks, bedsteads, mirrors, tables, clocks, and other articles. Focus is on furniture accessible to the collector, including simpler pieces and a larger than usual coverage of Empire style. Introductory chapters identify structural elements, characteristics of various styles, how to avoid fakes, etc. "We are frequently asked to name some book on American furniture that will meet the requirements of the novice collector, the beginning dealer, and . . . the general public. . . . We believe Mr. Miller's two volumes more completely satisfy this specification than any other work," *Antiques.* Appendix. Index. Total of vi + 1106pp. 7⅞ x 10¾.
21599-7, 21600-4 Two volume set, paperbound $10.00

THE BAD CHILD'S BOOK OF BEASTS, MORE BEASTS FOR WORSE CHILDREN, and A MORAL ALPHABET, *H. Belloc*
Hardly and anthology of humorous verse has appeared in the last 50 years without at least a couple of these famous nonsense verses. But one must see the entire volumes — with all the delightful original illustrations by Sir Basil Blackwood — to appreciate fully Belloc's charming and witty verses that play so subacidly on the platitudes of life and morals that beset his day — and ours. A great humor classic. Three books in one. Total of 157pp. 5⅜ x 8.
20749-8 Paperbound $1.25

THE DEVIL'S DICTIONARY, *Ambrose Bierce*
Sardonic and irreverent barbs puncturing the pomposities and absurdities of American politics, business, religion, literature, and arts, by the country's greatest satirist in the classic tradition. Epigrammatic as Shaw, piercing as Swift, American as Mark Twain, Will Rogers, and Fred Allen, Bierce will always remain the favorite of a small coterie of enthusiasts, and of writers and speakers whom he supplies with "some of the most gorgeous witticisms of the English language" (H. L. Mencken). Over 1000 entries in alphabetical order. 144pp. 5⅜ x 8. 20487-1 Paperbound $1.25

THE COMPLETE NONSENSE OF EDWARD LEAR.
This is the only complete edition of this master of gentle madness available at a popular price. *A Book of Nonsense, Nonsense Songs, More Nonsense Songs and Stories* in their entirety with all the old favorites that have delighted children and adults for years. The Dong With A Luminous Nose, The Jumblies, The Owl and the Pussycat, and hundreds of other bits of wonderful nonsense. 214 limericks, 3 sets of Nonsense Botany, 5 Nonsense Alphabets, 546 drawings by Lear himself, and much more. 320pp. 5⅜ x 8. 20167-8 Paperbound $1.75

THE WIT AND HUMOR OF OSCAR WILDE, *ed. by Alvin Redman*
Wilde at his most brilliant, in 1000 epigrams exposing weaknesses and hypocrisies of "civilized" society. Divided into 49 categories—sin, wealth, women, America, etc.—to aid writers, speakers. Includes excerpts from his trials, books, plays, criticism. Formerly "The Epigrams of Oscar Wilde." Introduction by Vyvyan Holland, Wilde's only living son. Introductory essay by editor. 260pp. 5⅜ x 8.
20602-5 Paperbound $1.50

A CHILD'S PRIMER OF NATURAL HISTORY, *Oliver Herford*
Scarcely an anthology of whimsy and humor has appeared in the last 50 years without a contribution from Oliver Herford. Yet the works from which these examples are drawn have been almost impossible to obtain! Here at last are Herford's improbable definitions of a menagerie of familiar and weird animals, each verse illustrated by the author's own drawings. 24 drawings in 2 colors; 24 additional drawings. vii + 95pp. 6½ x 6. 21647-0 Paperbound $1.00

THE BROWNIES: THEIR BOOK, *Palmer Cox*
The book that made the Brownies a household word. Generations of readers have enjoyed the antics, predicaments and adventures of these jovial sprites, who emerge from the forest at night to play or to come to the aid of a deserving human. Delightful illustrations by the author decorate nearly every page. 24 short verse tales with 266 illustrations. 155pp. 6⅝ x 9¼.
21265-3 Paperbound $1.50

THE PRINCIPLES OF PSYCHOLOGY,
William James

The full long-course, unabridged, of one of the great classics of Western literature and science. Wonderfully lucid descriptions of human mental activity, the stream of thought, consciousness, time perception, memory, imagination, emotions, reason, abnormal phenomena, and similar topics. Original contributions are integrated with the work of such men as Berkeley, Binet, Mills, Darwin, Hume, Kant, Royce, Schopenhauer, Spinoza, Locke, Descartes, Galton, Wundt, Lotze, Herbart, Fechner, and scores of others. All contrasting interpretations of mental phenomena are examined in detail—introspective analysis, philosophical interpretation, and experimental research. "A classic," *Journal of Consulting Psychology*. "The main lines are as valid as ever," *Psychoanalytical Quarterly*. "Standard reading . . . a classic of interpretation," *Psychiatric Quarterly*. 94 illustrations. 1408pp. 5⅜ x 8.
20381-6, 20382-4 Two volume set, paperbound $6.00

VISUAL ILLUSIONS: THEIR CAUSES, CHARACTERISTICS AND APPLICATIONS,
M. Luckiesh

"Seeing is deceiving," asserts the author of this introduction to virtually every type of optical illusion known. The text both describes and explains the principles involved in color illusions, figure-ground, distance illusions, etc. 100 photographs, drawings and diagrams prove how easy it is to fool the sense: circles that aren't round, parallel lines that seem to bend, stationary figures that seem to move as you stare at them – illustration after illustration strains our credulity at what we see. Fascinating book from many points of view, from applications for artists, in camouflage, etc. to the psychology of vision. New introduction by William Ittleson, Dept. of Psychology, Queens College. Index. Bibliography. xxi + 252pp. 5⅜ x 8½. 21530-X Paperbound $1.75

FADS AND FALLACIES IN THE NAME OF SCIENCE,
Martin Gardner

This is the standard account of various cults, quack systems, and delusions which have masqueraded as science: hollow earth fanatics. Reich and orgone sex energy, dianetics, Atlantis, multiple moons, Forteanism, flying saucers, medical fallacies like iridiagnosis, zone therapy, etc. A new chapter has been added on Bridey Murphy, psionics, and other recent manifestations in this field. This is a fair, reasoned appraisal of eccentric theory which provides excellent inoculation against cleverly masked nonsense. "Should be read by everyone, scientist and non-scientist alike," R. T. Birge, Prof. Emeritus of Physics, Univ. of California; Former President, American Physical Society. Index. x + 365pp. 5⅜ x 8. 20394-8 Paperbound $2.00

ILLUSIONS AND DELUSIONS OF THE SUPERNATURAL AND THE OCCULT,
D. H. Rawcliffe

Holds up to rational examination hundreds of persistent delusions including crystal gazing, automatic writing, table turning, mediumistic trances, mental healing, stigmata, lycanthropy, live burial, the Indian Rope Trick, spiritualism, dowsing, telepathy, clairvoyance, ghosts, ESP, etc. The author explains and exposes the mental and physical deceptions involved, making this not only an exposé of supernatural phenomena, but a valuable exposition of characteristic types of abnormal psychology. Originally titled "The Psychology of the Occult." 14 illustrations. Index. 551pp. 5⅜ x 8. 20503-7 Paperbound $3.50

FAIRY TALE COLLECTIONS, *edited by Andrew Lang*
Andrew Lang's fairy tale collections make up the richest shelf-full of traditional children's stories anywhere available. Lang supervised the translation of stories from all over the world—familiar European tales collected by Grimm, animal stories from Negro Africa, myths of primitive Australia, stories from Russia, Hungary, Iceland, Japan, and many other countries. Lang's selection of translations are unusually high; many authorities consider that the most familiar tales find their best versions in these volumes. All collections are richly decorated and illustrated by H. J. Ford and other artists.

THE BLUE FAIRY BOOK. 37 stories. 138 illustrations. ix + 390pp. 5⅜ x 8½.
21437-0 Paperbound $1.95

THE GREEN FAIRY BOOK. 42 stories. 100 illustrations. xiii + 366pp. 5⅜ x 8½.
21439-7 Paperbound $2.00

THE BROWN FAIRY BOOK. 32 stories. 50 illustrations, 8 in color. xii + 350pp. 5⅜ x 8½.
21438-9 Paperbound $1.95

THE BEST TALES OF HOFFMANN, *edited by E. F. Bleiler*
10 stories by E. T. A. Hoffmann, one of the greatest of all writers of fantasy. The tales include "The Golden Flower Pot," "Automata," "A New Year's Eve Adventure," "Nutcracker and the King of Mice," "Sand-Man," and others. Vigorous characterizations of highly eccentric personalities, remarkably imaginative situations, and intensely fast pacing has made these tales popular all over the world for 150 years. Editor's introduction. 7 drawings by Hoffmann. xxxiii + 419pp. 5⅜ x 8½.
21793-0 Paperbound $2.25

GHOST AND HORROR STORIES OF AMBROSE BIERCE, *edited by E. F. Bleiler*
Morbid, eerie, horrifying tales of possessed poets, shabby aristocrats, revived corpses, and haunted malefactors. Widely acknowledged as the best of their kind between Poe and the moderns, reflecting their author's inner torment and bitter view of life. Includes "Damned Thing," "The Middle Toe of the Right Foot," "The Eyes of the Panther," "Visions of the Night," "Moxon's Master," and over a dozen others. Editor's introduction. xxii + 199pp. 5⅜ x 8½.
20767-6 Paperbound $1.50

THREE GOTHIC NOVELS, *edited by E. F. Bleiler*
Originators of the still popular Gothic novel form, influential in ushering in early 19th-century Romanticism. Horace Walpole's *Castle of Otranto*, William Beckford's *Vathek*, John Polidori's *The Vampyre*, and a *Fragment* by Lord Byron are enjoyable as exciting reading or as documents in the history of English literature. Editor's introduction. xi + 291pp. 5⅜ x 8½.
21232-7 Paperbound $2.00

BEST GHOST STORIES OF LEFANU, *edited by E. F. Bleiler*
Though admired by such critics as V. S. Pritchett, Charles Dickens and Henry James, ghost stories by the Irish novelist Joseph Sheridan LeFanu have never become as widely known as his detective fiction. About half of the 16 stories in this collection have never before been available in America. Collection includes "Carmilla" (perhaps the best vampire story ever written), "The Haunted Baronet," "The Fortunes of Sir Robert Ardagh," and the classic "Green Tea." Editor's introduction. 7 contemporary illustrations. Portrait of LeFanu. xii + 467pp. 5⅜ x 8.
20415-4 Paperbound $2.50

EASY-TO-DO ENTERTAINMENTS AND DIVERSIONS WITH COINS, CARDS, STRING, PAPER AND MATCHES, *R. M. Abraham*
Over 300 tricks, games and puzzles will provide young readers with absorbing fun. Sections on card games; paper-folding; tricks with coins, matches and pieces of string; games for the agile; toy-making from common household objects; mathematical recreations; and 50 miscellaneous pastimes. Anyone in charge of groups of youngsters, including hard-pressed parents, and in need of suggestions on how to keep children sensibly amused and quietly content will find this book indispensable. Clear, simple text, copious number of delightful line drawings and illustrative diagrams. Originally titled "Winter Nights' Entertainments." Introduction by Lord Baden Powell. 329 illustrations. v + 186pp. 5⅜ x 8½. 20921-0 Paperbound $1.25

AN INTRODUCTION TO CHESS MOVES AND TACTICS SIMPLY EXPLAINED, *Leonard Barden*
Beginner's introduction to the royal game. Names, possible moves of the pieces, definitions of essential terms, how games are won, etc. explained in 30-odd pages. With this background you'll be able to sit right down and play. Balance of book teaches strategy – openings, middle game, typical endgame play, and suggestions for improving your game. A sample game is fully analyzed. True middle-level introduction, teaching you all the essentials without oversimplifying or losing you in a maze of detail. 58 figures. 102pp. 5⅜ x 8½. 21210-6 Paperbound $1.25

LASKER'S MANUAL OF CHESS, *Dr. Emanuel Lasker*
Probably the greatest chess player of modern times, Dr. Emanuel Lasker held the world championship 28 years, independent of passing schools or fashions. This unmatched study of the game, chiefly for intermediate to skilled players, analyzes basic methods, combinations, position play, the aesthetics of chess, dozens of different openings, etc., with constant reference to great modern games. Contains a brilliant exposition of Steinitz's important theories. Introduction by Fred Reinfeld. Tables of Lasker's tournament record. 3 indices. 308 diagrams. 1 photograph. xxx + 349pp. 5⅜ x 8. 20640-8 Paperbound $2.50

COMBINATIONS: THE HEART OF CHESS, *Irving Chernev*
Step-by-step from simple combinations to complex, this book, by a well-known chess writer, shows you the intricacies of pins, counter-pins, knight forks, and smothered mates. Other chapters show alternate lines of play to those taken in actual championship games; boomerang combinations; classic examples of brilliant combination play by Nimzovich, Rubinstein, Tarrasch, Botvinnik, Alekhine and Capablanca. Index. 356 diagrams. ix + 245pp. 5⅜ x 8½. 21744-2 Paperbound $2.00

HOW TO SOLVE CHESS PROBLEMS, *K. S. Howard*
Full of practical suggestions for the fan or the beginner – who knows only the moves of the chessmen. Contains preliminary section and 58 two-move, 46 three-move, and 8 four-move problems composed by 27 outstanding American problem creators in the last 30 years. Explanation of all terms and exhaustive index. "Just what is wanted for the student," Brian Harley. 112 problems, solutions. vi + 171pp. 5⅜ x 8. 20748-X Paperbound $1.50

SOCIAL THOUGHT FROM LORE TO SCIENCE, *H. E. Barnes and H. Becker*
An immense survey of sociological thought and ways of viewing, studying, planning, and reforming society from earliest times to the present. Includes thought on society of preliterate peoples, ancient non-Western cultures, and every great movement in Europe, America, and modern Japan. Analyzes hundreds of great thinkers: Plato, Augustine, Bodin, Vico, Montesquieu, Herder, Comte, Marx, etc. Weighs the contributions of utopians, sophists, fascists and communists; economists, jurists, philosophers, ecclesiastics, and every 19th and 20th century school of scientific sociology, anthropology, and social psychology throughout the world. Combines topical, chronological, and regional approaches, treating the evolution of social thought as a process rather than as a series of mere topics. "Impressive accuracy, competence, and discrimination . . . easily the best single survey," *Nation*. Thoroughly revised, with new material up to 1960. 2 indexes. Over 2200 bibliographical notes. Three volume set. Total of 1586pp. 5⅜ x 8.
20901-6, 20902-4, 20903-2 Three volume set, paperbound $10.50

A HISTORY OF HISTORICAL WRITING, *Harry Elmer Barnes*
Virtually the only adequate survey of the whole course of historical writing in a single volume. Surveys developments from the beginnings of historiography in the ancient Near East and the Classical World, up through the Cold War. Covers major historians in detail, shows interrelationship with cultural background, makes clear individual contributions, evaluates and estimates importance; also enormously rich upon minor authors and thinkers who are usually passed over. Packed with scholarship and learning, clear, easily written. Indispensable to every student of history. Revised and enlarged up to 1961. Index and bibliography. xv + 442pp. 5⅜ x 8½.
20104-X Paperbound $3.00

JOHANN SEBASTIAN BACH, *Philipp Spitta*
The complete and unabridged text of the definitive study of Bach. Written some 70 years ago, it is still unsurpassed for its coverage of nearly all aspects of Bach's life and work. There could hardly be a finer non-technical introduction to Bach's music than the detailed, lucid analyses which Spitta provides for hundreds of individual pieces. 26 solid pages are devoted to the B minor mass, for example, and 30 pages to the glorious St. Matthew Passion. This monumental set also includes a major analysis of the music of the 18th century: Buxtehude, Pachelbel, etc. "Unchallenged as the last word on one of the supreme geniuses of music," John Barkham, *Saturday Review Syndicate*. Total of 1819pp. Heavy cloth binding. 5⅜ x 8.
22278-0, 22279-9 Two volume set, clothbound $15.00

BEETHOVEN AND HIS NINE SYMPHONIES, *George Grove*
In this modern middle-level classic of musicology Grove not only analyzes all nine of Beethoven's symphonies very thoroughly in terms of their musical structure, but also discusses the circumstances under which they were written, Beethoven's stylistic development, and much other background material. This is an extremely rich book, yet very easily followed; it is highly recommended to anyone seriously interested in music. Over 250 musical passages. Index. viii + 407pp. 5⅜ x 8.
20334-4 Paperbound $2.50

THE TIME STREAM
John Taine
Acknowledged by many as the best SF writer of the 1920's, Taine (under the name Eric Temple Bell) was also a Professor of Mathematics of considerable renown. Reprinted here are *The Time Stream,* generally considered Taine's best, *The Greatest Game,* a biological-fiction novel, and *The Purple Sapphire,* involving a supercivilization of the past. Taine's stories tie fantastic narratives to frameworks of original and logical scientific concepts. Speculation is often profound on such questions as the nature of time, concept of entropy, cyclical universes, etc. 4 contemporary illustrations. v + 532pp. 5⅜ x 8⅜.
21180-0 Paperbound $3.00

SEVEN SCIENCE FICTION NOVELS,
H. G. Wells
Full unabridged texts of 7 science-fiction novels of the master. Ranging from biology, physics, chemistry, astronomy, to sociology and other studies, Mr. Wells extrapolates whole worlds of strange and intriguing character. "One will have to go far to match this for entertainment, excitement, and sheer pleasure . . ."*New York Times.* Contents: The Time Machine, The Island of Dr. Moreau, The First Men in the Moon, The Invisible Man, The War of the Worlds, The Food of the Gods, In The Days of the Comet. 1015pp. 5⅜ x 8.
20264-X Clothbound $5.00

28 SCIENCE FICTION STORIES OF H. G. WELLS.
Two full, unabridged novels, *Men Like Gods* and *Star Begotten,* plus 26 short stories by the master science-fiction writer of all time! Stories of space, time, invention, exploration, futuristic adventure. Partial contents: *The Country of the Blind, In the Abyss, The Crystal Egg, The Man Who Could Work Miracles, A Story of Days to Come, The Empire of the Ants, The Magic Shop, The Valley of the Spiders, A Story of the Stone Age, Under the Knife, Sea Raiders,* etc. An indispensable collection for the library of anyone interested in science fiction adventure. 928pp. 5⅜ x 8. 20265-8 Clothbound $5.00

THREE MARTIAN NOVELS,
Edgar Rice Burroughs
Complete, unabridged reprinting, in one volume, of Thuvia, Maid of Mars; Chessmen of Mars; The Master Mind of Mars. Hours of science-fiction adventure by a modern master storyteller. Reset in large clear type for easy reading. 16 illustrations by J. Allen St. John. vi + 490pp. 5⅜ x 8½.
20039-6. Paperbound $2.50

AN INTELLECTUAL AND CULTURAL HISTORY OF THE WESTERN WORLD,
Harry Elmer Barnes
Monumental 3-volume survey of intellectual development of Europe from primitive cultures to the present day. Every significant product of human intellect traced through history: art, literature, mathematics, physical sciences, medicine, music, technology, social sciences, religions, jurisprudence, education, etc. Presentation is lucid and specific, analyzing in detail specific discoveries, theories, literary works, and so on. Revised (1965) by recognized scholars in specialized fields under the direction of Prof. Barnes. Revised bibliography. Indexes. 24 illustrations. Total of xxix + 1318pp.
21275-0, 21276-9, 21277-7 Three volume set, paperbound $7.75

HEAR ME TALKIN' TO YA, *edited by Nat Shapiro and Nat Hentoff*
In their own words, Louis Armstrong, King Oliver, Fletcher Henderson, Bunk Johnson, Bix Beiderbecke, Billy Holiday, Fats Waller, Jelly Roll Morton, Duke Ellington, and many others comment on the origins of jazz in New Orleans and its growth in Chicago's South Side, Kansas City's jam sessions, Depression Harlem, and the modernism of the West Coast schools. Taken from taped conversations, letters, magazine articles, other first-hand sources. Editors' introduction. xvi + 429pp. 5⅜ x 8½. 21726-4 Paperbound $2.50

THE JOURNAL OF HENRY D. THOREAU
A 25-year record by the great American observer and critic, as complete a record of a great man's inner life as is anywhere available. Thoreau's Journals served him as raw material for his formal pieces, as a place where he could develop his ideas, as an outlet for his interests in wild life and plants, in writing as an art, in classics of literature, Walt Whitman and other contemporaries, in politics, slavery, individual's relation to the State, etc. The Journals present a portrait of a remarkable man, and are an observant social history. Unabridged republication of 1906 edition, Bradford Torrey and Francis H. Allen, editors. Illustrations. Total of 1888pp. 8⅜ x 12¼.
20312-3, 20313-1 Two volume set, clothbound $30.00

A SHAKESPEARIAN GRAMMAR, *E. A. Abbott*
Basic reference to Shakespeare and his contemporaries, explaining through thousands of quotations from Shakespeare, Jonson, Beaumont and Fletcher, North's *Plutarch* and other sources the grammatical usage differing from the modern. First published in 1870 and written by a scholar who spent much of his life isolating principles of Elizabethan language, the book is unlikely ever to be superseded. Indexes. xxiv + 511pp. 5⅜ x 8½. 21582-2 Paperbound $3.00

FOLK-LORE OF SHAKESPEARE, *T. F. Thistelton Dyer*
Classic study, drawing from Shakespeare a large body of references to supernatural beliefs, terminology of falconry and hunting, games and sports, good luck charms, marriage customs, folk medicines, superstitions about plants, animals, birds, argot of the underworld, sexual slang of London, proverbs, drinking customs, weather lore, and much else. From full compilation comes a mirror of the 17th-century popular mind. Index. ix + 526pp. 5⅜ x 8½.
21614-4 Paperbound $3.25

THE NEW VARIORUM SHAKESPEARE, *edited by H. H. Furness*
By far the richest editions of the plays ever produced in any country or language. Each volume contains complete text (usually First Folio) of the play, all variants in Quarto and other Folio texts, editorial changes by every major editor to Furness's own time (1900), footnotes to obscure references or language, extensive quotes from literature of Shakespearian criticism, essays on plot sources (often reprinting sources in full), and much more.

HAMLET, *edited by H. H. Furness*
Total of xxvi + 905pp. 5⅜ x 8½.
21004-9, 21005-7 Two volume set, paperbound $5.50

TWELFTH NIGHT, *edited by H. H. Furness*
Index. xxii + 434pp. 5⅜ x 8½. 21189-4 Paperbound $2.75

LA BOHEME BY GIACOMO PUCCINI,
translated and introduced by Ellen H. Bleiler

Complete handbook for the operagoer, with everything needed for full enjoyment except the musical score itself. Complete Italian libretto, with new, modern English line-by-line translation—the only libretto printing all repeats; biography of Puccini; the librettists; background to the opera, Murger's La Boheme, etc.; circumstances of composition and performances; plot summary; and pictorial section of 73 illustrations showing Puccini, famous singers and performances, etc. Large clear type for easy reading. 124pp. 5⅜ x 8½.
20404-9 Paperbound $1.50

ANTONIO STRADIVARI: HIS LIFE AND WORK (1644-1737),
W. Henry Hill, Arthur F. Hill, and Alfred E. Hill

Still the only book that really delves into life and art of the incomparable Italian craftsman, maker of the finest musical instruments in the world today. The authors, expert violin-makers themselves, discuss Stradivari's ancestry, his construction and finishing techniques, distinguished characteristics of many of his instruments and their locations. Included, too, is story of introduction of his instruments into France, England, first revelation of their supreme merit, and information on his labels, number of instruments made, prices, mystery of ingredients of his varnish, tone of pre-1684 Stradivari violin and changes between 1684 and 1690. An extremely interesting, informative account for all music lovers, from craftsman to concert-goer. Republication of original (1902) edition. New introduction by Sydney Beck, Head of Rare Book and Manuscript Collections, Music Division, New York Public Library. Analytical index by Rembert Wurlitzer. Appendixes. 68 illustrations. 30 full-page plates. 4 in color. xxvi + 315pp. 5⅜ x 8½. 20425-1 Paperbound $3.00

MUSICAL AUTOGRAPHS FROM MONTEVERDI TO HINDEMITH,
Emanuel Winternitz

For beauty, for intrinsic interest, for perspective on the composer's personality, for subtleties of phrasing, shading, emphasis indicated in the autograph but suppressed in the printed score, the mss. of musical composition are fascinating documents which repay close study in many different ways. This 2-volume work reprints facsimiles of mss. by virtually every major composer, and many minor figures—196 examples in all. A full text points out what can be learned from mss., analyzes each sample. Index. Bibliography. 18 figures. 196 plates. Total of 170pp. of text. 7⅞ x 10¾.
21312-9, 21313-7 Two volume set, paperbound $5.00

J. S. BACH,
Albert Schweitzer

One of the few great full-length studies of Bach's life and work, and the study upon which Schweitzer's renown as a musicologist rests. On first appearance (1911), revolutionized Bach performance. The only writer on Bach to be musicologist, performing musician, and student of history, theology and philosophy, Schweitzer contributes particularly full sections on history of German Protestant church music, theories on motivic pictorial representations in vocal music, and practical suggestions for performance. Translated by Ernest Newman. Indexes. 5 illustrations. 650 musical examples. Total of xix + 928pp. 5⅜ x 8½. 21631-4, 21632-2 Two volume set, paperbound $5.00

THE METHODS OF ETHICS, *Henry Sidgwick*
Propounding no organized system of its own, study subjects every major methodological approach to ethics to rigorous, objective analysis. Study discusses and relates ethical thought of Plato, Aristotle, Bentham, Clarke, Butler, Hobbes, Hume, Mill, Spencer, Kant, and dozens of others. Sidgwick retains conclusions from each system which follow from ethical premises, rejecting the faulty. Considered by many in the field to be among the most important treatises on ethical philosophy. Appendix. Index. xlvii + 528pp. 5⅜ x 8½.
21608-X Paperbound $3.00

TEUTONIC MYTHOLOGY, *Jakob Grimm*
A milestone in Western culture; the work which established on a modern basis the study of history of religions and comparative religions. 4-volume work assembles and interprets everything available on religious and folkloristic beliefs of Germanic people (including Scandinavians, Anglo-Saxons, etc.). Assembling material from such sources as Tacitus, surviving Old Norse and Icelandic texts, archeological remains, folktales, surviving superstitions, comparative traditions, linguistic analysis, etc. Grimm explores pagan deities, heroes, folklore of nature, religious practices, and every other area of pagan German belief. To this day, the unrivaled, definitive, exhaustive study. Translated by J. S. Stallybrass from 4th (1883) German edition. Indexes. Total of lxxvii + 1887pp. 5⅜ x 8½.
21602-0, 21603-9, 21604-7, 21605-5 Four volume set, paperbound $12.00

THE I CHING, *translated by James Legge*
Called "The Book of Changes" in English, this is one of the Five Classics edited by Confucius, basic and central to Chinese thought. Explains perhaps the most complex system of divination known, founded on the theory that all things happening at any one time have characteristic features which can be isolated and related. Significant in Oriental studies, in history of religions and philosophy, and also to Jungian psychoanalysis and other areas of modern European thought. Index. Appendixes. 6 plates. xxi + 448pp. 5⅜ x 8½.
21062-6 Paperbound $2.75

HISTORY OF ANCIENT PHILOSOPHY, *W. Windelband*
One of the clearest, most accurate comprehensive surveys of Greek and Roman philosophy. Discusses ancient philosophy in general, intellectual life in Greece in the 7th and 6th centuries B.C., Thales, Anaximander, Anaximenes, Heraclitus, the Eleatics, Empedocles, Anaxagoras, Leucippus, the Pythagoreans, the Sophists, Socrates, Democritus (20 pages), Plato (50 pages), Aristotle (70 pages), the Peripatetics, Stoics, Epicureans, Sceptics, Neo-platonists, Christian Apologists, etc. 2nd German edition translated by H. E. Cushman. xv + 393pp. 5⅜ x 8.
20357-3 Paperbound $3.00

THE PALACE OF PLEASURE, *William Painter*
Elizabethan versions of Italian and French novels from *The Decameron*, Cinthio, Straparola, Queen Margaret of Navarre, and other continental sources – the very work that provided Shakespeare and dozens of his contemporaries with many of their plots and sub-plots and, therefore, justly considered one of the most influential books in all English literature. It is also a book that any reader will still enjoy. Total of cviii + 1,224pp.
21691-8, 21692-6, 21693-4 Three volume set, paperbound $8.25

THE WONDERFUL WIZARD OF OZ, *L. F. Baum*
All the original W. W. Denslow illustrations in full color—as much a part of "The Wizard" as Tenniel's drawings are of "Alice in Wonderland." "The Wizard" is still America's best-loved fairy tale, in which, as the author expresses it, "The wonderment and joy are retained and the heartaches and nightmares left out." Now today's young readers can enjoy every word and wonderful picture of the original book. New introduction by Martin Gardner. A Baum bibliography. 23 full-page color plates. viii + 268pp. 5⅜ x 8.
20691-2 Paperbound $1.95

THE MARVELOUS LAND OF OZ, *L. F. Baum*
This is the equally enchanting sequel to the "Wizard," continuing the adventures of the Scarecrow and the Tin Woodman. The hero this time is a little boy named Tip, and all the delightful Oz magic is still present. This is the Oz book with the Animated Saw-Horse, the Woggle-Bug, and Jack Pumpkinhead. All the original John R. Neill illustrations, 10 in full color. 287pp. 5⅜ x 8.
20692-0 Paperbound $1.75

ALICE'S ADVENTURES UNDER GROUND, *Lewis Carroll*
The original *Alice in Wonderland*, hand-lettered and illustrated by Carroll himself, and originally presented as a Christmas gift to a child-friend. Adults as well as children will enjoy this charming volume, reproduced faithfully in this Dover edition. While the story is essentially the same, there are slight changes, and Carroll's spritely drawings present an intriguing alternative to the famous Tenniel illustrations. One of the most popular books in Dover's catalogue. Introduction by Martin Gardner. 38 illustrations. 128pp. 5⅜ x 8½.
21482-6 Paperbound $1.00

THE NURSERY "ALICE," *Lewis Carroll*
While most of us consider *Alice in Wonderland* a story for children of all ages, Carroll himself felt it was beyond younger children. He therefore provided this simplified version, illustrated with the famous Tenniel drawings enlarged and colored in delicate tints, for children aged "from Nought to Five." Dover's edition of this now rare classic is a faithful copy of the 1889 printing, including 20 illustrations by Tenniel, and front and back covers reproduced in full color. Introduction by Martin Gardner. xxiii + 67pp. 6⅛ x 9¼.
21610-1 Paperbound $1.75

THE STORY OF KING ARTHUR AND HIS KNIGHTS, *Howard Pyle*
A fast-paced, exciting retelling of the best known Arthurian legends for young readers by one of America's best story tellers and illustrators. The sword Excalibur, wooing of Guinevere, Merlin and his downfall, adventures of Sir Pellias and Gawaine, and others. The pen and ink illustrations are vividly imagined and wonderfully drawn. 41 illustrations. xviii + 313pp. 6⅛ x 9¼.
21445-1 Paperbound $2.00

Prices subject to change without notice.

Available at your book dealer or write for free catalogue to Dept. Adsci, Dover Publications, Inc., 180 Varick St., N.Y., N.Y. 10014. Dover publishes more than 150 books each year on science, elementary and advanced mathematics, biology, music, art, literary history, social sciences and other areas.